S0-AZV-189

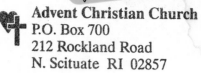

Advent Christian Church
P.O. Box 700
212 Rockland Road
N. Scituate RI 02857

CHRISTIANITY WITH POWER

Christianity
with Power
Your Worldview and Your
Experience of the Supernatural

Charles H. Kraft
with Christie Varney
and Ellen Kearney

Servant Publications
Ann Arbor, Michigan

Copyright © 1989 Charles H. Kraft
All rights reserved.

Vine Books is an imprint of Servant Publications especially
designed to serve Evangelical Christians.

Published by Servant Books
P.O. Box 8617
Ann Arbor, Michigan 48107

Cover illustration by Thomas Blackshear
Cover design by Michael Andaloro

Scripture texts used in this work, unless otherwise indicated,
are taken from *Good News Bible: The Bible in Today's English
Version*; copyright © 1976 for Old Testament, American Bible
Society, New York; copyright © 1966, 1971, and 1976 for
New Testament, American Bible Society, New York. The
Scripture texts are cited by permission of the copyright owner.

00 01 02 03 04 05 15 14 13 12 11 10

Printed in the United States of America
ISBN 0-89283-396-3

Library of Congress Cataloging-in-Publication Data

Kraft, Charles H.
    Christianity with power : your worldview and your
experience of the supernatural / by Charles H. Kraft.
    p. cm.
    Bibliography: p.
    Includes index.
    ISBN 0-89283-396-3
    1. Power (Christian theology)   2. Cosmology.
3. Christianity and culture.   4. Christian life—1960-
5. Evangelicalism.   6. Spiritual healing.   7. Miracles.
8. Kraft, Charles H.   I. Title.
BT738.25.K73   1989
231.7—dc19   88-36715
                                               CIP

Contents

Foreword

THERE ARE SEVERAL FEATURES of *Christianity with Power* which make it a good book, but there is one thing that in my judgment makes it a *great* book.

First, what makes the book a good one? For starters, Kraft points us to the balance and vibrancy which New Testament Christianity maintains between the divine Word and supernatural deed. Second, it is both inspiring and instructive to discover how Kraft's conversion on this point has transformed his own life, making his faith in God an exciting adventure and setting him on paths of much more effective service. Third, it is good to see this eminent Christian scholar continue what he began to do in his earlier work *Christianity in Culture*: namely, to address the need for applying authentic Christianity to real daily needs. These are three things that make this a good book well worth reading.

But there is something which makes *Christianity with Power* more than just another good book—something that makes it quite possibly great, maybe even a major publishing event to be noted some day when the history of the modern church is written. I refer to the way in which Kraft helps us as no one else has in understanding our Western worldview in relation to the way the Holy Spirit is working today. He tackles head on the blockage experienced by large numbers of North American Evangelicals who seek to open up to the power of the kingdom or even to accept with enthusiasm the remarkable revival of the Holy Spirit now in progress, especially in the Third World.

Now it is true that other pioneers of this new movement, often referred to as "the Third Wave of the Holy Spirit," have pointed to the worldview problem. John Wimber, for example, in chapter five of *Power Evangelism* speaks to the issue, basing his discussion partially on Kraft's previous work. So we will not be completely unaware of this concern when we encounter it in *Christianity with Power*. But until now no one with Kraft's credentials as a missionary anthropologist has analyzed the worldview problem in detail and explained how it can be surmounted by those who so choose.

He has both the expertise as a scholar and the proven experience as a Christian leader to instruct us concerning worldviews. In Kraft's compelling new book, we see how a secular Western worldview colors our perception of reality, in particular how it can blind our eyes from seeing what is otherwise plain scriptural truth. The autobiographical character of the book is also important, because it tells us that Kraft has taken his own medicine and broken through the barriers himself.

The heart of this book—the feature that makes it such a landmark publication—is the detailed way in which Kraft explains to the reader exactly what this Western mindset or perspective is. He tells us what it is like. We begin to see why such a worldview creates problems for us in taking Jesus' Word in the Gospels seriously. We glimpse the good news of how we, too, can break the habit of deeply ingrained unbelief, if we so choose. Like a skilled surgeon, Kraft lays bare our predicament and tells us exactly what needs to be done to escape our worldview limitations and to expand our horizons. What he has to say is surely crucial to effective ministry and world mission in the coming decades if the Lord tarries.

His stated aim is modestly put: to help North American Evangelicals, like himself, to face up to their culture and traditions so they can move beyond them into paths of more effective service that Jesus models for us. What he says, however, applies to Christians of every background. Evangelical or not, all of us need to hear the same ringing challenge.

For example, Kraft's analysis forcefully challenges many religious liberals today to critique their own modern prejudices, rather than to attempt to demythologize the New Testament. In a sense, his theme is even more relevant to many religious liberals than it is to Evangelicals, because at least Evangelicals do not deny that the religion of the New Testament was experienced with power, even if such is not their experience today.

Christianity with Power raises a question that clamors for a personal response on our part: What are we going to do about all of these new experiences and the new understandings of Christian truth that they lead to? Kraft has shown us where we stand. He has shown us how we have been hindered from operating in the power of God's kingdom. Perhaps, for the first time, we see how we have allowed ourselves to fall into sub-biblical patterns of Christian behavior.

Now we must ask ourselves, "Do we really want to get rid of these bad habits? Or do we want to keep clinging to them?" Is it really in our hearts to change? Do we really want to move forward in the direction that the Lord and his Word indicate? Or would we rather remain functional deists and live in a safe world of our own making with a God who has no real power to change our lives?

It really comes down to this: *Christianity with Power* is a dangerous and even revolutionary book to read. Reading it puts you right into the valley of decision. For it is one thing to have been ignorant of a truth and not to have thought much about it, but it is quite another to have faced it head on and then to have said "no." That puts one in a very different spiritual condition. Some Evangelicals, like Kraft, are opting today to join the growing pentecostal revival and create a united flame for Christ. Still others, however, are pulling away and retreating into a defensive bunker. This book requires that we decide which camp to belong to. Raising this issue could make this a critical hour of decision for Evangelicals.

In light of the challenge *Christianity with Power* presents, let me give you an exhortation as you examine this book. Brothers and sisters, our risen Lord has triumphed over the powers of evil. He now reigns at God's right hand, having all authority on heaven and earth. King Jesus now wills to save and heal human beings in every dimension of their fallen condition: in body, mind, and spirit.

Shall we not then exercise faith in the victorious power of Jesus to fight everything that enslaves and oppresses humankind? Shall we not take authority over all the power of the enemy? Shall we not determine to live our lives as those who expect miracles to come from the hand of God our Father—forsaking the paths of functional unbelief?

Fellow Christians, Jesus Christ is now challenging us to help set aright the disorder and pain of a fallen creation by going forth in his authority and power. He sends us forth in his name to proclaim the good news of the kingdom, to heal the sick, and to cast out demons.

As the author blesses you, his readers, at the end of this book, so I bless you at the beginning. My blessing is that this important and powerful book will have the same effect upon you that it has had upon me. May it lead you to commit yourself to the obedience of faith.

Dr. Clark H. Pinnock
McMaster Divinity College
Hamilton, Ontario

Introduction

THIS BOOK HAS BEEN A JOY TO WRITE. It recounts a series of discoveries about God and myself, chronicling how I and many others have moved from traditional Evangelicalism in which we simply talked about the authority and power Jesus demonstrated into an Evangelicalism in which we *do* the things Jesus said we would do (Jn 14:12). I have always asserted the authority and trustworthiness of the Bible as an inspired record of God's mighty works in the past. Now I am experiencing the validity of those claims by becoming a part of the continuance of those mighty works in the present.

This is then, in part, the story of a change in me. But I do not speak only for myself. I know many Evangelicals who are also experiencing a new working of the Holy Spirit in their lives. In the process, they are discovering that Christianity is much more than they had previously known. They and I are members of what my colleague Peter Wagner has begun to call "the Third Wave."[1] The first two waves of the Holy Spirit in this century were the Pentecostal and charismatic movements. This third wave is a movement of the Holy Spirit among Evangelicals who, by and large, choose to remain Evangelicals.

In general, we are quieter than those of the first two waves. We, with them, assert the validity of all of the gifts for today but focus more on healing and less on tongues. We applaud the increasing openness of many Evangelicals to a reasonable expression of the charismatic gifts and count on this, plus a lot of patience and love, to enable us to enrich Evangelicalism, rather than feeling we have to split off from it.

Moreover, we see ourselves moving away from an unbalanced Evangelicalism that has presented the word aspect of the gospel message without much of the power aspect (1 Cor 4:20). Not that that kind of Evangelicalism was or is bad. It has most of the important parts of Christianity in place. But we have found it unbalanced in that, though it provides abundant *knowledge about* the things of God, there is not a corresponding *demonstration of* the works of God. Therefore we seek a more balanced Christianity characterized both by knowledge about and practice of the things Jesus taught, including both the works and the fruits of the Spirit. Because the Third Wave seeks a balanced approach, it has even attracted quite a number of us who are academics.

In order to understand and appropriate New Testament power, though, we have had to fight a rather formidable enemy. The cultural conditioning passed on to us through family, school, and church has not been conducive to understanding and following our Master and his early followers in the area of spiritual power. This book aims first to help us Evangelicals to understand the blockage that has been caused in this area by our worldview. It then seeks to lay out what it is we need to do about this blockage to spiritual power if we want to move toward a more balanced, biblical expression and experience of Christianity.

I have not learned what I share here without help. Therefore I would like to thank God and John Wimber, the one God used to lead me into new understandings; Peter Wagner, my colleague and traveling companion on this journey; and my wife Marguerite, who has shared most of the journey with me and been patient through it all.

I would also like to thank Servant Publications and their editors, Ann Spangler and David Came, for encouraging me to write this book and for offering their comments along the way.

All biblical quotations are, unless otherwise noted, from The Good News Bible.

Charles H. Kraft
South Pasadena, California

ONE

Signs and Wonders Are for Evangelicals, Too

I T WAS A MONDAY EVENING IN JANUARY, 1982. I was sitting in on a class entitled *Signs, Wonders, and Church Growth* that we were offering on an experimental basis at the School of World Mission, a part of Fuller Seminary where I am a professor. We had invited John Wimber—a man we knew and trusted—to teach the course. We were aware that up until about 1976 John had been at least as skeptical as we were about so-called "faith healers." Yet clearly something had changed for him since now he was pastoring a rapidly growing church with a healing ministry.

Personally, I had been wanting for some time to learn about spiritual power. Therefore I strongly supported the offering of the course and even decided to attend the sessions. So I was in that classroom in January of 1982 because I wanted to be. But what I saw happening was quite different from what usually happened either in the classes or the churches I attended. People were getting healed in class! This smacked of Pentecostal or charismatic Christianity, and I was an Evangelical. Do I really belong here? I asked myself.

I remembered on occasion watching faith healers on TV. One picture especially kept coming back to me. It was of Kathryn Kuhlman. I remember watching and listening to her in a state of disbelief. She is weird! I concluded. And I never tuned in to her again. A stereotype developed from that experience that kept me from opening myself up to others who claimed to have a healing ministry. Why was I behaving differently now?

I had to a large extent overcome my early dispensational training against the possibility of God working through faith healers today. But I continued to interpret the Scriptures as I always had, assuming that Jesus' healing ministry was something he could do as God but that I could not do as a mere man. I still assumed that the "power and authority to drive out all demons and to cure diseases" that Jesus gave the disciples (Lk 9:1) was just for them and a few others in the early centuries of the Christian era. So though I now believed that a few today might also have been given the gift of healing, I had never seen such a gift in operation. Therefore I acted as if it didn't exist.

I had, however, been opening up to some extent. For example, I had ceased to tremble when I met a Pentecostal! I had learned that they were usually decent people. And at least in my presence, they didn't always act like Kathryn Kuhlman! In fact, I had even published statements to the effect that missionaries need to know how to pray effectively for healing if they are to adequately represent Jesus Christ to the peoples of the world.

But now my openness was being put to the test. An African student I knew well went forward for prayer one evening. He had just spent two weeks in the hospital where he had been taken with severe pain in his chest and shoulders. The doctors had put him through a series of tests but could find nothing medically wrong with him. Yet he hurt badly. John Wimber prayed for him right up in front of the class. And the pain left immediately! During the remaining months of his time with us, he told us that the pain never returned!

A similar thing happened to my colleague, C. Peter Wagner, who had been suffering from high blood pressure for several years. He requested and received prayer in class for the ailment. His doctor then, after several examinations, took him completely off the medicine he had been taking to control the blood pressure.

But this classroom experience involved more than just the manifestation of healings. Wimber and others kept having what they called "words of knowledge" concerning the physical conditions of various people in the class. Someone would see a picture in his or her mind, or feel a strange pain, or receive an impression concerning a physical problem someone was experiencing. When the "word" was announced, John would ask the person with that problem to stand or come forward to be prayed for. I remember a young woman in the class, who was not even one of the team members, telling us that she had been given a picture of someone's lower back with a very shiny object in the middle of it. It turned out to apply to another young woman who had a back problem and was wearing a brace with a shiny rivet in it!

My Evangelical Roots

You can imagine my reaction to all of this. I grew up in a more or less "typical" Evangelical church in Connecticut where I imbibed a dispensational approach to Christianity. We carried Scofield Bibles and learned the details of God's plan for the ages from that perspective. Our pastors and teachers contended strongly that the miracles recorded in the Bible had actually happened. Our dispensational interpretations, however, kept us from wondering why they did not seem to happen today.

My conversion to Christ took place at a Christian camp when I was twelve. My mother a few years earlier had given her life to the Lord in response to a letter received from a missionary cousin working in Africa. So she packed off my brother and me to the camp to find Jesus as our Lord and Savior.

Influenced by the ethos of the small church we attended, I soon became serious enough about my faith to volunteer for missionary service. As the end of high school approached, I applied to and was accepted at Wheaton College with three things in mind: 1) to prepare for missionary work in Africa; 2) to find a wife; and 3) to prove myself to my dad by becoming good at athletics.

My major was anthropology with a specialization in linguistics. My future wife and I then felt called to go to Africa as Bible translators. After college, we entered Ashland Theological Seminary. There we signed on with The Missionary Board of the Brethren Church to go to Nigeria to help establish a mission among a small tribal group known as the Higi. During our seminary days, we picked up an additional year of specialized anthropology and linguistic studies.

Taking a Powerless Christianity to Africa

Theologically and experientially, we were typical Evangelicals. As missionaries we were well prepared in theological, cultural, and linguistic studies. As Evangelicals, however, we were totally unprepared to deal with the one area the Nigerians considered most important—their relationships with the spirit world. Time after time Nigerians would turn our discussions to the disruption in their lives they claimed were caused by evil spirits. Such things as disease, accidents, death, the infertility of humans, animals, and fields, drought, and the disruption of relationships were all seen as the work of these evil entities.

Though the Nigerian church leaders decided that a primary strategy would be to focus on God's conquest of the spirits through Christ, I was in no position to assist them. I tried to believe in the reality of evil spirits, but I was just plain ignorant in this area. I was, the Nigerians told me, more open than my missionary colleagues to accepting the reality of the spirit world and appreciating its importance in their lives. Nevertheless, neither my anthropological nor my biblical and theological training had provided me with any constructive approaches to meet their felt need.

The power of God to heal and deliver from demons was a frequent theme of the Nigerian leaders in their preaching (I did not preach). But we never demonstrated what we claimed in this area. So those we sought to reach were not very impressed with that part of our message. There seemed to be more visible power in their old ways than in Christianity. As missionaries we had brought an essentially powerless message to a very power-conscious people.

In spite of this deficiency, many Nigerians still found other good reasons for becoming Christian, and the churches grew. Many found their new relationship to Jesus Christ fulfilling and rejoiced in his acceptance, forgiveness, and love. But they learned not to expect power—except in the material realm where we had brought Western medicine, schools, agriculture, and even a Western approach to Christianity—all in the name of Jesus.

The Nigerians "knew" that whatever power Christianity brought it wasn't adequate to deal with such things as tragedy, infertility, relational breakdowns, and troublesome weather. It didn't meet many of their deepest spiritual needs. Even though this was puzzling to them—given the fact that Christian leaders talked such a good game—they simply accommodated by developing a kind of dual allegiance: a loyalty to Christianity to handle certain needs paralleled by a continuing loyalty to traditional religious practitioners to handle their power needs. As missionaries we decried this practice, but we had no effective antidote.

Though we talked a great deal about spiritual things, the Nigerians understood most aspects of spirituality much better than we did. I'm afraid we were doing what Paul accuses the Galatians of doing: starting in the Spirit but then turning to human power (Gal 3:3). In the name of Christ, as if this was the best he could offer, we had simply reproduced Western secularized approaches to illness, accident, education, fertility, agriculture, and every other problem of life. We acted as though Western scientific methods were more effective than prayer.

We did pray, of course, calmly for ordinary things and fervently when things got really bad. But Western secular techniques were our first choice, God was our last resort. Without meaning to, we taught our African converts that the Christian God works only through Western cultural ways (though they soon learned that our methods couldn't handle many of their needs). We claimed that we were working in the name and power of God, that it was because of his blessing that these techniques were successful.

But by observing Western doctors, agriculturalists, and teachers who were not Christian, they discovered that there seemed to be little difference in the results of what was done by Christians and what was done by non-Christians—beyond the fact that Christians often applied the same techniques more lovingly. This was an important difference in approach, but the power seemed to be in the techniques and not in the God we talked about. The God of power portrayed in the Scriptures seemed to have died.

This is not to belittle the transforming power of God's love at all. In fact, once the village medicine man became so impressed with the love of the Christians that he began to attend church. His wife had died and a group of the local Christians joined him and his family in mourning her loss. They had so identified with him in his sorrow that he decided to check out Christianity. After a few weeks of church attendance, however, he no longer came.

Though I can't be sure of his reasons for dropping out, my suspicion is that, though he heard in the sermons about an amazing miracle worker who once lived and manifested great power, the local Christians had none of that power themselves. As a matter of fact, these Christians—along with everyone else—came to *him* (not to the pastor) when they needed healing (often after they had tried the medicine recommended by the Christian leaders and found little or no relief from it). Though the love of Christians was impressive, his primary interest was in spiritual power. And if there was no greater power among the Christians than he already possessed, then why join them?

Taking a New Look at Charismatics and Pentecostals

We returned from Nigeria and tended to the business of making a living and raising a family. But during the ensuing years, both my wife and I lived with a certain uneasiness over whether we had been experiencing all there is to Christianity. We both completed graduate study programs and launched into teaching careers (though hers was delayed until our children were on their own).

We remembered fondly the successes of our Nigerian experiences, but our inability to deal adequately with Nigerian spirituality was bothersome. This memory provided a constant, though still fairly weak, motivation for looking into the charismatic movement. But we were so put off by the charismatics and Pentecostals we were acquainted with that we tended to turn away.

Once I became a part of the faculty at Fuller in 1969, however, I had two additional reasons for seeking to learn more about spiritual power. First, faculty discussions of church growth often led us to note that the most rapid growth in worldwide Christianity was taking place among Pentecostal and charismatic churches. My initial reaction was to explain this growth as primarily related to emotionalism, for many of the peoples of the world seek a more emotional expression of their relationship with God than that provided by Evangelicalism.

Yet it soon became obvious that there was more to it than that. With my colleagues, I came to believe that the primary reason for the amazing growth rate of the Pentecostal and charismatic churches was quite simply their ability to address people's need for spiritual power. Though I had no firsthand understanding of what this might mean, I was thus led for the first time to take Pentecostal and charismatic Christianity seriously.

A second nudge came when, through the growth of our student body at Fuller, more and more Pentecostals and charismatics began to come to campus. My unfavorable television exposure to certain Pentecostals and charismatics, like Kathryn Kuhlman, made it difficult for me to accept these students as "normal." Yet greater exposure to people with this perspective added to my growing respect for what God was doing through them around the world. It led me to be more open with them as Christians and to their points of view on ministry.

These were the years during which I was writing *Christianity in Culture* (published in 1979 by Orbis Books). As I read through that book now, I am surprised to note that there are a substantial number of statements that indicate my changing perspective and lay a foundation for what has happened to me during the last seven years. I allude several times to the importance of the spirit world to most peoples and note the greater effectiveness of Pentecostals in dealing with this issue. I also assert the inadequacy and partialness of any presentation of Christianity that does not address healing and deliverance. Further, I suggest that, for most of the peoples of the world, healing is a theological problem and not simply a technological one. Beyond these contentions, I had—without any conscious influence from Pentecostals—endorsed a view of revelation much like theirs. It just seemed to me that if God is alive, he must still be revealing himself.

Such positions have, of course, taken on new meaning for me now. I still consider myself an Evangelical, but I see the hand of God clearly leading me through such events into further truth (Jn 16:13)—truth and experience that have been all too often ignored by Evangelicals.

A Credible Witness

It was, however, the *Signs and Wonders* course conducted by John Wimber in 1982 that brought these things into sharper focus. I had met John on several occasions between 1975 and 1977 while he was working with Peter Wagner in what was then known as the Fuller Evangelistic Association (FEA). I did not know him well at the time, but I came to respect him as a church growth analyst. He was not involved in a healing ministry at that point and was, it seemed, even skeptical of the degree of openness we on the missions faculty had to the miraculous. When I heard then that he had left FEA to start a church with a focus on healing, I became curious. Through Wagner, who had maintained contact with him, I was assured that Wimber was not "going off the deep end." Therefore when his name was proposed as the adjunct professor for the course, I was more curious than troubled.

Thus Wimber became for me what communication theorists call "a credible witness." His background and mine were very similar. I could identify with both his experience of Evangelical Christianity and the unfulfilled need he had for real spiritual power. His rational and unemotional, yet clearly powerful and scripturally based approach made a lot of sense to me. It wasn't long before I was following his lead and experiencing Christianity with power for the first time in my life.

This Christianity with Power Is for Evangelicals

This is why I'm writing primarily to Evangelicals—my own kind. Just as Wimber was able to speak to me through his background and experience, so I am writing as an Evangelical to Evangelicals about a new understanding and experience of Christianity. I have long been part of a branch of Christianity that I feel has believed correctly and accomplished much for God in nearly all areas except that of spiritual power. So I am not about to give up the good things that have been a part of my own Evangelical Christian experience for nearly half a century. Indeed, these good things are more meaningful to me than ever before. But I have now experienced more of what Jesus expected of us than my Evangelical heritage had provided for me. So I offer that to my fellow Evangelicals.

I want all that God has for us in this area, but in a balanced, reasonable way. The extremes in power ministry still bother me greatly. I have no desire to move toward those extremes. As I attempt to analyze my own experience, I see genuine growth in an area of legitimate Christian experience that I had previously not explored. "Why," I ask, "should this area be the exclusive preserve of Pentecostals and charismatics?" If—as I believe God has been showing me over the last seven years—spiritual power is the birthright of all Christians, why are we Evangelicals not appropriating this part of our inheritance?

Ministering in spiritual power was integral to Jesus' ministry. And he didn't seem to be very emotional about it. Jesus simply took the authority and exercised the power his Father gave him. Then he deliberately gave the same power and authority to his disciples (Lk 9:1) and later in his ministry instructed them to "teach [your own disciples] to obey everything I have commanded you" (Mt 28:20).

I want to obey whatever Jesus meant by "everything." And I want the same for you. For years I have been working at parts of that "everything" that include such things as love, forgiveness, repentance, and communicating the gospel—all those things that as Evangelicals we have rightly committed ourselves to. Now God has added to my experience another part of that "everything": the spiritual power dimension. With all my heart I want the same for you so that you, too, may practice a more complete Christianity—a Christianity with power as well as with love.

To move into this more complete understanding of Christianity, however, you will need to overcome the blockages caused by our Western Evangelical worldview. I pray God's blessing on you as you join me in trying to understand and work through those obstacles.

Take heart, though! Experiencing Christianity with real power is worth the effort.

TWO

Puzzling Reflections in a Mirror

I N 1 CORINTHIANS 13:12, PAUL WRITES, "What we see now is like a dim image in a mirror; then we shall see face-to-face. What I know now is only partial; then it will be complete—as complete as God's knowledge of me."

God alone sees reality as it actually is. For God, everything is seen and known absolutely. Whether we think of those things that make up the physical realm—like mountains and rivers—or those aspects of life we call social or psychological or spiritual, God knows and understands exactly and perfectly.

But it is not that way with humans. We observe much of the same reality that God sees. But we perceive it in a limited and biased way because of our humanity. We see but dimly and know only partially—even when we look at the same things God is looking at. Our view, unlike God's, is fuzzy and partial. In our human state, no matter how sincere and trustworthy we may be, we never see the whole picture as it really is.

The well-known story of the blind men and the elephant[1] points out the same truth. Each blind man experienced a different part of the elephant and then generalized from that experience that the *whole animal* was like that part. One concluded that he was dealing with a hose, because the part he was holding—the trunk—seemed like a hose. Another concluded he was in contact with a tree-like being because he had grasped a leg. The others drew their conclusions from impressions of the elephant's tail, his side, his ear, or his tusks.

And each was right when he concluded that *this part* of the elephant is like a tree, a wall, a hose, a rope, a fan, or a spear. But each was wrong when he generalized about the whole animal on the basis of his limited experience with but one part of the beast.

Now this story has been used in many ways, to prove many points. I am not buying into any of those uses of the story—except for one. I simply want to make the point that there is a reality—symbolized in the story by an elephant—that different people on the basis of differing experiences of that reality interpret differently. They then go on to assume that their limited experiences enable them to conclude with certainty what the whole animal is like. Each one identifies his or her own perception of the part of reality he or she has experienced with the total reality, though none of them has either seen or touched most of the elephant. As the apostle Paul has pointed out, all human beings are like those blind men—seeing and experiencing only in part and dimly at that.

This fact raises at least two problems when we consider the possibility of changing from one perspective to another:

1. As we grew up, we learned only one view on most issues. Our view then seems to be the only one, since it is without competitors.

2. Even if we become aware of other views, we assume that our view is the right one since we trust those who taught it to us. How could our view be mistaken? It was taught to us by our parents and other trustworthy people.

In fact, many of us become dogmatic concerning perspectives we have learned. Only these seem logical and right to us. If our views are logical and right, any other views, any alternative view of reality, must be illogical and wrong. Scholars such as Ian Barbour[2] and Peter Berger[3] have written a good deal about this matter.

Alternative Views of Reality

There are at least four ways of approaching the differences between how human beings understand things, which I will call *reality* with a small "r," and what is actually there (as God sees it), which I will call *REALITY* or Reality with a capital "R."

1. **Denying there is any difference between one's own position and what is absolutely right.** The first approach is to deny that there is any difference. To refer back to the blind men and the elephant story, suppose the first of the blind men had limited experience with the

elephant but had great prestige. He might well have argued that all the rest were wrong, saying *only he understood correctly.* He could contend that he alone "sees" REALITY as God sees it. And since his prestige is high, the others might acquiesce, not realizing that his lack of experience makes it likely that his judgment is wrong.

Such a dogmatic attitude is commonly taken in real life by people whose exposure to ideas different from their own is minimal. Some of these claim God's authority for their ideas. This is also the usual attitude of those who are insecure about their own beliefs and understandings. It is technically called *naive realism.*[4]

This view basically assumes that "my reality" is identical with God's REALITY. Anyone, therefore, who questions my point of view is clearly wrong. I once heard a pastor with this kind of attitude present his views concerning Jesus' second coming. At the end, he stated, "If you disagree with what I am saying, you're not disagreeing with me; you're disagreeing with God!" Though there are some things we as Christians will want to assert strongly and even commit our lives to, we need to be very careful that we don't claim to know the mind of God absolutely in very many areas—especially those (such as the second coming) where equally committed Christians have differing interpretations.

We in Western society are often guilty of taking this kind of a dogmatic point of view about things. After all, we're in charge of the world because we have learned so much through science, aren't we? And science leads people into absolute truth, doesn't it? Or does it? When Western Christians take this position, asserting that it is God who has put us Westerners in charge, they are likely to make dangerous assumptions concerning their understandings of REALITY.

The record of Western science is indeed impressive in certain areas. Western scientists have enabled their societies to gain much more control over the material world than was ever before possible. But one might argue that the world is worse off than ever before in areas not so well handled by science: for example, human relationships, morality, and spirituality. Furthermore, many of our most competent scientists are today questioning the absolute validity of certain basic insights of their disciplines.

2. **Nobody's completely wrong or right.** A second approach to the reality problem is to go to the opposite extreme from the dogmatic attitude. "Anyone's way of doing things is just as good as anyone

else's," some say. "Who are we to judge? Are we God to assert that we can decide which beliefs, customs, and perspectives are right and which are wrong?"

People who take this approach recognize (rightly, I think) that the way one person or one group understands things is not necessarily totally right, while the way another person or group understands the same things is not necessarily all wrong. But then they go to the extreme of postulating that any view of reality is valid as long as it is held sincerely. Their contention is that reality is not a given. That is, there is no REALITY or, if there is, it is irrelevant. Reality with a capital "R" is but a mental construct produced by people in their minds. Such a position has been labeled *idealistic or intuitive*.

The extreme position such as that held by many of the peoples of India maintains that whatever reality is attributed to psychological, spiritual, or even material things exists only because humans have created it, not because it really exists. Moral standards and religious and philosophical beliefs, for example, are only psychological constructs produced by people to meet certain needs. They are not to be taken as perceptions of something more real than something else.

For many Indians even material objects such as mountains or elephants are seen as illusory. If someone thinks an elephant is a kind of tree, it *is* a kind of tree for that person. If someone else thinks it is a rope, it *is* a rope for him or her. To one person it's a tree, to another a rope, to another a wall, because the only reality is what is in our minds. The same holds true with moral standards.

Many Westerners, including philosophers and social scientists who consider themselves relativists, would go a long way toward this extreme position in the conceptual and nonmaterial realm. They would contend that values, morals, and religious or philosophical ideas are merely the products of human thought. Such Westerners would, however, typically believe that material things such as mountains and elephants actually exist.

3. The Agnostic. Some people have adopted an *agnostic* position, contending that if there is a REALITY lying behind perceived reality, we cannot know it.

4. The Two-Realities Position. The position I consider most accurate attempts to avoid all of the extremes just cited. It is technically referred to as *critical realism*. It holds that there are two realities. There is a REALITY "out there." The world outside ourselves does exist both materially and nonmaterially. It is REAL. But there is also a perceptual reality inside our minds. That, too, is real, but it is different in nature from REALITY as God knows it to be.

REALITY and **reality**

There is then both an objective REALITY and a subjective reality. We look at external REALITY and take a kind of photograph of it with our minds. Then we operate on the basis of that mental picture. Thus the REALITY "out there" is mediated to our minds through a mental picture that we ourselves construct.

This view would explain both the differences between our perceptions and God's (1 Cor 13:12) and the changes that take place as God leads us into clearer insight and further truth. Though material, psychological, social, and spiritual REALITY exist and are seen clearly by God, the mental pictures we construct of those parts of REALITY that we observe and analyze may not correspond with God's complete and clear view of it. Our pictures are constructed on the basis of limited and distorted understandings provided by such things as our present and past experience, our psychological makeup, and our sociocultural training—all affected by sin.

Note that we do observe "big R" REALITY, but we perceive or picture it as "small r" reality. Our perception is always subjective, focused, limited, and partial. We always relate it to our own interests and usually embellish it with our imaginations.

We do not see *absolutely*. Yet if human beings do not perceive and respond to their perceptions *adequately*, they will not survive long or well. Inadequate responses to REALITY may lead to such things as physical death, psychological dysfunction, sociological destruction, and spiritual ruin. In the physical realm, those who violate the rules of REALITY by trying to fly without an airplane or by drinking poison tend to not live long or well. Those who violate psychological, social, or spiritual rules likewise forfeit the kind of existence they were meant to have.

Though we cannot understand absolutely, we need to learn as much as possible about REALITY and to adjust our perception of reality accordingly. To do this we must learn to be open to understandings that lie beyond those we now have. We need to keep searching for new insight into REALITY and adjusting our perceptions to those new insights. This involves constant comparison between our present views and those we become aware of through other people and new experiences, including books.

One main source of such comparison is, of course, the Bible. Another is the experience people gain as they relate to God and put the teaching of the Bible into practice. The biblical revelation is a part of "big R" REALITY. Though we do not interpret even the Bible absolutely, God has provided that revelation, plus the guidance and empowerment of the Holy Spirit, to enable us to adjust our perceptions so that we can live adequately in the spiritual area.

In some areas of life, such comparisons—and the adjustments they require when we discover an error in perception—are relatively easy. Several years ago, for example, I was rushed to the hospital with an intense pain in my abdomen. The doctors diagnosed my problem as a ruptured peptic ulcer and proceeded to operate. During the operation, they discovered that their diagnosis had been wrong. But they were close enough to the real problem to ascertain it and to remove a gangrenous appendix. Their perception had been wrong, but they were open to correction, adjusted their approach, and saved my life. Their adjusted perception turned out to be very close to the REALITY of my predicament—perhaps as close as is humanly possible.

In many other areas of life, it is unfortunately not so easy to know whether what we are perceiving is as close to the REAL as was the perception of my doctors. In human relationships, for example, how can we know for sure how a person really feels about us? Or in the realm of ideas, how can we know for sure just what is truth in any given area of thought? Or in the spiritual realm, can we really know what angels or demons are like? Or can we really know whether our interpretation of a given passage of Scripture is the only absolutely correct one? Even Jesus claimed absolute truth only for his personal identity and mission (Jn 14:6), certainly not for our perceptions of him.

Though some will accept this position with regard to natural things, they will claim that God has solved the problem in spiritual matters by providing us with his written Word. Certainly there we can be absolutely certain, they contend. I wish this were so. Unfortunately, even the fact that the Scriptures themselves are inspired does not assure that our interpretations of them are always accurate. In fact, the wide diversity of interpretations of Scripture testifies to the fact that even the REALITY of God's inspired Word is subject to the perceptual reality of human interpretation.

Though God's written revelation may be labeled capital "R" REALITY, the human interpretations of it on which we depend are subject to all of the limitations that have just been discussed. We simply cannot legitimately assume with the naive realist that any human interpretation, even of Scripture, is exactly the same as God's understanding. Yet there are certain human understandings that we regard as trustworthy enough that we commit our lives to them in faith. For example, God loves us. He has redeemed us through his Son. Jesus is the Son of God. And we can be saved through faith in him.

We have to settle for greater or lesser approximations and strive toward ever more adequate perceptions and responses without getting discouraged over the fact that we dare not claim absolute understandings, even of many things that we are willing to die for. I, for example, am giving my life to God on the basis of my understanding of who God is, what he has done, and what he expects of me. I have a high degree of certainty in each of these areas—a certainty I believe to be adequate to undergird my commitment. But I cannot claim the kind of absolute understanding that only God has of anything, even of the God I've given myself to.

Advantages to This Position

There are at least two great advantages to this position:

1. One is the potential for a lessening of dogmatism. The dogmatic person demands that one interpretation be set up as a "party line" that everyone follows. For that alone is truth. But if we recognize that—as Paul says in 1 Corinthians 13:12—we always understand in a fuzzy, partial way, we should be much less tempted to assert our interpretations as if we are absolutely certain that they correspond with God's view.

2. Another advantage is that this position provides us freedom to learn from others. If, for example, you and I disagree on a certain position, we can sit down and discuss the differences and learn from each other. As we both attempt to understand the REALITY that lies beyond our positions, we may decide that your position seems more accurate than mine in certain details, while mine seems to have the advantage in others. We can learn by discussing and comparing, thereby possibly bringing both of our understandings into closer correspondence to REALITY, as well as growing spiritually in the process.

We See Largely What We Are Taught to See

We see then that perception influences all of our interpretations and responses. But how did it happen that we interpret in the way we do, rather than in some other way? Our elders taught it to us, to put it simply. Through the process of being taught our culture, and especially the worldview of our culture, we are trained to see as the other members of our society see. We are strongly indoctrinated long before we seek to make any of our own choices in perceiving reality.

1. **We are taught to interpret in culturally approved ways and rewarded when we conform.** Though a certain number of people choose to be nonconformists, most people go along with the tide. In secular Western society, those who get excited about religion tend to fall into the nonconformist category and pay a social penalty for it. Artistic people also pay a penalty because they tend not to conform to our society's focus on rational, mechanical, and scientific ("left brain") pursuits.

2. **We are taught to see selectively.** There are certain things in focus in any given society and certain things that are out of focus. Material, economic, and political things tend to be very much in focus for Westerners. The existence and influence of spiritual beings, however, is an aspect of REALITY that most Anglo-Americans learn to ignore or deny. Until recently, the destructive influence of industrial pollutants on the atmosphere was also ignored—as was the fact that the high mobility and urban sprawl required of the American workforce is destructive to family life. An aspect of our life that is still largely blurred is the fact that contemporary schooling usually trains the mind without teaching us how to live. Thus we tend to produce adults who may know how to think but often don't know how to live.

3. **Accepting things that confirm what we've been taught.** In considering how to relate to new experience or information, we almost always accept those things that confirm what we have been taught. We usually reject most or all of any position that would raise questions about our present perspective. Because the perspective we have been taught is usually naturalistic, even many committed and

spiritually minded Christians reject contemporary miracles. Yet they typically contend quite emphatically that the biblical accounts of miracles are factual. To hold this view, they have developed the theory that God has changed his method of operation since the first couple of centuries of the church. He must work differently today than he did in biblical times.

4. **As pointed out by Paul, we see REALITY only dimly and partially** (1 Cor 13:12), that is, we see through "lenses" or "filters." The following diagram attempts to portray some of these lenses and to label them. Note that the number of influences, which are indicated by the number of arrows, lessens as we go from one side of the chart to the other. There are, for example, a much greater number of things that happen than there are things we are taught to believe possible. What we eventually focus on to analyze and construct our view of reality comes from much less than what we believe or have experienced.

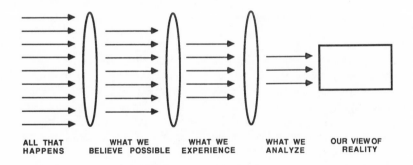

| ALL THAT HAPPENS | WHAT WE BELIEVE POSSIBLE | WHAT WE EXPERIENCE | WHAT WE ANALYZE | OUR VIEW OF REALITY |

Factors Influencing Our View of REALITY

What are the factors, then, that influence our view of REALITY? Among them are the following:

1. **Our Worldview.** By far the most important is *worldview*. We are taught by those who raise us certain socially acceptable patterns concerning what to focus on and how to interpret things. The basis for these patterns is a large number of underlying assumptions that

channel, limit, and focus our perspective. These assumptions and the channels or guidelines we form based on them make up what we call worldview.

We will here define worldview as the *culturally structured assumptions, values, and commitments underlying a people's perception of REALITY.* Worldview is the major influence on how we perceive REALITY. In terms of its worldview assumptions, values, and commitments, a society structures such things as what its people are to believe, how they are to picture reality, and how and what they are to analyze. People interpret and react on this basis reflexively without thinking.

For example, on the assumption that gasoline cans without any apparent liquid in them are "empty," a certain number of Americans have been badly injured by lighting a match too close to them. The American worldview assumption is that a container with liquid in it contains something but that one without liquid in it does not contain anything. The gaseous fumes that can produce an explosion when ignited are not taken into account because we have unconsciously learned to ignore them. Unthinkingly, then, one may light a match too close to such a container, though one is unlikely to light it very close to a container full of liquid gas—a much less dangerous situation.

In Acts 14:8-18, we find another interesting reflexive reaction based on a worldview assumption. This one led to a crosscultural misunderstanding since there were two sets oɪ worldview assumptions in operation. Paul and Barnabas responded in the name of Jesus to the need of a crippled man. From their point of view, they simply used the authority and power Jesus had given them to demonstrate God's love and concern for the lame man. The Lystrans, who were observing the healing, interpreted this event differently, however. Based on their worldview perspective, they made the statement, "The gods have become like men and have come down to us!" (v. 11). One event was interpreted in two quite different ways by those who had learned different worldviews. And Paul and Barnabas had great difficulty in getting the Lystrans to understand that they weren't gods who should be sacrificed to (v. 18).

Worldview, then, is the primary influence on our perception of REALITY. We are taught to view REALITY in socially prescribed ways and are constantly under pressure from the other members of our society to maintain those perspectives. Should we begin to view things differently, we become subject to forms of social ostracism and even ridicule. Worse yet, the socially patterned aspect of our own consciences condemns us and damages our self images. There is great social pressure coming from both external and internal sources to keep us perceiving REALITY according to the worldview of our society. We will come back to this fact later when we deal in more detail with worldview.

2. The Limitations of Our Experience. A second factor influencing our view of REALITY is the *limitations of our experience.* A young boy, for example, may simply not believe how babies come into the world. Though his worldview allows for such understanding, the boy is hindered in his acceptance of even a factual explanation due to his lack of experience with this aspect of life. The certainty of salvation experienced by Christians is another thing that is often difficult to convey to those who have never experienced it. Likewise, those who have never had the experience of seeing a person healed as the result of prayer may deny that it can happen. All of us are hampered to a greater or lesser extent in our attempts to understand the experiences of others that we ourselves have not had.

3. A Person's Personality or Temperament. A third factor influencing the perception of REALITY is *a person's personality or temperament.* Our viewpoints are affected by a series of characteristics that may be partly psychological and partly cultural. Among these are such things as predisposition, motivation, degree of openness to new ideas, a conservative or liberal view of life, an optimistic or pessimistic outlook on life. It is obvious that REALITY looks different to a pessimistic person than to one who is optimistic. A more conservative person takes quite a different attitude toward change than a more liberal person.

4. Our Will. Then there is *the will factor.* We choose to view any given thing either as we have been taught to view it or differently. When confronted with new information or a new experience that may challenge our present views, we will either reconsider our position or remain unchanged in our opinion. In the face of such conflicting data we will be likely to defend our position if we aren't open to change. As we will see later, the place of the will is very important in maintaining or changing one's worldview.

5. The Sin Factor. Woven in with all of these factors is the *presence of sin*. Whether sin is manifested in a rebellious will, in unholy motives, or simply in adding confusion to an already fuzzy perspective, we can be certain that human sinfulness affects every aspect of the way people perceive and respond to the glimpses of REALITY they see.

For all of these reasons, the views we have of REALITY are partial and fuzzy. And when we compare them with the partial and fuzzy understandings of others, we become even more puzzled. This fact is troublesome enough when we ponder its implications for our understandings of the nonessentials of life. But it also applies to the way we perceive God and spiritual things. Is there anything we can do about it? Do we have any choice in the matter?

THREE

How Do Westerners
Picture the World?

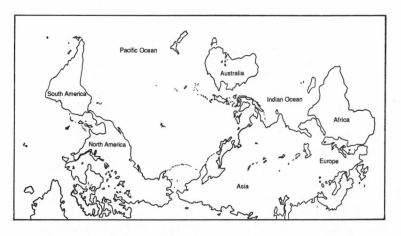

I WAS BROWSING IN AN AUSTRALIAN NEWS SHOP ONE DAY and came across an interesting map. It is entitled "McArthur's Universal Corrective Map of the World." Not to be taken lightly, it is a map that makes a serious statement about the world. One accustomed to traditional maps that picture northern countries at the top of the map with southern countries at the bottom is shocked to find the tips of South America and Africa pointing up! For the map is arranged with the south at the top and the north at the bottom!

But whoever said there could only be one right way of picturing the world? We see the world (both physical and all other aspects of it) as we have been taught to see it. It is a part of our worldview to assume that our way of seeing the world is right. Viewing it in any other way seems both strange and wrong to us as Westerners.

And whoever implied that any given worldview would picture everything correctly? Those who taught us, that's who. We from the Western nations bordering the North Atlantic have been taught or allowed to assume that our perception of reality is the same as absolute REALITY itself. And this impression is strengthened by the fact that our societies seem to be in charge in the world. How could we be wrong when we are so powerful?

This is the problem of worldview. As pointed out in the previous chapter, we see as we have been taught to see. And we have been taught to see only one way. North is always up! Study the map I have included. See if you don't experience some shock at this altogether different view of the world.

The Influence of "The Enlightenment" on Western Worldviews

Just as surely as we from European and American societies have learned that north is always up, we have also learned that there are no invisible beings in the universe. We are taught to believe only in visible things. "Seeing is believing," we are told. If we can see it, then it must exist. If we can't see it, it must not exist. We are allowed to believe in certain invisible things only if our scientists tell us they exist. Radio waves fall into this category (though we may have trouble believing in radio waves even with the authority of scientists backing their existence).

For centuries a supernaturalistic perspective was an important part of the worldview of the peoples of northern Europe and those from among them who fled to America to escape religious persecution. People were, to be sure, often quite superstitious and uncritical concerning accounts of purported miracles. Accounts of demonic manifestations and of witchcraft often even produced panic. And unscrupulous religious leaders and others were often quick to take advantage of such credulity. In fact, an important part of the reason for Luther's revolt against the Roman Catholic church lay in his deep concern about some abuses in church practice that played on certain superstitions.

Yet during the centuries following the Reformation, this revolt broadened into one against any institutionalized religion and then one against any expression of supernaturalism. By the end of the eighteenth century, the so-called "Enlightenment" was in full swing, prompting the great thinker Immanuel Kant in 1784 to write an article contending:

[The] Enlightenment was man's coming of age. It was man's emergence from the immaturity which caused him to rely on such external authorities as the Bible, the church, and the state to tell him what to think and do. No generation should be bound by the creeds and customs of bygone ages. To be so bound is an offense against human nature, whose destiny lies in progress.[1]

Such Enlightenment thinkers included Kant, Newton, Rousseau, Voltaire, and American founders Franklin and Jefferson. In general they held "a deistic view of God, acknowledging his existence as Creator but leaving the conduct of life to man and his reason"[2] This was the age in which modern science was being born. Humans became very impressed with themselves and with their ability to work things out rationally. The mechanistic view of the universe commonly held by Euro-Americans is a product of these times, as are the basic ideas on which much of our schooling depends. Scientific thinking and reason became the keys to release us from enslavement to disagreeable social, political, and religious bondages.

The quest for a so-called superior, more rational view of life led Enlightenment thinkers to be:

highly critical of the traditional appeal, made by Christian apologists, to fulfilled prophecy and miracles as proof of divine attestation of Christianity. They argued that the Old Testament passages that were alleged to be fulfilled did not really predict the events concerned and that the New Testament miracles did not really happen.[3]

So out went the baby with the bath water. In reacting against the excesses of extreme religious credulity, Enlightenment thinkers threw out, or at least raised serious questions about, belief in anything that could not be rationally understood. And these assumptions have become a part of our worldview so that quite unconsciously we have all imbibed their influence from birth.

Because such Enlightenment influence has become so strong in our societies, modern Westerners—both non-Christian and Christian—now find it extremely difficult to believe in angels, Satan, demons, and even God. Whether or not real spiritual power can be exercised through prayer, then, is seriously questioned both outside and inside our churches. For the spiritual real is not considered scientifically or rationally verifiable. It is no longer considered a part of the Western understanding of the REAL.

Many, of course, stand against part of the worldview pressure and do believe in the existence of God. Yet he is usually perceived, even by many committed Christians, as some vague and distant figure—an absentee landlord who used to do wonderful things and who someday may do them again. But he seems largely irrelevant or at least inactive to most people.

Characteristics of Western Worldviews

Most of us are quite unconscious of the majority of our basic underlying worldview assumptions and values. We learn them unconsciously as we grow up, largely by imitating our elders. And, unless we travel to or read about other societies who picture life differently, we may never question those assumptions. It is important, therefore, right at the beginning of our discussion, to look at some of that unconscious part of us that so totally affects our vision and behavior.

It is interesting (and discouraging) to note that even though we are Christians, our basic assumptions are usually more like those of the non-Christian Westerners around us than we like to admit. We have, as Christians, made certain modifications. But even though there is often a wide discrepancy between the teachings of Scripture and the common Western assumptions listed below, we often find ourselves more Western than scriptural. At least we find the greatest tensions between our Western cultural/worldview assumptions and values and those of Christ, to whom we have committed ourselves. This tension is especially acute if we seek to be more open in the area of spiritual power.

The purpose of listing the following Western worldview assumptions is not to condemn us or to put down our way of life. Our culture and worldview are in most respects neither worse nor better than others. Due to human limitations and sinfulness, however, we find that every human product (such as a worldview) embodies features that make God's action difficult. Though there are in Western worldviews certain features that can be quite helpful to the cause of Christ, we seek here to become more aware of those that may obstruct it.

1. Our worldview is naturalistic. In comparison to other societies, Americans and other North Atlantic peoples are *naturalistic*. Non-Western peoples are frequently concerned about the activities of supernatural beings. Though many Westerners retain a vague belief in God, most deny that other supernatural beings even exist. The wide-ranging supernaturalism of most of the societies of the world is absent for most of our people.

Indeed, unlike most of the peoples of the world, we divide the world into what we call "natural" and what we call "supernatural." And then we largely disregard the supernatural. Our focus is squarely on the natural world, with little or no attention paid to the supernatural world.

For example, when someone gets sick, our first question is a naturalistic one: *What* caused it? We assume that the cause was a germ or some other such natural substance. Or if there is an automobile accident, we ask: *What* went wrong? Our assumption is that something mechanical failed, or some chance occurrence resulted in the two vehicles being at the same point at the same time.

Most non-Western peoples—including the Nigerians I worked with—would have asked a "supernaturalistic question" instead. They might have asked: "Which spirit caused me to get ill or to have an accident?" Or, "Who might I have offended? Is this person taking revenge on me by having a spirit afflict me?" Not that their question is any better than ours. But the contrast points out the difference between the two types of assumptions.

Most of us as Western Christians would not make these kinds of assumptions about the workings of spirits. But we do claim to assume that God is involved in all of our everyday activities. And yet we often base our thinking and behavior on naturalistic assumptions almost as much as do our non-Christian neighbors and friends. We, too, are likely to explain disease, accidents, and most other occurrences of life as if God doesn't exist.

A generation ago a prominent anthropologist named Clyde Kluckhohn included in an introductory text a perceptive chapter on the United States viewed from an anthropological point of view. With no Christian commitment that I know of and seemingly no axe to grind—he states that American society is profoundly irreligious:

> More than half of our people still occasionally go through the forms . . . But very few of our leaders . . . are convinced that prayer or the observance of church codes will affect the course of human events. . . . belief in God's judgments and punishments as a motive for behavior is limited to a decreasing minority. Feelings of *guilt* are common but a sense of *sin* is rare.[4]

Western societies have specialized in producing scientists, engineers, and technicians to develop new theories and plans for action to control the substances and processes of nature. We seem to have listened to God's command in Genesis 1:28 for humans to conquer and control the earth. And we have gone at it with a vengeance.

We have done well at it, too—some might say too well. Never has any people gained so much control over the natural world and its processes. We can lift heavier loads, move people and goods, and project voices and pictures farther and faster than has ever been done before. The production of new machines and techniques to keep up with such inventiveness is truly amazing. Innovations in food technology, medicine, engineering, the creation of synthetic substances, the refining of natural substances, and the like have far outstripped even the wildest imaginings of our ancestors.

In the process, however, Western peoples have developed what might be termed a "technological mindset." We seem to see the universe and all within it as machines, operating according to rules that we call "natural laws" without reference to God or other beings or powers that exist and operate outside the realm of what we consider "natural" or "normal." If we do admit the existence of such beings, we tend to regard them as having little, if any, influence on the "normal" processes according to which the universe and all within it operate.

Westerners, including most Christians, act as if God is largely unconcerned with day-to-day affairs. Though our doctrinal statements speak of his sustaining activity, we seem to assume that he simply set the universe going and has left it to continue on its own power, operating according to "natural laws." (See chapter four for more on this subject.) Occasionally we interpret something that happens as a miracle, but by definition we see such an act as a matter of God's *interference in normalcy*. This seems to contrast with Jesus' view that such acts ought to be considered normal in the kingdom of God.

Westerners frequently even see humans as machines, governed by physical rules that we have largely mastered and by psychological rules that we're just beginning to understand. When something goes wrong in our bodies or our minds, we go to a doctor or a psychologist to get fixed, as if we were machines and they were the repairmen. Only when their mechanical diagnoses don't seem to work do we explore the possibility that what ails us might be helped by something other than "natural" healing techniques. Even Christians often do not think of praying for healing until all naturalistic measures have been exhausted.

I was discussing this matter with a group of missionaries once. To illustrate my point, I asked for a show of hands on the question, "When an illness or accident occurs, how many of you think of a doctor or medicine first before you think of prayer?" Both they and I were amazed to see nearly every hand raised to indicate they thought of the naturalistic solution first! Indeed, the one person in the group who was openly charismatic sheepishly illustrated the point; he shared that he too had turned to medicine before prayer recently when he had sprained his ankle.

The majority of the creative minds in Western societies largely ignore the spiritual nature of humans or confuse it with our psychological makeup. And the possibility of nonhuman spiritual beings in the universe who can really make a difference is generally considered fiction. As humans, we are understood to be the products of natural processes such as evolution and sexual relations. The concept of humans made in the "image of God" seems puzzling, even to many Christians.

2. **Materialism dominates Western society.** Is it any wonder, then, that we are *materialistic*? As the bumper sticker states, "The one who collects the most goodies wins." "Goodies" are the things we can see. They make us more comfortable because we believe they enable us to be more in control of our physical surroundings. They are the things that can be seen and used to gauge our superiority over others in the race to get even more goodies.

When we look at a scene or a situation, what catches our eye? People of another society might comment on the relationships of the people in the situation. But we tend to focus on material objects. In our daily life we seek such objects—especially if we feel they will bring us more comfort, more security, more of a cushion against an unfriendly world. When we think of achievement, we tend to measure it in terms of the material wealth that accompanies it. Unlike many of the other peoples of the world, we define wealth and poverty purely in material terms. Usually we measure it by the amount of money we have.

"How poor you are," says the rural Filipino to his American acquaintance, "you have no relatives." Yet the American feels he's "made it." He can't quite figure out what the Filipino means. He has enough material wealth to travel around the world to visit this Filipino peasant whom he pities, because he lacks so many of the material things the American values so highly. And just look at the number of children running around the Filipino's house. "Don't they know anything about birth control?" the American thinks to himself, not knowing that from the rural Filipino point of view, those children are his social security—his wealth and protection against the uncertainties of old age.

The bottom line is that we sell our energy and our time to gain as much of a surplus of buying power as possible in order to fill our lives with the seeming security of material things. With our eyes focused on the visible, then, we classify that as "real" and the invisible as "unreal." To quote Kluckhohn again:

> Money comes closer with us than with any other people to being the universal standard of value. . . . Possession of gadgets is esteemed as a mark of success to the extent that persons are judged not by the integrity of their characters or by the originality of their minds but by what they seem to be—so far as that can be measured by the salaries they earn or by the variety and expensiveness of the material goods which they display.[5]

3. Western society is humanistic. Since we believe our achievements have come through unaided human effort, we focus on human accomplishments and abilities. We become *humanistic* in our outlook. Though human accomplishment is indeed impressive, many seem to believe that there are no limits to it; and, of course, no outside spiritual assistance is needed.

It is just a matter of time and effort, we believe, before we conquer such-and-such a disease or learn how to control the weather. And if we can just create an organization big and powerful enough to handle the whole world, we will at last have attained peace. Though in previous stages of Western societies humans were considered inherently evil, large numbers of our contemporaries seem to assume—in spite of much evidence to the contrary—that those who have achieved so much in conquering the natural world, those who have produced so many impressive material things, are surely not evil.

It is the structures that cause the problems, they say. If we could only throw off these constraining structures and become genuinely free, we would certainly be good. And if we could only apply our technical expertise to the social problems around us, we would certainly be able to conquer them just as we have conquered nature. Just as scientific education was the means to conquest of the natural world, so it will be the means to conquest in the human realm. Humans can do it, we say, for we are invincible! Nothing is impossible.

So we freeze corpses, awaiting the day when our scientists will discover a cure for whatever the person died of. And we expect the quick development of some miracle cure for whatever disease we may have. And we go to the psychiatrist to get a quick fix on some psychological or relational problem we can't seem to handle alone. Or we read the latest expert's advice on how to improve our body or our mind to live up to society's unrealistic expectations for achieving the "perfect you."

It was not always thus. Our societies became humanistic gradually. In the Middle Ages, Western peoples acknowledged God as so much in control of the universe that many had become quite fatalistic. All that happened was understood to be God's will. Over several centuries, however, as wealth began to be used to encourage creativity, as knowledge began to be shared, as states merged into nations, and universities, commerce, exploration, and empires came into vogue, fatalism diminished.

Western societies passed through the Renaissance, the Reformation, the Enlightenment, and a wide variety of ripples and spinoffs from these movements. Scientists such as Bacon, Galileo, and Newton, and philosophers such as Hume, Descartes, Hegel, and Kant emerged—often paying a high social price for their ideas and inventions. The result: God and the church were dethroned, and the human mind came to be seen as savior. It is ignorance, not Satan we are to fight. And our weapons are human minds and technology. God, if there be a God, only helps those who do it all themselves.

Thus, by the nineteenth century, God had become irrelevant to most Westerners.

Now our real religion is science, and our priests are the scientists. For it is science that gives us control over the material universe and the promise of future control over everything else.

4. Reason has become our primary way of understanding REALITY. The key to such developments culminating in our present control over the material universe is the way we have used our intellects to gain knowledge—knowledge of what we can see, touch, and feel. This knowledge is gained through reason. So Westerners came to seek explanations for all things based on human logic and reason. We call such an approach *rationalism*. Having taken the natural, material world as the central focus of our lives, the application of our kind of logic and reason to that data became our primary approach to understanding. Thus intuition came to be scorned as did any claim to knowledge of nonmaterial things.

At the height of the eighteenth-century movement called the Enlightenment, objective truth and even ethics were thought to be discoverable through the rational analysis of experience. It was, therefore, the task of philosophers and theologians to apply the same kind of intellectual approach to these problems as the physical scientists applied to the realm of material entities and processes. In philosophy and theology as in the natural sciences, the very important part played by human intuition and imagination in the discovery process was ignored and scorned. So was any recognition of unseen beings and powers, since they were not subject to the rigors of rational analysis.

5. We highly value individualism and independence. To us, unlike most contemporary traditional peoples and the biblical Hebrews, the individual is the reality and groups are but abstractions made up of collections of individuals. We seem to have little of the sense of corporateness that we see so often in the Old Testament, where the behavior of one person brings blessing or punishment on a whole group.

Besides the self-centeredness this engenders and legitimizes, it creates for us a kind of private world within which we are captives, alone and hiding from others. We often experience little real relating to others or to God. Frequently we are so unaware of what others think and experience that we feel we are the only ones struggling with many of the most common problems of everyday life.

Such social isolation makes us hunger for the satisfaction of our innate need for substantial relationships with others and with God. We have even made Christianity into an individualistic, private affair. It is often our Christian acquaintances—those we should be able to share ourselves with—that we hide from the most, afraid that if they find out what we really are like, they will condemn us. We may even fear to go to them when we are in difficulty. And the "live and let live" philosophy of the non-Christians around us becomes a part of us as well.

This determination to "go it alone" also makes both Christians and non-Christians very vulnerable to Satan in the deepest recesses of our being. This is particularly true in emotional areas since we tend to focus so completely on the externals of life in our social relationships. This means that emotion is a private thing and to be dealt with privately. Problems such as anger, bitterness, unforgiveness, worry, fear, and lust are to be kept out of sight, even though they fester within us and make us sick. Satan is then free to gnaw away at our emotional problems like a rat working under cover of darkness.

Many of my experiences during the past few years praying with emotionally damaged people bear out this tragedy. Typical is a young man I will call Bill. Bill, like many American men, had suffered great emotional pain in relation to his father. He never felt his father cared whether he lived or died. The only times he can remember his father even noticing him were when he did something wrong. But Bill learned early on that real men don't get emotional or upset at such things. They keep it all within. As rugged individualists, men stand on their own two feet, never mentioning their anger and bitterness. Then such men are puzzled over the fact that they find it difficult to relate openly and warmly to their wives and children. Nor can they explain why their sons also feel they have a father who doesn't care about them.

Yet, ironically, we are expected by our society to use our individualism to conform! Our isolation and lack of understanding about others and their experience of life engenders a fear of being different, even as we loudly proclaim our right to be different. So we feel driven to join groups. Someone has called the United States a nation of joiners. We seek to be in association with others to try to prove that we are not alone in the world, that at least some people agree with us. In point of fact, we are expected to use our individual freedom to conform to our peers. Even in rebellion we conform, as did the hippies and the Jesus people, and now the "me generation."

But individualism does have a bright side. In our public world we are expected to conform. Our faith in such things as rationality, democracy, and science are public matters. Any serious questioning concerning the validity of these values is therefore not likely to be taken lightly by those around us. Yet we are allowed some leeway in our private world. If we feel secure enough to risk the negative opinions of others, we can make changes in such private affairs as our religious ideas. A person can get away with some "deviance" from the norm in the area of such beliefs, opinions, and values if he or she is careful enough. (This fact will become relevant in a later chapter when we discuss the possibilities for change in one's perspectives concerning spiritual power.)

6. **Westerners do tend to be open to change.** Another hopeful aspect of Western worldviews is their openness to *change*. We have experienced so much that we consider beneficial through changes in life resulting from scientific and technological achievements that we tend to welcome change in most areas of life.

Yet Westerners tend to be much more hesitant when it comes to change in religious ideas or allegiances. The feeling seems to be that since so much change is going on in nearly every other area of life, we should keep change in religious traditions to a minimum. This area of life is to provide an anchor, a solid footing, security, and protection from the relativity around us. Not that conservatism in religion is all bad. We need to commit ourselves to God and his purposes. But an unthinking, culturally inculcated commitment to mere religious traditions is shown over and over again in the Bible to keep people from God's best.

Nevertheless, Western peoples are potentially open to change, even in the area of religion. The major question seems to be, "On what basis will they be open?"

Felt Needs

Those who study the conditions under which people change like to speak of "felt needs." These are needs or wants that people have a strong urge to satisfy. When hungry, a person experiences the need for food. When unable to pay the bills, he or she desires more money. When lonely, a person feels the need for companionship. The key idea here is that when the answers of science, materialism, humanism, and naturalism fall short, people then begin to look for spiritual answers.

An increasing number of Western peoples seem to be coming to feel that our traditional naturalistic perspectives are not providing them with satisfactory answers to at least some of life's problems. Many are turning to the occult. One does not have to travel far in any of our cities to discover that palm readers, spirit mediums, and the purveyors of the "New Age" are very active. Within Christianity itself, charismatic and Pentecostal expressions are becoming more visible and acceptable.

In addition to the hunger being generated by dissatisfaction within our societies, more and more people are traveling and discovering that north doesn't necessarily have to be pictured as "up." There are other answers out there if the ones we have been taught aren't any longer satisfying.

One of the felt needs many Evangelicals experience is the sense that there must be more to Christianity than we have witnessed so far. "Why is our experience of Christianity so different from what we read about in the New Testament?" we ask. "What is wrong with our brand of Christianity? Is there more?"

FOUR

Enlightenment Christianity Is Powerless

IT WAS ABOUT 4:30 A.M. The call at our door was insistent. "Mr. Kraft! Mr. Kraft! Wake up! Vangawa is very ill!" Sleepily I came to and went with my Nigerian co-workers to the home where Vangawa, a young village church leader, lived. We found him curled up on his sleeping mat burning with fever and not in his right mind. The medicine provided by his friend who ran the local clinic hadn't reduced the fever. The only thing left was to take him in my Jeep over an hour's worth of rain-gutted dirt roads to the mission hospital.

We prayed, of course, "Oh Lord, if it be your will, please heal Vangawa." But there was no seeking the Lord to discern how he wanted to minister to his ill servant, no authority in our prayers, no claiming the power he has given us to minister healing. We thought we knew how to handle the situation. It is God who has given us modern medicine, isn't it? Since he is a God of common sense, then, of course he would want us to take Vangawa to the hospital immediately and let him heal through medicine. So we didn't seek God for direct intervention with real earnestness. We simply bundled the sick young man up and headed for the hospital, asking God to bless *our* strategy.

God was merciful. He healed Vangawa from spinal meningitis through the medical treatment he received. Vangawa was so grateful, he gave himself to learning the kind of medicine that had helped to heal him and thereafter ran village medical clinics himself.

My point is not that by praying authoritatively we surely could have induced God to heal Vangawa. Nor could we be sure that enough faith on our part would have done the job. And it certainly would have been foolish to simply pray and not take him to the hospital. What I am saying, rather, is that our attitude was such that we only gave God one option—that of healing through medicine. I don't believe we really honored God in that situation. Without even taking the time to consult him we turned to a human facility that we knew we could trust.

Such behavior on our part was quite confusing to the local Christians, however. On Sundays they would hear messages about a wonderful healer named Jesus who used to do wonderful things in a faraway land long ago. Then they would be told that he had risen from the dead and was still alive. They were to pledge allegiance to him as Savior and Lord and God, for only thus could they gain eternal life. But he no longer healed or spoke. Healing came now through secular medicine, and Jesus' voice could only be heard by those who went to school and learned to read the Bible.

We missionaries had taught them what we knew of Christianity. For this is how we had learned to treat the sick at home. If someone got sick, our reflex action was to turn to medicine and doctors, praying as fervently as we dared that God would use these secular means to get his will done. For we had been taught that somehow the power and authority to heal that Jesus had given his disciples had petered out after the early centuries of Christianity. Our professors taught that these early centuries had been a time of special grace to get the church off and running. Signs and wonders were needed then, but now we don't need that kind of power.

It was as if we had imitated the Galatians, to whom Paul says, "How can you be so foolish! You began by God's Spirit; do you now want to finish by your own power?" (Gal 3:3). What it amounted to is that we were really practicing a form of Christianity so strongly influenced by our Western Enlightenment worldview that we knew little else to do but to turn to naturalistic, human technique-centered methods for solving problems.

In our own way, we were like the medicine man referred to in chapter one. We, like him, experienced no spiritual power to resolve problems within Christianity, so we turned to our socially approved source of power. For us this source of power lay in secular medicine; for him it lay in the spiritual power of evil spirits.

Practicing Deists

In many ways our Evangelicalism was more like deism than like biblical Christianity. In the New Testament we find Christians appealing to God immediately and insistently whenever a problem occurred. Then, in the guidance, authority, and power received from God they ministered boldly. They believed God was near and always ready to respond graciously in love and power through his servants to those in need. Where in our ministries is the boldness and confidence manifested by Paul and Barnabas in the Acts 14 incident when they healed the lame man to the astonishment of the Lystrans?

As Chuck Swindoll has said, "Our God is some distant deity sitting around in heaven answering theological questions."[1] To the extent that such a comment is true, it shows that we have thrown ourselves right into the arms of deism—a Christian heresy spawned by the Enlightenment. Deists believe that God created the universe and set up unchangeable, universal laws that preclude him from getting directly involved in the running of the universe in any way. As Michael MacDonald puts it in the *Evangelical Dictionary of Theology*:

> [Deism] reduce[s] God's function in creation to that of first cause only. According to the classical comparison of God with a clockmaker . . . God wound up the clock of the world once and for all at the beginning, so that it now proceeds as world history without the need for his further involvement.[2]

As we have seen in chapter three, this deistic view came into vogue as a product of the Enlightenment during the eighteenth century. Though we Evangelicals would contend that deism embodies an unacceptable, even heretical understanding of God's relation to the universe, I'm afraid we may have been infected. I have found altogether too much similarity between my own basic assumptions and those of the deists.

That is why professor, theologian, and pastor Don Williams speaks of the need to "exorcise the ghost of Newton" in order to have a truly supernaturalistic perspective on Christianity. He says:

> What is important to note here is that I was raised with the modern myths of white middle-class, twentieth-century America. My education, the media, and my social relationships all tended to reinforce these unchallenged assumptions about reality. I bought

that part of the American dream determined by progress, service to society, and the discovery of its underlying rational order. Like my father, it was important for me to be in control and to maintain control. My . . . arena was the life of the mind. Here reason was king and I could control people and situations through my intellect. . . .

In my "enlightenment" theological education I was trained to control everything. Paul's dictum to do all things "decently and in order" is lived out by us Presbyterians to a fault. Thus I was given exegetical tools with which to manage the Bible, theological tools with which to manage the faith, homiletical tools with which to manage my sermons, psychological and sociological tools with which to manage people and business tools with which to manage the church. Today's seminary curriculum is far advanced in this application of the scientific method to the professional clergy.[3]

Williams' analysis of his upbringing and education highlights the problem perceptively, especially as it affects Christian ministry today. Under the unconscious influence of the worldview we have been taught, we naturally gravitate toward attempting to control whatever is around us, just as we've been taught to do in scientific investigation. Even in Christian matters, unless we know enough to curb our natural (that is, cultural) inclinations, control is usually the aim and reason is the means—just as is the case in science.

Sadly even very committed Christians—including those in the ministry—regularly fall into this seductive trap. They often resort to it unwittingly by attempting to make even God predictable and controllable. That is the way we have been taught to handle every aspect of life, so it is not surprising that we have carried it over into our practice of Christianity.

The deistic influence surfaces when we seem to assume that God is far away and not really involved in a day-to-day, moment-by-moment way with his creation. He may, on occasion, "interfere" in "natural" processes—especially if we his people are in big trouble and beg him hard enough. But we, like the deists, often act as if *we* have to start anything that needs to be started and carry out whatever is to be carried out. We ask him to bless our plans, of course. But the plans and the control are basically *ours*, not his.

Solving this problem is, of course, not easy. We will turn to that issue after a bit more discussion of certain symptoms of the problem.

Symptoms of Enlightenment Christianity

1. A Pervasive Rationalism. Our Enlightenment heritage has left us with a rationalistic, mind-oriented approach to everything. Even the Scriptures have come to be approached in a purely rational way.[4] Evangelicals haven't carried this to quite the extreme of liberalism—rejecting as "pre-scientific," naive, and nonhistorical all supernatural elements of the Bible, though attempting to retain Scripture's moral teaching. Liberals, in their quest to make the Scriptures palatable to contemporary people, have often made human reason and/or experience supreme.

Instead of attempting to return to at least the more reasonable aspects of the supernaturalism that the Enlightenment overturned, Evangelicals have often argued against the liberal positions from the *same* rationalistic basis. We, like they, have often seen little of God's hand in the present and conducted our defense purely on the basis of what God used to do. We have maintained stoutly that God once did miraculous things—the things recorded in Scripture—and will again do such things at the close of the age.

In the present day, however, Evangelicals tend to believe that God has stopped talking and doing the incredible things we read about in Scripture. Now we see God limiting himself to working through the Bible (the inspired record of what he used to do), plus an occasional contemporary "interference" in the natural course of events. What we usually call a miracle—the power God used to manifest in healing—has been largely replaced by secular medicine. The speaking he used to do now comes indirectly through rationalistic reasoning in books, lectures, and sermons—similar to the process used by the secular sciences.

We pray for guidance and then mostly reason it out. We train people to do God's work by sending them to schools where they learn to reason and think philosophically. But we seldom teach them to relate that philosophical thinking either to God or to the human beings they are supposedly learning to minister to. We have learned from the world how to educate by giving our students knowledge, but the art of training in character has been largely lost. We teach church leaders how to think *about* God and, to a lesser extent, human relationships. But we do not usually teach them how to *relate* to God and to other humans. They learn to lecture rather than to communicate on the assumption—engendered by our experience with science—that what is most needed is more information rather than better relationships on both divine and human levels.

2. **Doing Things Decently and in Order.** In describing his upbringing and education, Williams speaks of the fact that he learned to do things "decently and in order" as we are commanded to do in 1 Corinthians 14:40 (RSV). Well and good. We ought to obey Scripture. The question is how one defines "decently and in order." As Evangelicals, we automatically define it in such a way as to support our own preferred practices. As noncharismatics we even use that verse to justify our disobedience to the command in the previous verse: "Do not forbid the speaking in strange tongues!"

Could it be that God has a different definition of "decently and in order" than Evangelicals do? Obviously he does. For the preceding context in 1 Corinthians 14 makes it clear that Paul is suggesting orderliness in a kind of worship that is more like what charismatics do than like what is found in most Evangelical churches.

In the churches I have attended over the years, for example, we never had to deal with problems such as everyone speaking in tongues (1 Cor 14:23) or everyone prophesying (v. 24) or people getting disorderly as they bring hymns, teaching, revelation, messages in tongues, or interpretations (v. 26)—because everything was controlled from up front. Would the Holy Spirit have been allowed to work in these ways? I wonder. If not, is it because we have learned to control church meetings as we would secular meetings, rather than inviting the Holy Spirit to come do whatever he would like to do?

3. **Centering Our Church Meetings on a Lecture.** Where did our present practice of centering our church meetings on a lecture (called a sermon) come from? It was imported from the surrounding society, especially from the schools. The Reformers—Luther, Calvin, and others—were academics. They were trained by listening to lectures. They judged correctly that their followers needed more information. So, using the pattern current in Western society, they made their lectures/sermons the focal point of the church meetings they led.

Not that all lecturing is bad—though Jesus seldom used this method, preferring a more personal and effective approach in which he always accompanied his words with deeds. And that is the tragedy of our modern custom of centering our meetings around sermons (lectures). It is based on the Enlightenment assumption that what people need most is more information, and the way that information is gotten across is via lecture. This assumption wasn't that far off a couple of centuries ago. But in a generation characterized by an "information glut," people need to *do* something and not just think about what they or others ought to do. Knowing this, Jesus and his followers taught primarily through a combination of example and interpretive discussion. Our almost total dependence on a monologue in teaching should be at least as seriously reevaluated in church as it is now being questioned in schools.

The New Testament shows us a much wider range of church expression. Furthermore, it speaks a lot about worship. Yet most of our churches seem so focused on sermonizing that whatever worship there may be gets pushed into the corners of our time and attention. The songs ("hymns") we sing tend to be antiquated attempts to convey intellectual concepts. True worship takes time and gets the emotions into operation. It cannot be effectively done if it is merely another intellectual exercise. Nor can it be effective when used simply to smooth out transitions between other parts of the meeting in whatever bits of time can be allotted without interfering too much with the lecture/sermon.

Again, have we become captive to Enlightenment assumptions concerning the supreme importance of rational, logical, often academic presentations? And have we agreed with the rationalists that reason is more important than emotion—and virtually the only means God seeks to use to appeal to human wills?

4. Downplaying the Value of Experience. In keeping with the approach of the society around us, then, our focus both in listening to sermons and in Bible study tends to be on the information that can be gained from such study—preferably new information. We often assert that our aim is to "listen to God." And God does break through quite often. But it is the accumulation of information about the things of God that we are good at. We are often much less apt at really experiencing the relationship with God we talk about and value so highly.

We rightly learn biblical facts to enable us to describe what used to happen in order to be able to predict what will happen today. But the real criterion for accepting or rejecting biblical teaching may be something quite different than what we intend. It may unwittingly be simply a desire to rationally understand what is taught rather than to obey God and genuinely experience what we hear or read from the Bible.

It is reason and learning about God that tends to be in focus, even in our private devotional times—rather than relating, listening, and responding to him. Indeed, we often tend to downgrade experience as if it were somehow inferior to knowledge. "Don't base your theology on experience," we hear, "base it on biblical fact." But, in spite of our suspicions of the validity of experience as a measure of truth, we accept as fact very little that does not fit our experience. Indeed, whether or not we have experienced something the Bible deals with may be the real underlying reason for accepting or ignoring it. If we have not experienced it, we often resort to believing it is not valid for today. Since we have often not experienced much that is truly supernatural, our Christianity is seen as having a marvelous past and a great future, but the present often seems disturbingly void of the kinds of things the Scriptures usually dwell on.

For we interpret the Bible rationalistically and, without our realizing it, our own culturally conditioned human experience becomes the measure of all things. We assert that God's thoughts and ways are far above our thoughts and ways (Is 55:8-9). And we subscribe to doctrines that tell us that we cannot really understand God. But we tend to reject as not from God those things that we cannot understand on the basis of our own experience.

Again, as victims of Enlightenment ideas, we have learned that reason and intellectual processing of information can be trusted. Experience cannot, especially if there is any emotion involved. In spite of much evidence to the contrary, our worldview holds that reason is the surest way to appeal to human will. Though we would not want to go completely to the opposite extreme of enthroning experience and emotion, could it be that we need to seek a better understanding of the place and importance of experience in the way we interpret REALITY?

5. Our Tendency Is to Think of God's Word Only as Something Written. A further problem stems from our attachment to literacy. Whenever we see or hear the phrase "the Word of God," we tend to think of writing rather than of speaking. The phrase "the Word of God" turns our thoughts then to the Bible rather than to the voice of God. Yet throughout the Bible when that phrase is used, it usually refers to God *speaking* to us rather than to the written record of his words and deeds.

Evangelicals have rightly defended the importance of God's

written Word. That written Word is God's inspired gift to us. But we must never allow it to take the place of God himself. When, therefore, God says, "The word that I speak ... will do everything I send it to do" (Is 55:11), we should not interpret this as simply a reference to the written Word. Likewise, in Hebrews 4:12, where the author speaks of God's word as "alive and active, sharper than any double-edged sword," we should not assume that it is simply the Bible as the written Word that is being referred to.

Our Western respect for literacy, coupled with a deistic distancing of God has, I'm afraid, resulted in a fairly static view of how he interacts with us today. If he is "the same yesterday, today, and forever" (Heb 13:8), God must still be speaking to and interacting with people today as he used to in biblical times—not in contradiction of the written Word but as a fulfillment of how he has revealed himself in that written Word.

Our Evangelical fear of subjectivity and mistrust of our ability to control what people believe they have heard from God come, I fear, from our Enlightenment brand of Christianity rather than from the Scriptures. Shouldn't we seek release from such shackles?

6. Is Our Approach to Evangelism and Missions Primarily a Matter of Knowledge and Technique?

What about our approaches to evangelism and missions? How often do we give the impression that these are primarily a matter of knowledge and technique? Yes, we pray. But the analysis and emphasis on strategy, the way we communicate, the way we arrange our message, the many plans and methods we employ—these take up most of our attention. As Don Williams has said, we are "far advanced" in learning and training others to apply scientific methodology to the work of the ministry.

As a missionary strategist and theoretician, I myself am quite guilty of starting spiritual and immediately going secular! I have for years been teaching the importance of learning cultural and communication skills so that we may more effectively apply them to the ministry. And I still believe we need those things. I believe in developing understandings and strategies. I believe we need to use our reasoning powers, even when we are trying to escape the worst effects of rationalism.

However, I'm now seeking to discover how to keep from running ahead of God in the use of such insights. When we understand human things, are we thereby obligated to replace God's power with our plans? Can we learn to seek and wait for him to show us his will *before* and not after we work out the strategy?

This is a particularly tricky area for me. For though I believe in the necessity of hearing from God first, I often forget to really commit my problem to him and to wait for him to answer. And even when I do remember to listen, I often do not hear him clearly. What is the right combination between listening to God and using the knowledge and insight that have come to us through cultural and educational channels? I'm still struggling to discover the balance myself.

7. We Tend to Think of Medicine and Doctors before We Think of God. As pointed out above, we have a tendency as Western Christians to think of medicine and doctors before we think of God when someone needs healing. Perhaps we feel more in control of such techniques. Or perhaps it is simply unconscious habit that leads us to feel that though God can heal, medicine and doctors are more dependable. For God does not always do what we ask him to do. We can't control him. But we can rationalize that it is God who has given us the medicine and doctors and that we should not bother him but simply turn to the means he has provided. That is, unless the problem is too big for the usual secular means. In such a case, we "entreat God fervently" to bring about the healing because he is our *last* resort.

But is a father ever pleased to be simply a last resort? It doesn't please me at all if I hear that my children have gone to someone else to obtain what I could have provided. I like them to ask me first. For I love them and enjoy helping them. It is the deism built into our worldview that teaches us that God is basically uncaring—except as a last resort. The God made visible in Jesus Christ is gentle, open, and healing to those who hurt. He often does choose to work through medicine and doctors. But the choice should be his, not ours. He likes to be consulted first.

8. Secular Social Programs. We understand that God wants to help the poor and the malnourished. So we set up well-organized programs that collect from the rich and give to the poor and hungry, programs that are as efficient as possible. But such programs are often very impersonal and lacking in the kind of spiritual solutions Jesus would have used. Thus those who are helped frequently end up less poor and less hungry, but they are often still in bondage to whatever keeps them spiritually poor and hungry.

Jesus spoke of "setting free the oppressed" (Lk 4:18). We speak of "holistic ministry," serving the whole person. But a scripturally based holistic ministry needs to focus on more than the simple supplying of material needs. It needs to both start and continue with seeking God's plan and purpose and doing only what the Father desires to do (Jn 5:19).

I'm afraid our approach in this and other areas is often that of Moses when he struck the rock the second time (Nm 20:11). He had learned from his previous experience (Ex 17:1-6) to first listen to God, then to obey. The second time, however, he only partly listened, because he presumed he had the technique down pat by that time. I can imagine him saying in his heart, "Okay, I know what to do. I learned how to do it last time." He then made one of the biggest mistakes of his life simply because he didn't listen for fresh directions.

Just like Moses, we are likely to listen once and use the techniques that worked the first time forever after. Or worse, we may imitate someone who succeeded because he or she listened to God, assuming that the success was due to the technique rather than to the participation of God himself in every aspect of each specific situation. Oh, that we could learn to seek his presence as well as we know how to adopt the latest program in seeking to help others.

What Do We Do About This Problem?

I feel personally rebuked when I contemplate how much of my Christian life seems to have fallen into that Galatians 3:3 pitfall. My intentions have usually been good; I have usually really intended to walk and serve according to the Spirit's guidance. But how often I quickly turn to human power to carry out what I believe to be God's plans!

Further, I'm not always sure I can even imagine how to solve the problem. I am rationalistic through and through. On top of this, I am well versed in exerting as much control as possible over whatever situations I find myself in. Surely not all I have learned to think and do will be rejected by God as I try to learn to walk in the Spirit. But what changes do I need to make to escape from this controlling, rationalistic, and secular mindset? I have been trained in it, and I have habitually followed it all my life.

As I analyze the issue, two important components come into focus: 1) our drive to understand and thereby control whatever the situation may be and 2) our difficulty in really listening to and hearing clearly from God.

1. **Our Need to Understand.** Frequently, in ministering to people, I find that it is necessary for them to be released from bondage to the need to understand. Like me, they feel driven to understand everything that is going on before they can accept it. Even though we freely admit that God and his works are beyond our comprehension, there is something within us that won't quite accept that as the final conclusion. We want to *know*.

I was asked on one occasion to pray for an Anglican pastor who was experiencing deep discouragement in trying to open up more to the work of the Spirit. I felt led to pray against a spirit of "needing to understand." As I did, he was visibly moved and helped. Later he shared with me that right at that moment he realized as never before how blocked he had been by his mind's need to understand. "My mind," he said, "simply will not allow me to accept something I cannot understand." This had been a problem for as long as he could remember.

Not that mind and reason are to be altogether rejected. Our drive to understand is not evil in and of itself. But when that part of us is too much in control, we are not able to appropriate faith. Too much of a drive to understand robs us of our ability to trust God and to release ourselves to receive whatever he has for us, whether or not we can understand it.

Many of us are unconsciously demanding—as was our Anglican brother—that whatever God is doing in and around us be understandable. As long as this need to understand dominates us, we are crippled in our ability to accept and move into anything that falls outside the boundaries of our understanding. "How could what those charismatics do and what they believe be from God?" we ask. "It just doesn't fit into what we understand as biblical orthodoxy." We can't explain it so we reject it. And then we avoid being in places where we will have to take the charismatic approach seriously.

God's ways are above our ways (Is 55:9), we say. But then we expect to understand them! That's something I had to deal with head on in early 1982 when attending John Wimber's course. In order to accept what I was seeing and hearing in the *Signs and Wonders* class, I found I had to give up at least part of my right to understand. When I finally relaxed, accepted the situation, and gave up my right to understand what was happening, I found that God was able to break into my life in a new and exciting way. I discovered that Satan can be very clever in the way he takes such good things as our ability to reason and uses them to cripple us.

2. **Listening to God.** The other component to this problem is the difficulty many of us have in really listening to God. This never used to bother me much. I assumed that my usual offhand prayer for God's guidance was enough to assure that whatever circumstances occurred next were his will for me.

But whether I was praying or worshiping, I always seemed to structure things like one end of a telephone conversation.[5] I would talk to God in prayer. And, as soon as I finished talking, I would "hang up." Or I would sing a hymn to him, hang up, and call that worship. I trusted that he would talk to me through the Scriptures and frequently he did. But his voice was often muffled by the fact that I was focused largely on the information I was receiving, rather than on whatever he might want to say to me about my own life and attitudes. I expected and frequently got messages from him through preachers, teachers, or others. But when he wanted to speak to me directly, I had the phone on the hook and didn't even hear it ringing.

I'm still struggling in this area. Often when I try to listen to God during my prayer times, I simply fall asleep! I'm not a good meditator. But I now expect him to show me his will directly as well as indirectly. And such direct communication takes place most often so far when I am faithful to him by ministering his love in power to others.

Though I still have much to learn about hearing God, it is clearer than ever before that he is still alive and that he's still talking. Listening to someone whom we can't see is not a rational thing to do. But when I listen and then minister, I discover over and over again that God leads me into understandings far beyond my natural ability to know. I can't count the number of times God has led me to minister to a person in some area of great need I had no idea about until the Lord revealed it to me as I ministered. It then becomes clear that it was God's voice I heard and obeyed. Further, it becomes clear again and again that there is a REALITY beyond the rational, which we are able to tune into.

I've discovered that there is much more to Christianity than the powerless brand I used to know. But how does an Evangelical who has been affected by Western rationalism and powerless Christianity come into that kind of Christianity without getting "weird"? Is it really possible to be a faithful Evangelical and have a ministry of signs and wonders like John, Peter, and Paul in the New Testament? Can it really happen to me?

FIVE

What Empowers Culture?

A S I SAT IN THE *SIGNS AND WONDERS* COURSE IN 1982, my mind was being stretched. I knew from my studies of communication theory that the most effective communication takes place through demonstration. And this was demonstration par excellence! Each week we could expect God to move in power and do things that reminded us of New Testament times—things far beyond what we had anticipated in at least two ways. The events were obviously supernatural, not explainable by chance. And they were usually immediate and not of the "maybe God will answer our prayers" type.

My mind was being stretched as I observed healings and even more as I began to hear words of knowledge and to see how God used them to identify those he sought to bless. At that time I had been a Christian for thirty-eight years and in professional Christian work as a missionary and a seminary professor for twenty-six of those years. But I had never seen anything like this! It soon became obvious that I had been missing an important dimension of Christianity for all those years.

I had been teaching on the subject of worldview for several years and already understood intellectually most of what I am sharing here concerning the differences between worldviews. I even knew that Western worldviews are naturalistic in contrast with the supernaturalistic perspectives of biblical peoples and most of the rest of the world.

But I, too, had been under the lifelong influence of a worldview perspective that allowed me to see very little of the present supernatural activity of God. And that perspective affected both my viewpoints and my life experience. Perhaps God had been doing marvelous things near me all the time. But my perspective on life, including my view of Christian things, conditioned me against taking very much notice of anything that might be called miraculous.

I prayed, of course, but seldom saw answers that could unambiguously be classed as miracles. I believed in miracles, sort of. But I expected them to happen only rarely if at all.

Yet now we were seeing many healings each evening the class met! There were about eighty-five in the class, and a number of them would always seek healing. There were others as well who walked in just for the ministry time. Contrary to my expectations, the time of ministry was quite unemotional and not geared to ordering God to do anything. Wimber and his team simply claimed the authority Jesus gave his disciples (Lk 9:1) and ordered whatever was wrong to get better! To my surprise, the conditions usually got better—sometimes immediately, sometimes slowly.

I had wanted to move cautiously, even after I committed myself to attend the class. There was altogether too much "kookiness" associated with healing ministries. And, after all, I was and am an intellectual—a "left brain" type who keeps his distance from the emotional "lunatic fringe." But ever since my Nigerian days, I began to realize that I had been seeking something like this. So while part of me was amazed at what I was experiencing, another part of me was greatly relieved.

What I was hearing and experiencing was, however, filling so many gaps in my understanding that I soon relaxed and "just let it happen." It had been a concern of mine for some time that the Jesus I knew didn't seem to be the same today as he was yesterday, as promised in Hebrews 13:8. Though I had heard he was still doing miracles, I could not recall ever having seen a "real," unambiguous one. Looking back, though, I think I had always suspected that there was more to Christianity than I had yet experienced. And I was sure God was willing and able to do more than I had yet seen. So I did not resist the perspective being developed. I found it convincing and embraced it more and more as I saw powerful deeds that backed up the words.

The words of knowledge, though, were not only an experiential challenge but also an intellectual and doctrinal one. For I was being asked to accept that God was making known to people today specific insights concerning physical, emotional, psychological, and spiritual problems. If this was true, however, it called into question a strongly held Evangelical conviction that God had stopped revealing himself back in the first century. True, I had questioned this view in *Christianity in Culture,* concluding that a living God must still be a revealing God. So these contemporary revelations fit into an experience gap that I had already allowed for. And I began to get uncomfortable with my habit of behaving as if God does not reveal things today. But to believe something is one thing, to see and hear it actually happening is quite another.

What I was experiencing was a classic "paradigm shift," a major change in perspective. I had opened myself up to the possibility of change by exposing myself to new experiences. Now in response to these new experiences, I was turning from skepticism to belief. An important part of me became like a child again, hardly able to wait for the next Monday evening to arrive so I could see what God would do next!

What was happening to my Evangelical worldview? All of a sudden I was choosing to believe and behave quite differently from my Evangelical peer group.

Cultural Structuring

As implied in what I have already said, culture is a complex thing. First of all, culture consists of two levels: surface and deep levels. The surface level is largely visible and consists of the patterns according to which people behave. These behavior patterns are, however, closely linked to a deep level of largely unconscious and invisible assumptions we call worldview.

For example, if we observe people wearing clothes, we would guess that this surface-level custom relates to some deep-level assumption that wearing clothing is proper, right, even moral. If we see the people of a society regularly going naked—as I once did in northeastern Nigeria—we would guess that their deep-level worldview belief supports the rightness of that behavior.

Likewise, if we see people behaving as if God is not important in their everyday lives, we would guess that their behavior is supported by their worldview assumptions concerning the relevance of God. With regard, therefore, to what and how we eat, whom and how we marry, what we avoid and what we commit ourselves to, and all the rest of our surface-level behavior, we can be sure that there is deep-level worldview support.

Second, culture, including worldview, is simply a matter of structures and patterns. It is not like a person. It cannot do things. Culture, including worldview, is a set of patterns taught to people. We may define it as *that complex set of patterns in terms of which people think and behave*. When we do something, it is ordinarily in keeping with a cultural pattern. As I write, I am acting according to cultural conventions. When I walk, sleep, teach, drive my car, shave, shower, eat, kiss my wife, sit at a table—nearly all of the thousands of things I do, say, and think daily are according to cultural patterns. And even should I innovate by, say, shaving while hanging by my feet, I would ordinarily only change part of my customary daily pattern.

Third, culture, including worldview, is complex. Not a single "simple" culture has so far been discovered. All are very complicated, with each custom closely related to and interdependent with many other customs. I have illustrated above the close relationship between surface and deep culture. But the interrelationships are also close between the various customs that make up surface-level behavior and also between the various assumptions and values that make up deep-level behavior.

What clothes we wear and how we wear them, for example, relate to other surface culture patterns such as use of wealth, bodily cleanliness, bodily comfort, washing of clothes, ironing, hanging and storage, aesthetics, and the like. A change in what we wear may therefore affect any or all of those other patterns. Likewise, in deep-level culture, assumptions concerning individualism will closely relate to other worldview assumptions concerning freedom, naturalism, rationalism, and the like. Thus, if a person changes his or her understandings in one of these areas, there will be greater or lesser change in the other areas as well.

Fourth, culture, including worldview, is comprehensive. It covers all of life. Economics, politics, family relationships, language, religion, aesthetics, and every other aspect of human life are structured according to cultural patterns. We know how to behave in ways considered proper by our society because we have learned the cultural rules in each area of life. A toddler wets his pants, or throws food on the floor, or eats something that has been on the floor, or wakes up and starts playing in the middle of the night because he hasn't yet learned the rules—or, perhaps, chooses to ignore them. As he learns and agrees to follow each set of rules, his behavior becomes more and more acceptable to those around him who learned in the same way to follow all the patterns he is just learning.

Fifth, as I've already pointed out, culture, including worldview, is learned. Culture is neither transmitted biologically nor determined by the physical environment. The patterns are taught to the young by their elders, often quite unconsciously, and usually learned unconsciously as well. I learned to behave like my father behaves with little consciousness of what I was learning.

I raise these five issues concerning the nature of culture and worldview from a much longer list that could have been presented to form a backdrop for our discussion first of persons and then of change. Highlighting such issues gives us a better idea of what we face as we attempt to make changes in our cultural perspectives and practices. If, for example, culture were a kind of being that forces us to behave in certain ways, there would be no hope of making the kind of changes here recommended. The fact that we are talking of patterns that have no determining power in and of themselves, however, raises hope that changes can be made. For patterns can be changed by persons.

The recognition of the complexity and comprehensiveness of culture, though, may somewhat dim our hopes for changing things. These characteristics alert us to the fact that change at anything more than a trivial level is not simply a matter of neatly removing one pattern and replacing it with another. Whenever any substantial change is made, we can expect wide-ranging ramifications throughout many other areas of the life of those who change. This is especially true if a change is made at the worldview level. A person who changes his perspective on the importance of diet to health, for example, is likely to change his whole lifestyle—and those of everyone close to him. Likewise, one who decides to make a commitment to Christ central in his life will allow that change to affect his whole approach to life.

Nominal, superficial changes can be made without much disruption to the rest of one's cultural patterns. But major changes, such as embracing a brand of Christianity with real power, run into complications related to the complexity and comprehensiveness of one's culture.

Perhaps the most difficult problems associated with worldview change arise from the way in which culture is learned. We are very young as these patterns are imprinted in our minds. We are, furthermore, quite unconscious of the fact that there may be any flaw in what we learn. We trust the people who teach us and are often quite dependent on them for physical and emotional needs. So we are anxious to accept whatever they offer and are usually quite unaware that there may be alternative points of view. Thus our worldview beliefs and surface-level cultural behavior are deeply etched into our lives.

What is etched into us is, however, still a matter of patterns and structures. And if this is true, we are talking about something over which we can exert some measure of control. Why, then, do we find it so difficult to change them? Where does their power come from? Why aren't people more free to change their ways of thinking and behaving?

People and Culture

To deal with these questions, it is extremely important to distinguish between culture, including worldview, and people. Many speak as if culture is a pseudo-personal entity that goes around doing things to people. Some will say or imply, for example, that "a person's culture forces him or her to understand and behave in a certain way." This kind of statement is, however, very misleading, for it attributes to culture the power to determine individual choices.

But culture is not a person. It does not "do" anything. Only people do things. The fact that people ordinarily do what they do by following the cultural "tracks" laid down for them should not lead us to treat culture itself as something possessing a life of its own. Culture is like the script an actor uses. He follows it most of the time. But occasionally, either because he has forgotten his lines or because he thinks he has a better way of reaching the goal, he departs from the script and does something else.

The "power" that keeps people following the script of their culture is the power of habit, not any power that culture possesses in itself. People do ordinarily follow the patterns of their culture, but not always. Cultural patterns are like the roads on which we drive. We habitually drive on the road, but we sometimes deviate from our course. I was riding with a driver in France once who skirted a traffic jam by driving on the sidewalk for several hundred yards! It was a bit frightening, and I expected a policeman to arrive at any time to enforce the "drive only on the road" rule. But our driver got away with it.

The same is true of the cultural roads that are laid out for us. We, like the French driver, ordinarily follow them. But sometimes we change our behavior. For example, I learned in northern Nigeria that it is insulting for an adult to receive something from another person if it is offered with the left hand. This is the "road" or "script" they customarily follow in such situations, so I had to learn to follow it while living in that part of the world. In fact, I have often found myself practicing that custom in America where it is not required! There is no penalty I have to pay for this slight deviation, except for the inconvenience of shifting things from my left to right hand when it is not necessary to do so. If the French driver or I should choose to always drive on sidewalks, though, that would be considered a large and unacceptable deviation. We would quickly find ourselves in trouble with the police.

Cultural (including worldview) patterns, then, do not force people to follow them. *It is force of habit that keeps us following custom.* But even a habit can be changed with some effort. If the change is considered serious, however, others in the society will exert great pressure on the one who is deviating to get him or her to conform. If the deviation is not considered serious, little or no pressure may be exerted to get the person back in line.

When I decided to deviate from my lifelong practice of shaving and to grow a beard and mustache, little pressure was exerted on me (except by my wife) to return to the usual custom of my peer group. The change was considered important enough for me to pay a slight social penalty, but not a large one. My move into spiritual power, however, is regarded as much more serious by my peers, and I have been, and still am, subjected to much greater pressure to "come to my senses" and return to my previous beliefs and behavior.

As with culture as a whole, so with worldview. People perceive reality habitually according to culturally defined patterns. For instance, those whose viewpoints differ widely from the majority in American society—rebels, communists, and certain artists—are likely to be penalized except by those within their own select groups. They may be treated as "different," strange, or weird by the wider society. That is, they are "marginalized" by society in an attempt to get them to conform. The pressure society exerts to get Pentecostals and charismatics to leave their "weird" practices and conform is a case in point. Note, for example, that nearly every reference to these groups by the news media is negative or sarcastic.

Since culture and worldview cannot totally determine behavior and since people are more than simply bundles of habit, people are constantly making changes in the way they perceive REALITY. One kind of change occurs as we grow up. Children who may be skeptical about the facts of human reproduction eventually change their views as their experience widens. People who are at a loss to understand and comfort those suffering bereavement learn the meaning of bereavement when someone close to them dies.

Other changes are made in response to less typical experiences. A person may read someone else's thinking on a given issue and change his or her perspective out of deference to the other's viewpoint. Or a trusted friend may let someone down, leading the one who is hurt to respond in bitterness toward other people. A person who feels frustrated over not achieving certain goals may develop a fatalistic or negative perspective toward life in general. One who witnesses what appears to be a miraculous intervention of God may choose to believe in miracles.

In each case there may or may not be social penalties to pay. In individualistic American society, there is great latitude in most areas as long as people keep pretty much to themselves. But trying to convert others to one's perspective can prove troublesome, especially if one's new perspective seems to question the authority or accuracy of science and conventional perspectives.

It is the will to change a perspective that becomes crucial. One must decide to stand against inbred habit and social pressure to make an unpopular change of perspective permanent. This is difficult but not impossible. For what we are determined to do is ultimately more important than the cultural structures, the deeply ingrained habits, or the social pressures in our lives. We will see this more clearly later.

It Is Habit That Empowers Cultural Patterns

Our culture and worldview are empowered then by force of habit. Humans are creatures of habit. We do things in certain ways not simply because we have been taught to do them in those ways, but because we have gotten into the habit of doing them in certain ways. Worldview structuring provides the patterns, and those who are significant in our lives provide the modeling from which we learn the patterns, usually quite unconsciously. Most of these patterns we adopt and "habituate" with or without modification. Some of what is modeled or explained we reject. Not much of what we learn in our early years is rejected, however. It is largely assimilated at the unconscious level and practiced automatically without our being conscious of the presence of the patterns and habits that keep us following cultural tracks.

Among the most important habits we develop are those that push us to seek intimacy and recognition in social relationships. There seems to be a deep personal need for attention, preferably accompanied by acceptance and approval by the "significant others" in our lives. And we soon develop habits that conform our behavior to seeking such approval. As we note when observing children with their parents, if acceptance and approval are not forthcoming, they develop habits designed to gain attention from their parents.

Even as an adult, however, with great job security and a measure of prestige, I found it frightening to open myself up to the Holy Spirit. "What if I pray for someone and he or she doesn't get well?" I asked. "Will people still respect me?" Or what would people say if they thought I had become charismatic? Would they say I had "gone off the deep end"? Or worse yet, that I had joined the enemy? For Evangelicals are "us," charismatics are "them." And I am paying a social price. There are certain places I am not invited any more and certain people who now hold me at arm's length.

Social approval is ordinarily conditioned on a person's behaving in ways that show a high degree of conformity to the cultural patterns followed by his or her significant others. Social "enticements" are exerted to reward conformity and greater or lesser pressure is exerted to prevent deviance. These enticements and pressures, have a powerful effect on habit development and maintenance.

Note, for example, the strength of social pressure concerning church membership. The first line of pressure is exerted by the "normal" people of our society to not belong to a church at all. If one must belong to a church, however, the pressure is very strong in favor of those churches whose patterns of behavior are most like that of non-Christians. Society, even church society, exerts pressure for people to belong to certain "respectable" denominations— Presbyterian, Episcopal, Methodist, and certain Baptist groups. In this way it exerts pressure to keep even dedicated Christians from doing anything defined by the society at large as "weird."

Christian groups such as Pentecostals or charismatics are, of course, by society's definition "weird." They are typically either pressured to change, if not away from Christianity, at least to join a "respectable" group. If they do not submit to that pressure, then they are ignored and pushed to the margins of society by those defined as "normal" by the society. So they produce their own "ghetto," made up totally of their own kind of people in order to survive. But many within such ghettos live with a good bit of psychological uneasiness in the knowledge that they don't count in mainstream society. And many either leave the ghetto or seek to conform their church practices to those considered more socially respectable. There are now, for example, certain Pentecostal congregations that have, under the influence of such social pressure, come to behave and worship very much like Presbyterians!

In a society like ours, we learn from birth to view the universe naturalistically, think rationally, and follow the other patterns of our worldview until they have the force of habit. We habitually interpret and respond to all of life from these standpoints and find that our commitment to them runs very deep. This commitment makes it quite difficult to change worldview patterns. If we break out of such habits enough to commit ourselves to Christ, we stand in tension with a certain amount of the deistic view of life built into our Western worldview. Given the tension and the challenge of altering habits, we often change much less than we ought.

But, in spite of the depth and strength of such habits, the situation is not hopeless. Contrary to the opinions of behavioral psychologists, such as B.F. Skinner, who claim that there is no such thing as free will,[1] there is always some "room to wiggle." If human behavior is 90 percent habitual, it is still 10 percent creative. Or if it's even 95 percent habitual, there is still a 5 percent margin for creativity. I cannot estimate the percentages with any confidence. But whatever the ratio, I know that habitual behavior can be changed. I have seen it happen both in myself and in others! I have seen myself change from a traditional Evangelical to one who regularly and effectively prays with people for healing—something I would have thought impossible over seven years ago.

We are not 100 percent determined by the perspectives and customs we have learned from our society. We can—by exercising our wills with the aid of the power of God—make changes both in our perspectives and in our behavior. In fact, much of the material in this book is designed to assist us in using our wills to break lifelong worldview perspectives and engrained habits so we can minister in spiritual power.

As an Evangelical I Chose to Step Out

Observing what was going on in the *Signs and Wonders* class was fun. Though the healings, the words of knowledge, and several other aspects of the class challenged my Evangelical worldview and Christian practice, the experience was quite enjoyable. But then something quite unexpected happened. I found the experiences in class so exciting that I couldn't stop talking about them. The trouble was that by telling the stories, I was unwittingly leading people to think I myself could do the things I was describing! So I kept getting asked to pray for people—both in and out of class. And I did pray for them. But not much happened—which is what I expected. And I wasn't getting words of knowledge.

My thinking had changed. What was happening now was a challenge to my practice. For though I now believed in my head, I still acted as though God only healed through others. Our teacher, however, kept acting as though: 1) *we*—not just he—should be ministering healing to others; and 2) that we should be practicing both in class and on our own. This kind of ministry is not, he said, a matter of "gifting" nearly so much as it is a matter of obedience.

We accept, Wimber pointed out, Jesus' command to preach (Lk 9:2; 10:9), but we ignore the fact that the same verses command us to heal. They say we are to *preach and heal.* Learning *about* and even seeing healing demonstrated was only a start. We are called to do it. So once Wimber had demonstrated how he goes about this kind of ministry, he turned to us and said, "Now you do it!" At that point, I strongly considered retreating into Enlightenment Evangelicalism!

This was scary! I remember inwardly trembling in my seat as he would say, "If anyone near you stands up (for prayer), *you* lay hands on that person and pray for him or her." I remember actually praying that God would not let anyone near me stand up! I was fairly certain that it wouldn't work if I was involved. In spite of the teaching, I assumed that I didn't "have the gift." Worse yet, I thought I was too sinful for God to use me in this way. And I rationalized that I certainly didn't want to hurt anyone's chances of getting healed by exposing them to the second-class attempts at prayer of someone who would in reality only block God's blessing. Better, I reasoned, to let someone who knew what he or she was doing pray for the person. And besides that, I, as a professor, was so visible in the class that everyone would know I was a failure!

Usually God seemed to honor my prayer that I not be required to minister to someone. But sometimes he seemed to forget! What should I do then? Cleverly, I devised a method of standing back from the person to be prayed for. With a smile on my face, I would try to mislead people into thinking I really knew what to do but was allowing the students to get experience. I would simply watch! Inwardly, though, it was fear that held me back, in spite of the fact that Wimber attempted to make the class a safe place for us to practice.

He pointed out from his own experience that it is only by "hands on" practice in spite of fear and discouragement that we ever will become good at this kind of ministry. This teaching also proved to be a problem for me. I assumed that God simply "zapped" certain people with the gift. When that happened, they would immediately become successful. I began to reflect on how I came to have my gift of teaching. It came with a lot of hard work. But somewhere along the line, I believe God had confirmed it as a spiritual gift. We were learning that people become "gifted" at praying for healing in the same way—by claiming God's help and by working hard at it.

The class had run from January to March of 1982. My wife and I attended every session that year. It ran during the same time slot in 1983, and I got to about half of the sessions that year. I kept busy with my usual duties, but I was beginning to enjoy a new sense of God's presence in my everyday life. Yet I had not fully moved into an active prayer ministry, in spite of the fact that I really wanted to.

Beginning in early 1984, however, two full years after I had changed my perspective, opportunities began to come my way that put my newfound conviction to the test. First, I was invited by the pastor of our church to lead a ministry team after the evening services to pray for people with "specific needs." Though not many people usually came, I got to pray with someone nearly every week. This gave me some practice and enough happened to give me some confidence.

Second, I began to teach on healing in my own Sunday school class and soon began to be invited elsewhere for the same purpose. I found it easy to teach on healing without seeking to actually pray for anyone. I got away with this at first. But as time went on, I developed the boldness to ask God to provide opportunities to demonstrate what I was talking about right in front of the class. On a couple of occasions, the results were dramatic.

During the spring of 1984, I even experienced a healing of my own from a heart problem and saw more and more small things begin to happen. Then came the experience that propelled me from a shift in perspective into what I call my "practice shift." (I'll share more about that experience in chapter seven.)

Keep in mind that I was no "superstar" at praying with people for healing. On the contrary, I believe many can follow this same path, a path full of fits and starts, of ordinary fears, of disappointments, and limited successes. Yet in spite of my humanness, God was able to use me in increasingly effective ways as I yielded to him.

Let's now turn to what may be the greatest hindrance to our attempts to make this kind of change in perspective and practice.

SIX

The "What We Think We Know" Problem

IT IS NOT SO MUCH WHAT WE DON'T KNOW, but what we think we know
that obstructs our vision, says Harvard theologian Krister
Stendahl.[1] This piece of wisdom has certainly described accurately
quite a number of situations in human history. It also points out the
basic problem in a large number of the conflicts that have taken place
in the history of Christianity. Every time there is renewal, for
example, the "what we think we know" problem arises. Typically, the
traditionalists who think they know how God behaves become the
opponents of the new things God wants to do.

This was true in the first century when a council of early Christian
leaders met in Jerusalem to resolve the controversy about Gentile
believers being required to convert to Jewish culture (Acts 15). The
Jewish traditionalists thought they knew God's answer. But fortunately for us, he had a different idea! (Entrance into Christianity
wasn't to require that Gentiles become Jews but that they commit
themselves to Jesus Christ.)

During the Protestant Reformation, the new wave of God's Spirit
was opposed by those who thought they knew that God would only
work through certain kinds of structures and in only one language.
Still later, those who thought they knew God's will attempted to
squelch revival movements in Britain and the United States. In our
day, others who think they know the mind of God stand in opposition
to the movements of the Holy Spirit that have produced Pente-
costalism and the charismatic movement.

The problem seems to be a human tendency to make rules for God! We learn certain things about how he works, arrive at the principles we think to be appropriate, and then impose those principles on those who seek to follow him as if God himself had endorsed them. We then virtually forbid him to work in any other way. In Acts 15, the early Hebrew Christians fell into this trap. They assumed that since God had used their culture to reveal himself, it was his intent to require everyone—even Gentiles—to become Hebrew and follow Hebrew customs in order to relate to God. This was one of their rules for God. But God broke the rule and gave his Holy Spirit to Gentiles as soon as they believed—without their submitting to circumcision and the other requirements of Hebrew society.

God simply refuses to be bound by "what we think we know," even if that knowledge is about him. For he knows the severe limitations of that knowledge. It is always constrained by our humanity and derived from our interpretations of but a small selection of God's acts. And all of those interpretations are influenced by our worldview, our experience, our predisposition, our sin, and all our other human limitations. *We dare not trust that knowledge.* As the writer of Proverbs warns us, we should "never rely on what [we] think [we] know" (3:5).

Knowledge can be a very helpful thing. Indeed, one of my aims in writing this book and one of yours in reading it is an increase of knowledge about the power of God. But the knowledge we seek here is intended to help us in countering some of the "what we think we know" kind of knowledge that comes through our cultural conditioning. Otherwise, we will continue to be victimized by it when we try to think of or relate to supernatural beings and power.

"We Know This Man Could not Have Healed You"

The "what we think we know" kind of knowledge and its consequences are well illustrated in the incident in John 9 concerning the healing of the man born blind. First of all, the disciples "knew" that the reason why a person would be born blind is either his sin or that of his parents (v. 2). The Pharisees "knew" then that "the man who [healed him] cannot be from God, for he does not obey the Sabbath law" (v. 16).

Because of this "knowledge," the Pharisees "were not willing to believe that he had been blind and could now see" (v. 18). Nor were they willing to believe that Jesus was the Messiah (v. 22). For they said, "We know that this man who cured you is a sinner" (v. 24). Jesus was not to be compared with their rabbi, Moses, whom they "knew" God had spoken to—implying that Jesus was not acting on a word he had heard from God (v. 28). They also "knew" that they themselves were not blind when it came to recognizing whether someone like Jesus was from God (v. 41).

By way of contrast, the man born blind, working from experience and inference, arrived at some true knowledge. He states, "I do not know if he is a sinner or not. One thing I do know: I was blind, and now I see" (v. 25). Interestingly, in response to what the Pharisees claimed to know, he then says,

> What a strange thing that is! You do not know where he comes from, but he cured me of my blindness! We know that God does not listen to sinners; he does listen to people who respect him and do what he wants them to do.... Unless this man came from God, he would not be able to do a thing. (vv. 30-33)

What both the disciples and the Pharisees claimed to "know" came from their worldview conditioning. They—and the blind man himself—shared both the assumption that blindness was the direct result of specific sin and the assumption that anyone who deliberately transgressed the Sabbath law could not be from God. This was embedded in the Judaic worldview they shared.

But the events recorded in this passage led to different reactions on the part of the participants. The disciples showed themselves willing to learn and to change their assumption in response to Jesus' words and deed. The blind man also changed his assumption on the basis of his experience. But the Pharisees, even though participating in the same event, refused to change their assumption and became morally and spiritually blind.

Worldview conditioning is something we all have to put up with. In a sense, we are all victims of that conditioning like the blind man, the disciples, and the Pharisees. It is not a sin to be the victim of a worldview. But as we go through life, we experience certain things that challenge what we have been taught to believe. The Hebrews experienced a major challenge to their worldview every time God allowed them to be defeated in war. For they believed they could not lose. The same thing happened to Americans when we couldn't win in Vietnam.

A miraculous event, especially by one the Pharisees did not respect and wouldn't accept, was an enormous challenge to their worldview. And they chose to retain their worldview assumptions and to ignore the evidence provided by their own experience. They "thought they knew" better.

We have such experiences every so often. And we have wills with which to choose whether to defend an old perspective or to change our perspective. The habits of belief that have sustained our worldview are strong enough, even when we are unconscious of them. When, however, those habits are further reinforced by the conscious exercise of our will, there will be no change in view at all. We become trapped in our worldview.

We May Lack the Categories to Accept an Experience of God's Power

Why do we find ourselves trapped in our worldview? Sometimes it's because we lack the categories to accept an experience of God's power. A worldview provides a way of classifying reality so we can understand it. The way we evaluate categories and their contents is patterned by our worldview. Western societies, for example, are conditioned to evaluate the category "visible material goods" as important, while the category "invisible supernatural beings" is for most people the same category that contains the characters we read about in "fairy tales." These things are evaluated as "unreal." Perhaps they are interesting, but we are not to take them seriously. Thus we become victims of our conditioning by using these categories.

Yet many are able to make some sort of an exception for God. One member of the unreal "invisible being" category is then taken seriously. But our conception of beings such as angels, demons, and Satan is left in limbo. The problem then becomes not the lack of a category but the lack of a serious regard for most of the members of a particular category.

In the categorization of power, we find that many Euro-Americans completely lack an awareness of such spiritual things as blessings and healings. And yet we do have names for them, just as we have names for other spiritual beings besides God. We can easily think of power wielded by humans, by nature, and even by such things as political and economic structures. But to conceive of real power being generated when a person says, "I bless you," or "Be healed," or

"Demon, come out" may be more than most of the members of our society can handle.

A young Fuller student, I'll call Jim, experienced this very thing as he watched a colleague and myself attempting to get a demon out of a young woman. As we challenged the demon and it responded, Jim became more and more uncomfortable. Finally he got up and left. He told us later, "I simply had no categories in my mind that would allow me to handle what I was seeing." It "blew his mind" to see spiritual power wielded by a demon and then countered by God's power in response to our words. Jim could accept the existence of demons in the abstract. But it was more than he could handle to see the effects of the battle between the invisible, though quite tangible power of a demonic being and the even more tangible, invisible power of God.

Jim probably tried to explain the event by referring to the categories already in his worldview. "Perhaps that woman is having some sort of a seizure," he might have thought. "Or possibly she has a serious psychological disorder." But the fact that several times violent behavior—including choking—was stopped by a command from one of us in the name of Jesus made it well-nigh impossible for him to continue to hold to what he thought he knew. Jim felt let down by those who had taught him how to interpret the world around him, the victim of an inadequate worldview.

Nor will Jim be able to handle such confrontations in the future unless—probably stimulated by repeated experience—he "grows" a new mental compartment. He will need to exercise his will to do that. And he will have similar difficulty if he experiences the actual conferring of a blessing through what sounds to him like "mere words." For the perspective that invisible transactions take place in the spiritual realm in response to such words is not part of the worldview he has been taught.

The Will Problem

But what if Jim had walked away having made the decision 1) not to accept our interpretation of the event and 2) not to expose himself any longer to an event that was forcing him to reconsider his previous perspectives? Worst of all, suppose he had decided not to face the possibility that he was going to have to develop new categories of thinking? Jim might have felt it was easier to just walk away and forget the whole thing. It is just plain hard work to revise and expand one's worldview, and he might simply have opted out. But it's more than just a question of hard work.

Our worldview paradigms or perspectives are precious to us. They are like our language, having been passed on to us by people in whom we have trusted over the years. So our first reaction is ordinarily to defend and protect them when they are challenged. This is especially true if we suspect that by changing a certain paradigm, we may run afoul of the opinions of our group. The potential of a loss of prestige is usually sufficient to keep us in line, especially if we are feeling socially insecure.

Of course, as already pointed out, there are changes in worldview perspectives that are socially approved. As we move from childhood into adulthood, we change many perceptions to accommodate to new experience. These changes of paradigms underlie the changes Paul speaks of when he says, "When I was a child, my speech, feelings, and thinking were all those of a child; now that I am a man, I have no more use for childish ways" (1 Cor 13:11).

The youngster referred to earlier who asked his mother how babies come into the world is a case in point. The mother explained in more detail than the boy could comprehend at the time. So he vehemently refused to believe what his mother had told him. As he grew up, however, he changed his perspective in keeping with rather than against social pressure.

Notice the prominent place of a person's will in changing a worldview. The child willed to change his understanding of human reproduction and was supported in that change by the society around him. We commonly call that "growth." As we grow up, certain socially approved changes in perspective are advocated through schooling and in a variety of informal (family and peer group relationships, for example) and semi-formal ways (scouting, athletics, music groups, for example). When we adopt such changes, they are valued positively by our society and are often referred to as "progress" and "maturation." We decide to go along with them and receive social approval as we do.

Jim, observing our attempts to free the woman from the demon, probably had altogether different thoughts. The church society in which he grew up and in which he was planning to minister would certainly not approve of him becoming open to our interpretation of what was going on. That group—though thoroughly Evangelical and deeply committed to serving Christ—is in general very attached to the kind of understandings of Christianity that do not allow for such displays of supernatural power. He may well have been asking himself, "What would happen to my relationship with those I respect in my denomination if I got into this stuff?" And he would guess that the result would be negative. Such considerations tend to affect one's willingness even to entertain the possibility of changing a perspective.

The Pharisees had a similar problem with their wills. Not that they didn't believe in spiritual power. Unlike most in Western societies, they had no problem in that respect. But from their point of view, Jesus did things the wrong way and at the wrong times. He made the wrong claims. Most disturbing of all, he was a threat to their positions and power (Mk 11:18; Jn 11:48). If Jesus had been just another charlatan, attracting and leading another group of common people, the Jewish religious leaders would not have been so upset. But many—even from among their own numbers—had become at least secret believers and were exercising their wills against the social pressure to endorse Jesus' claims (Jn 12:42).

When Jesus discusses his use of parables, he points out that the secrets of the kingdom will be open to those who commit themselves to the kingdom but closed to those who choose to "look but . . . not see, . . . [to] listen but . . . not hear or understand" (Mt 13:13). He then quotes Isaiah 6:9-10 to reinforce his critique of those who deliberately choose to remain blind in spite of the evidence, because they refuse to change their worldview perspectives:

> This people will listen and listen, but not understand; they will look and look, but not see, because their minds are dull, and they have stopped up their ears and have closed their eyes. (Mt 13:14-15)

If they had only opened their minds to a new perspective: "Their eyes would see, their ears would hear, their minds would understand, and they would turn to me, says God, and I would heal them" (Mt 13:16).

Willful reluctance to open oneself up to what God wants to reveal in the spiritual realm can carry with it serious consequences. We may be victims of a worldview conditioning that makes such openness difficult, but we should carefully avoid allowing ourselves willfully to choose blindness like the Pharisees. For they *could not see because, through their own choice, they would not see.*

Knowledge as a Will Weakener

As we have seen, will plays a major role in determining whether one will or will not change a perspective. Our choice is often to stick with what we think we know. It's easier that way. So if change is to come, we need to will new understandings and habits.

Easier said than done. For our wills are often weakened in indirect as well as direct ways. We have been taught not to be serious about spiritual beings and power. That influence is direct. We have also been taught a series of other things that have resulted in habitual perceptions, attitudes, and practices that provide less direct and more subtle hindrances to openness in this area.

Let's take a look at a few of these habitual perceptions and attitudes:

1. **Frequently our wills are weakened by some stereotype that those in healing ministries are weird.** I myself developed such a point of view, even before I saw Kathryn Kuhlman on television. But it was especially after watching her that a stereotyped image would come to mind and leave me with a very negative impression whenever I thought of faith healing. Yet this impression was not based on any real firsthand experience. It was all based on hearsay, along with that single viewing of Kathryn Kuhlman on TV. It was sufficient, however, to keep me from investigating further, even though there was a part of me that longed to experience more of God's power.

My will was weak until a "credible witness," someone I could trust, came along—John Wimber. I knew he was a stable and trustworthy person long before he had embarked on a healing ministry. When such a balanced person offered to show us what he had learned about spiritual power, I opened myself to him in a way that I would not, had he come from a traditionally Pentecostal or charismatic background. Even so, if Wimber had focused strongly on speaking in tongues as a requirement for moving into God's power, I would probably have "turned sadly away" and left.

2. **A second type of "will weakener" is the teaching that occurs in many churches, Bible schools, and seminaries. Simply put, it is that the exercise of such gifts as healing, tongues, and prophecy "is not for today."** Much of such teaching is associated with a theological perspective called Dispensationalism. Many Fundamentalist and Evangelical Bible schools and some seminaries teach this position. The notes in the widely used Scofield Reference Bible also articulate this position.

Such teaching is a product of Enlightenment perspectives applied to theology by those who have not had the kind of spiritual experience that might lead them to question such a belief. I don't mean to belittle those who hold this belief. I have been guilty of it myself for most of my Christian life. Such lack of experience in the area of spiritual power leads even very sincere and committed people to rationalize this lack. They will assert that "Jesus Christ is the same yesterday, today and forever" (Heb 13:8) but also assert that the constancy of Jesus does not apply to spiritual power—even though he gave his disciples authority and power (Lk 9:1) and told them to teach their followers "to obey everything I have commanded you" (Mt 28:20).

3. A third perspective that contributes to a weak will in this area is the unbalanced emphasis on Jesus as divine in contrast to his humanity. Though his favorite name for himself was the Son of Man (meaning human being), and though we assert that he was "fully human" as well as fully divine, it has been my experience that his divinity gets a disproportionate amount of emphasis in Evangelicalism. Perhaps it is largely a legacy of the debates with modernists over the deity of Christ. However, it is also strongly affected by the fact that much of what Jesus did seems to be more easily explained if we see him as God than if we see him as a human being.

Before I had seen and experienced "words of knowledge," for example, I could only come up with one explanation for the times in Jesus' ministry when he knew what people were thinking (see Matthew 9:4; 12:25; John 4:17, 18). I assumed that Jesus could know such things only because he was God. Likewise, I explained his miracles as evidences of his divinity. But I had no good explanation for the times when he didn't seem to know (see Luke 8:45; Mark 9:16, 21; 10:51), or for the fact that it seems he did not know until the end of his ministry that Judas would betray him.

I asserted that he had emptied himself of his divinity and glory as stated in Philippians 2:6-8, but I really felt that he cheated a lot! Yet seeing and experiencing how God reveals things to human beings through words of knowledge enabled me for the first time to understand how Jesus could have been fully human and yet on occasion know things he had not been told. I now saw that through living in total dependence on the Father, he could get certain insights from the Father (Jn 8:28-29), even though as a human being he often had to ask people for information. He was not cheating but, rather, demonstrating how God wants to work with all human beings.

4. A fourth type of perspective that can weaken the will is a wrong view of God. As one woman put it, "I always see God with a stick in his hand." This woman was so conscious of her sin and the condemnation she deserved that she could not identify with the oppressed in the Gospels and recognize that Jesus' gentleness toward them shows the real attitude of God toward victims like her. The love, forgiveness, and gentleness of God is hard to accept when one hates and condemns oneself. In ministry, God met and released this woman both from bondage to oppression and from bondage to a serious misunderstanding about the nature of God.

God is a lover, an accepter, a forgiver. He delights to free people from captivity to sin, the self, and Satan. His gentleness and tenderness demonstrated in Jesus toward ordinary people—and especially toward victims—are some of his main characteristics. To be sure, he is hard on hypocrites such as the Pharisees who use their power and position to add to the oppression of others. But, as with the adulteress in John 8, he reads our motives, not our desperate attempts to survive, even when the latter are misdirected and sinful.

He discerns the heart and knows the difference between a mistake or series of mistakes and confirmed, rebellious willfulness. He is loving, gentle, and ready to bless people who have been "chewed up" in the system and have made mistakes in their attempts to survive. So he accepts the unworthy, since that's really the only kind of people there are once we face ourselves and our sin. For some incredible reason he is in love with humans in spite of all the experience he has had with us! But a wrong view of God can keep us from understanding that he wants to minister to and heal people today, including each one of us.

5. Another will weakener is the feeling that one is spiritually inadequate to minister in power. It is easy to develop a mentality that assumes that God will only use "spiritual giants" or that he will only bless our efforts when we are spiritually on top of the world. If we have sinned or grown cold in our love for him, if we don't feel spiritual or have neglected daily Bible study and prayer—we assume that God will certainly punish us by withholding his blessing.

Though there is some truth to these feelings, we tend to exaggerate the importance of external behavior. Again, God is most concerned with our intent, not merely surface-level acts. More often than not he rewards those who "risk" in faith, even though they frequently make mistakes. Think of the many mistakes the apostle Peter made, for instance! As many who have launched out into a ministry of spiritual power can testify, it is often when one feels least adequate that God does the most spectacular things. Not that one should be unconcerned over his or her spiritual state. God forbid! But to allow concern over one's spiritual state to weaken one's will to minister in power is to play into the hands of the enemy.

6. **A sixth weakener of the will is fear, whether it be personal or social.** "What if I pray for someone and it doesn't work?" we ask ourselves. "It will be very embarrassing for me and disappointing for the person being prayed for." Right! I can testify to the embarrassment and the disappointment. And I still fear both whenever I attempt to minister to anyone. But I can also testify that something amazing and wonderful happened to me when I finally came to the point where I said to God, "I don't care if you allow me to be embarrassed, I just want to do what I believe you would do if you were here in the flesh." As Wimber says, faith is spelled R-I-S-K!

So, by an act of my will, I decided not to hold back. I decided to take risks in ministering as often as possible, while letting people know that I have no power to coerce God into doing my will. I only try to understand what he might want to do and then take the authority that he has given me to try to bring it about. I then go at it with an enormous amount of curiosity to see what God will choose to do. And it is that curiosity, perhaps more than anything else, that for me combats the fear that still remains.

Don't Be a Captive to Your Worldview

The bottom line is: don't be captives either to your worldview or to your will. Let's learn a lesson from the amazing story of Gideon. God will come to you just as he did to Gideon who—out of fear of the Midianites—"was threshing some wheat secretly in a wine press." For the Lord says to us, as his angel said to Gideon, "The Lord is with you, brave and mighty man!" (Jgs 6:11-12).

Gideon did not see himself as possessing the authority and power the angel described. His courage was small and his will weak. He was fearful and felt that God was far away. So he asked, "If I may ask, sir, why has all this happened to us if the Lord is with us? What happened to all the wonderful things that our fathers told us the Lord used to do. . . ? The Lord has abandoned us and left us to the mercy of the Midianites" (Jgs 6:13).

Gideon had heard all the wonderful stories of the things God used to do for his people. But he had not seen anything except the trouble that he and his people were in. He believed that God had abandoned them. Such an understanding is quite common among God's people today.

But the God of Gideon still lives! And all of the power that enabled Gideon to defeat the Midianites with an impossibly small army is still available to do mighty works today. God still wants to do such works. And just as in Gideon's day, he wants to do them on his own terms—in his own way—lest we think we did them by ourselves and give him no credit (Jgs 7:2). In fact, a major part of his strategy is to choose and work through weak and fearful people such as us who—like Gideon—he calls out of hiding and declares to be "brave and mighty!"

SEVEN

From a Change in Perspective to a Change in Practice

I T WAS ABOUT AS FRIGHTENING an experience as I have ever had! I had come to believe that God heals today through seeing it happen over and over in the *Signs and Wonders* class. If anyone had asked me then if I believed in healing, I would have answered something like, "Indeed I do, I've seen it!" And I would tell a story or two showing how I had come to such a belief.

In fact, this was one of the reasons I was now in difficulty. I had been telling young people at a church camp stories of the amazing things I had seen. I wanted them to learn how to open up to God's action at an earlier age than I had. And some of them were marvelously responsive. We had even prayed over one of the worship leaders and seen her healed of chest congestion almost immediately.

I had come through a change of perspective (my paradigm shift) to the point where I now thoroughly believed that God does heal people today. I had even come to the point where I was willing to join with others as they prayed for someone. But it was a frightening thing for me to imagine launching out and taking authority over an illness myself. I still thought of myself as not gifted and too sinful to be used by God in bringing healing to others.

But now, a young woman, whom I'll call Sharon, had collided with someone on the softball field and was calling for me to come and pray for her! I had been chatting with some of the young people sitting on a hillside overlooking the softball field. We had seen the collision and now saw Sharon lying on her back, with the camp director—a specialist in first aid—making preparations to get her onto a stretcher and then into his station wagon to take her to the hospital. The injury appeared to be in her left shoulder or in her neck, and the camp director judged it serious enough to warrant using a neck brace when she was moved.

Telling stories about healing and even praying in a group is one thing, but being asked to pray by yourself for a serious injury is quite another! So I was frightened! But there was no way out. She had specifically requested that I be the one to pray. Trembling, I went down to the ballfield where she was lying on the ground, visibly distraught. Sharon was an athlete, used to the rough and tumble of basketball and softball. But this was more pain than she could handle. As I gently placed my hand on her left arm to pray for her, she winced in pain and began to sob.

The prayer was nothing special. I simply tried to imitate what I had heard others say. And nothing seemed to happen! This disturbed me, but I wasn't surprised. After all, who was I to think I had any special "in" with God in spite of the things I had been seeing and hearing recently?

Then the prayer was over. The first aid expert, who had been rather impatiently waiting for us to complete our little ritual, put a stretcher underneath Sharon and the neck brace around her neck. He then supervised her transfer into the back of his station wagon so she could be taken to the hospital. We prayed again as they left, our spirits dampened considerably. When we returned to our game, it just wasn't the same. Sharon was on all of our minds.

No word came from the hospital during supper or the worship time that followed. And I began my evening message. Then after a few minutes, the back door opened and in walked Sharon with the friend who had accompanied her to the hospital. I remember looking to see what kind of bandage or splint she would be wearing. Nothing was evident. "Tell us the news," I said.

What she told us was as exciting as the experience had been frightening. She told of an extremely painful ride to the hospital. When she had arrived, an experienced doctor took one look at her and ordered that she be x-rayed for a possible broken neck. That x-ray showed nothing amiss, so he had the technicians take a picture of her shoulder. Nothing there either, so he asked them to take an x-ray of her collarbone. Still they found nothing.

At that she had suddenly realized that the pain was all gone! This amazed the doctor who remarked something like, "I've been around long enough to know when someone is badly hurt. When you came in here, I could tell that something was radically wrong. But the x-rays show nothing. And now you say there's no more pain! I can't explain it, but you may as well go home." And he released her.

We, too, were amazed and rejoiced. And I made a decision. If God was going to allow me to participate in making people well, I would simply "go for it." I would pray for everybody he brought my way.

Not everyone I have prayed for since then has received healing. Indeed, probably under half have received from God what I have asked for. But I was learning, growing in faith, and becoming more bold. I learned, for example, that in spite of the fact that everyone I prayed for did not get healed, everyone seemed to receive some blessing from the Lord. And my boldness increased to the point that I remember telling God I didn't even care if he let me be embarrassed, just as long as the Lord accomplished whatever he had in mind. As for me, I was going to be active in seeking opportunities to minister to people in this way, rather than ignoring or avoiding opportunities as I had been doing previously.

It was this decision to be faithful to God in this kind of ministry, no matter what the consequences, that I point to as my "practice shift." This was a second step. It was the crucial step that confirmed my change of perspective.

In this chapter I want to deal with how perspective and practice shifts take place. But first, let's attempt to clarify a few points concerning worldview.

Clarifying the Concept of Worldview

It has recently become fashionable for people to use the term worldview in popular writing and speaking with a much more restricted and imprecise meaning than is here in view. Many are seeking to discover and to live according to what they term "*the* Christian worldview."[1] Others use the term synonymously with religion and speak of Hindu, Buddhist, Muslim, and secular humanist worldviews.[2] Though it is fairly clear what such authors and speakers intend, the imprecision of their usage can result in a good bit of confusion, especially if one person is using the term anthropologically while another is using it in a more popular sense.

Is there a single Christian worldview? If so, why is it that committed, mature Christians from Africa, Asia, and North America do not all view things in the same way? While not denying that their Christian commitment has had a profound impact on their beliefs and behavior, we need to ask why it is that in most ways the members of a given society still look and think more like the other members of their society than like the Christians of any other society. It is also obvious that not even all Christians in any given society understand and act out their Christian principles in the same way. Is there, then, more than one Christian worldview?

Or if the term worldview is synonymous with religion, how should we talk about secular societies, such as those of Europe and America in which religious perspectives play a fairly minor role? Are dominant secular and scientific perspectives to be regarded as both religion and worldview? Or should we call what we traditionally term religion by that name and label secularism as a worldview? If so, how are we to understand the perspectives of those in such societies whose values and assumptions seem to be partly secular and partly Christian? Are they part one thing and part another?

It can all get very confusing and technical. My aim here is to help reduce the potential confusion without getting too technical. I have provided a more technical and detailed approach to worldview in the appendices for those who want to pursue the matter further.

1. First, note from our earlier definition that **a worldview includes all of the basic understandings of REALITY in terms of which the members of a society organize and live out their lives.** The term should not be used simply to refer to religious or even specifically Christian assumptions, as important as those are. The people of any given society, for example, will have specific assumptions, values, and commitments in areas of government, social control, economics, concepts of beauty, technology, and the like. Thousands of such assumptions underlie the behavior of a social group and are largely neutral with respect to religion in general and Christianity in particular.

2. Second, **though a person who becomes a Christian will need to make significant changes in his or her worldview, that person never exchanges his or her whole worldview for another one.** The term worldview does not merely refer to the things that we change in the process of growing in Christ. It refers to the whole cultural phenomenon *within* which Christian perspectives are to be planted.

If, then, Christian principles and values can operate within any given worldview, it is misleading to use a term such as "Christian worldview." For if God were advocating a totally Christian world-view, the implication would be that there is one divinely endorsed set of assumptions, values, and commitments designed to compete with those of every cultural worldview. But a worldview covers more territory than God seeks to change when someone becomes a Christian.

3. Third, **though there are many worldview assumptions that need to change as a person grows in the Christian faith, most of them—like most of the cultural behavior based on them—don't need changing.** For most of these assumptions simply represent an alternative that is preferred by a given social group in a particular area of life. Such assumptions would include whether a people assumes that time is to be conceived of as linear (the Western view) or spiraling (the Hebrew view), or whether they see the universe as divisible into two parts (earth and sky) or more than two, or whether they classify plants and animals according to Western scientific criteria or in some other way, or whether their society is arranged hierarchically or is more egalitarian, to name only a few. I will try to clarify this point further later on.

4. Fourth, **the term worldview may be used at different levels.** At one end of the spectrum, we can speak of an individual's worldview. At the other end of the spectrum, a term like "Western worldview" can be used to indicate a set of broadly construed assumptions shared by a number of Euro-American societies. Though these societies share such assumptions, they also differ in many other assumptions. Between individual worldviews, on the one hand, and those broad conglomerate worldviews that we call Western or African or Latin American, lie a large number of worldviews underlying the behavior of specific societies and subsocieties. We might speak of American Anglos or American Hispanics, for example, or a subgroup within such a society—such as "TexMex" Hispanic, rural Black, or Mid-western Anglo.

An individual's worldview is made up of his or her own set of assumptions, values, and commitments which will differ at least slightly from those of any other individual. Just so the worldview of a society or a subsociety is made up of those assumptions that are typical of a very high percentage of its individual members. And the worldview of a group of societies will be even more generalized and involve still more variation.

The worldviews of various societies—even of individuals for that matter—often differ from each other precisely at those points that are crucial in any attempt to communicate effectively across cultural boundaries. This fact is of great importance both to those who would want to communicate from one society to another and to those who would understand a crosscultural book such as the Bible. Differing perceptions of how a human being should be defined, for example, can greatly frustrate a would-be crosscultural communicator. In many societies of Papua New Guinea, for example, one cannot be regarded as a full human being unless one owns pigs. A person who owns no pigs finds no one listening to him. In traditional Korea and many other societies, it is the fact that one is a part of a family that makes one a human. Orphans are despised and treated as subhuman. Even more important for Christians are such things as different understandings of the proper relationship between humans and nature, humans and God, humans and material possessions, humans and other humans in the same group, humans and members of those outside the group. The nature of such relationships is often of considerable importance to God, as is evident from many of Jesus' parables. For instance, the parable of the prodigal son deals with a father's attitude toward a son who is first wayward and then repentant as symbolic of God's attitude toward his wayward children. It also is instructive concerning the attitude we should adopt toward fellow repentant sinners. The parable warns against the attitude of the elder son who harbors resentment against the younger son and the father's willingness to receive him back into the family.

The "Paradigm Shift": Seeing Becomes Believing

As I've mentioned, people never change their whole worldview. Yet worldviews change because people change parts of them. The reason for this is that a worldview is made up of a large number of distinguishable perspectives or "paradigms." It is these perspectives that can be changed. Indeed, many of them do get changed over the course of a person's lifetime.

A "*paradigm*" is a perspective on a sizable segment of reality. Each worldview is an organization of thousands of such semi-independent "picturings" or renderings of reality. The fact that such perspectives on reality can differ from person to person and from group to group explains why so much diversity can exist, even within a single society.

A perspective that is part of one's worldview might be the assumption that there are a large number of spiritual beings in the universe headed by a supreme Deity. Such a view is usually labeled "supernaturalism." Within that worldview assumption, then, there will be a large subset of perspectives or views (paradigms) about various beings. What kind of beings are they? What kinds of powers and responsibilities do they have? How can they influence or affect my life?

Likewise, if we suggest a worldview-level perspective such as the Western concept of individualism, we could point to paradigms that picture how the role of the individual is to be defined. Different paradigms enable us to understand how our society expects an individual to act in various circumstances when one is alone and when one relates to his or her family. We will have paradigms indicating what are the rights of an individual vis-a-vis the rights of other individuals of equal, greater, or lesser status.

We have spoken of the fact that paradigms are changed as we grow up and replace earlier perspectives with more developed ones. An even more radical type of paradigm shift takes place, however, when—through less predictable circumstances of life—we are brought face to face with the inadequacy of a previously held perspective. A tragic death in the family confronts us, for example, with an experience in which we feel at a loss to explain why. Or we witness something previously thought to be impossible like a physical healing by prayer and laying on of hands. Such events can shake us up and exert pressure on us to change our points of view. At such times people often make changes in the way they picture some aspect of reality.

Paradigms, then, are the segments of a worldview that should attract most of our attention both as we attempt to describe worldviews and as we discuss changing them. One important payoff of this kind of focus is the ability to sort out and recommend paradigms that Jesus taught as replacements for those taught by one's society.

The people of Jesus' day, for example, believed a paradigm that held that if the all-holy God got close they would die (see Isaiah 6:5). Jesus demonstrated, however, that when God gets close things go well for victims, though not for oppressors (see the series of stories in

Luke 5:1-32). Similarly, first-century Jews held that one should love his neighbors but hate his enemies. Jesus, of course, taught a paradigm that advocated love for everyone, even enemies (Lk 6:27, 35). Jesus also advocated forgiveness in place of unforgiveness and acceptance rather than rejection of outsiders—paradigms that contrasted with those of the people of his day.

In our day, we have our own set of challenging contrasts to deal with, such as that between the view that God is actively involved in world affairs and the understanding many of us were taught—that God is far away and uninvolved. Likewise, in the area of spiritual power, Jesus held that spirit beings such as angels and demons are alive and active; whereas, the paradigm we have been taught treats such beings as fictitious. Such "kingdom paradigms" (see chapter nine) call for a radical response when one becomes a kingdom Christian.

Conversion to and growth in Christianity thus becomes a series of paradigm shifts from one perspective to another in a number of areas. The first is a change in one's ultimate allegiance from the world and its values to God and his kingdom. It continues in a series of further paradigm shifts as one grows in the Christian faith. These are changes within one's worldview from certain of the native worldview perspectives to those mandated in Scripture. These changes or shifts are indeed crucial, but the vast majority of our paradigms that make up the assumptions and values distinguishing our worldview undergo little if any change. These remain pretty much the same as those of the non-Christians around us. This is why I refuse to speak of a single Christian worldview.

Within paradigms, there are still smaller, less complex picturings of reality, technically called *models*. These are often in the form of analogies. Jesus' representation of his relationship to God as that of a son to a father is such a model. So are the pictures Jesus drew of himself in his teachings as the Good Shepherd, the Bread of Life, the Lamb of God, the Water of Life, the Vine, the Word and others.

Though we will not go into detail at this level of worldview, it is valuable to know that such smaller "models" of reality are also subject to change in the process of worldview change. New experiences of God's closeness and loving concern will, for example, transform one's understandings of such models as Jesus the Good Shepherd and our relationship to him as that of branches to the Vine. Likewise, a deepened appreciation of Jesus as the expression of God, coupled with the recognition that when the word "Word" is employed in Scripture it almost always refers to God speaking to us, can transform our understanding of the model in view when Jesus is referred to as the "Word" (Jn 1). Under the influence of our Western veneration of literacy, the Jesus-as-Word analogy has tended to lead us into a concept of Jesus and of God's revealing activity in general as much more restricted and static than we see it presented in Scripture. Yet when we realize what the biblical authors really had in mind with this model, we witness afresh the dynamic activity of God in revealing himself—an activity that continues throughout history. Thus this model and, hopefully, our whole understanding about the present-day active involvement of God with his people becomes transformed. We see with new eyes.

Practice Confirms Perspective

With any change in our basic assumptions, there are at least two levels of change we need to be aware of. These are the level of *belief*—including worldview, paradigms, and models—and the surface level of cultural *practice*. It is quite common for a person to take at least some steps toward changing basic assumptions and beliefs before any attempt is made to change their practice. This was my experience in moving into belief in and practice of spiritual power. Yet there are other situations in which a person seems to change his or her practice first. For example, some people have been known to pray to God when they are in some kind of serious trouble, even before they fully believe he really exists. Likewise, many have had the experience of praying for healing with little or no belief that God heals today only to discover that he does indeed heal today! Yet believing either of these things does have to come fairly soon after the discovery in practice if there is to be a true change in one's worldview. The real key, though, is that change in both belief and practice are necessary if true worldview change is to take place. Whether the changes come in one order or the other is not particularly important.

The thing that cemented the new perspective for me was not when I changed my basic assumptions but when I changed my *practice*. Changing one's thinking does not in and of itself bring about the kind of radical change in worldview I am recommending. Only launching out and acting on the basis of new understandings will do the job.

Jesus dealt with this problem in response to a question about his credentials. "How does this man know so much when he has never been to school?" the Jewish leaders asked (Jn 7:15). He hasn't been to the right schools! How can he know so much? The answer Jesus gave was, I learned by *doing*. "What I teach . . . comes from God" (Jn 7:16). Then he told his hearers how they could be certain about the authenticity of his teaching: "Whoever is willing to *do* what God wants will know whether what I teach comes from God" (v. 17).

Jesus did not ignore the importance of doing, as opposed to merely thinking about how to do things, as is the case in much Western educational practice. For us, teaching is usually reduced to the intellectual exercise of simply passing information from one brain to another. Knowledge is defined as the information thus passed on. But for Jesus, teaching and knowing are primarily concerned with enabling people to *do* things, not simply to think things. *He knew that knowledge of something or someone is not really knowledge until it is cemented by a change in a person's behavior.*

The way to get to know God, then, is to obey him by doing his will. Just as person after person throughout the Old and New Testaments stepped out in risky obedience to God and thereby discovered who God really is, so we are to decide to do God's will and thus come to a certainty about who he is.

All other kinds of knowledge come this way as well. If we are ever to really know whether a healing ministry is for today, we will need to get beyond the theoretical discussions and even beyond the observation stage. We need to *try it*. Only after we have practiced something is our thinking structured and our knowledge confirmed according to our worldview. Because we assume what we have been taught, we interpret our practice as confirming our beliefs.

For years, I assumed that a particular cold remedy would help me get well when I had a cold. I had been taught that it was a good medicine, and my knowledge was based on the assumption I held. In fact, the medicine did seem to work. My practice confirmed my assumption. I *knew* the value of that remedy and recommended it to all my friends when they had colds.

But there came a time when I read an article in a popular consumers' magazine that questioned the value of all but one ingredient in the medicine I had faith in. That ingredient was aspirin. The article went on to suggest that it would be less expensive and just as effective to buy and use only aspirin. I believed the article and began to use only aspirin as a cold remedy. Several years of practice have now confirmed the new understanding I received from that article. When I read the article, I began to change my views on effective cold remedies. My theory changed. But the important part of the change, bringing with it the assurance of new knowledge, did not happen until I had put what I claimed to believe into practice.

As James warns, we should not deceive ourselves:

> By just listening to his word; instead, put it into practice.... But whoever looks closely into the perfect law that sets people free, who keeps on paying attention to it and does not simply listen and then forget it, but puts it into practice—that person will be blessed by God in what he does. (Jas 1:22, 25)

Practice confirms belief. Jesus taught his disciples first through example. He demonstrated what he talked about. Then he sent them out to practice it for themselves (Lk 9:1-6; 10:1-12). They were to "do it" with the power and authority he gave them. They were then to report back to him, and he would help them to do it better next time. So as Jesus left the earth and ascended to the Father, he instructed his disciples to teach—presumably in the same ways he taught them—all those they discipled "to obey everything I have commanded you" (Mt 28:19-20). As those who have become disciples of Jesus, we, too, are to learn through practice to obey all his commands.

Worldview Focus in Relation to Spiritual Power

As I've indicated elsewhere, different societies focus on different aspects of REALITY. Though all peoples need to deal with the material world, the human world, and the spirit world, different societies choose to emphasize one or two of these areas to the exclusion of the other(s).

One of the major differences between Western peoples and most of the rest of the peoples of the world lies in the contrast between our cultural focus and theirs. Whereas most of the rest of the world is primarily concerned with how to deal with the spirit and human worlds, we in the West are almost exclusively concerned with how to conquer and manipulate the material world. Our worldview assumptions keep our eyes focused on that area of life, while the worldviews of other peoples keep their eyes focused on that area they consider most important. In this respect, biblical peoples were much more like contemporary non-Western peoples than like Euro-Americans.

Since belief and practice go together, then, it is predictable that the worldview focus will be apparent in a society's surface-level behavior. This is why those whose focus is on the spirit world behave quite differently from those whose focus is elsewhere. Those who—like most Westerners—virtually ignore the spirit world demonstrate this in what they believe and how they live their lives. In actual practice, they act as if the spirit world doesn't exist, although they may pay some lip service to it. Instead, the emphasis is on material concerns to which human concerns are usually subservient. Spirit world concerns are, then, virtually nonexistent.

This being true, it is not by accident that technologically oriented Americans easily find themselves treating people, the universe, and even God as if they were machines. We expect well-nigh total predictability and surefire methods for fixing anything that gets broken—even humans and God. In fact, I believe that much of our desire to develop precise theological formulations and dependable rules of human behavior derives from our belief that God and people are like machines.

On the other hand, many non-Western peoples are more person-oriented and therefore tend to picture the universe as largely personal. They see such things as the weather and what Westerners call the "laws of nature" as capricious—as being more like people rather than almost totally predictable like machines. Such peoples seldom speak with the kind of certainty typical of Westerners about how humans, God, or nature will behave. Whereas Westerners tend to see their environment—both natural and human—as controllable, such peoples feel themselves largely under the control of an environment that may be quite unpredictable. Though this attitude may be expressed in a fatalistic response to such events as storms, floods, and droughts—they are often less "uptight" and angry than Westerners with respect to circumstances beyond their control.

Such peoples do, however, often seek to attain some control over their environment by focusing on the spirit world. They devote a large share of their attention to relating to the spirit world in hopes of keeping capricious beings and forces of the universe from harming them. With little understanding of causal factors that we term the "laws of nature" or of human life, they tend to explain most negative events as due to the activity of supernatural beings or powers. For many such peoples any accident, premature death, or "natural" disaster is automatically interpreted as caused by malevolent spirits. They seek then to discover why the spirits took revenge and try to appease them.

On the other hand, Western peoples tend to settle for understandings that focus on what may be called "intermediate causes." Explanations of reasonably predictable events by more ultimate causes such as God or evil spirits have for the last several generations seldom been appealed to by the majority of Westerners. Disease or accidents of all kinds, for example, are typically attributed to germs or "physical laws," rather than to more ultimate beings such as God or spirits.

My point is not that our Western approach is all wrong and that of some non-Western people is all right. As a matter of fact, each approach, though tending to be strong in the area of focus, is inadequate as a total approach. Each approach deals with only some of the variables. Non-Western societies with a supernatural perspective tend to focus only on ultimate causes, often ignoring important intermediate factors. On the other hand, Western peoples specialize in attempting to understand intermediate causes, usually ignoring ultimate ones.

Yet the rapid rise of the occult and "New Age" religion in Western societies shows that an increasing number of Westerners no longer believe our focus on intermediate causes is sufficient to explain everything that we want to know. Out of a sense of the inadequacy of the worldview answers we have been taught, both Christian and non-Christian Westerners are groping toward better understandings of a world of spirit beings and powers heretofore ignored by our societies. In this discovery, they are finding more ultimate explanations than those provided by science alone, plus enough spiritual power to satisfy some of their cravings and to overcome at least certain of their problems.

Moving Toward a Balance

I believe the realm of supernatural beings is a part of REALITY. That realm is not simply the invention of the peoples that believe in it. The fact that a concern for this area of life has biblical sanction leads me to believe that we are dealing with more than simply perceived reality at this point.

My mention of the fact that many contemporary peoples make the spirit world their central focus should not, however, be taken as an endorsement of their views. Their concern in this area simply indicates that certain contemporary peoples are not as blind as Westerners tend to be in this area. Their interpretations in this area of life are just as likely to be deficient as our or their interpretations in any other area. But the fact that the Bible takes supernatural beings and power seriously alerts us to the need for us to develop better insight into this part of REALITY. We should, therefore, give ourselves to learning as much as possible about spiritual beings and power, even from other peoples, in spite of the limitations imposed by our society.

I am not denigrating Western societies for their focus on gaining power over the material world. This quest is not wrong in and of itself. The problem comes when either our society or any other becomes so focused on one or the other of these aspects of life that balance is lost.

A society needs to tend to every important aspect of life if it is to be as helpful to its people as God intended. Otherwise, it is imbalanced. When non-Western or Western societies fail to develop adequate approaches to either material, human, or spiritual worlds, they get into difficulty. The appeal is for balance on the part of both types of societies. And there is hope for change. For though our worldviews are powerful forces in our lives, we are not totally determined by them. *It may be difficult, but we are able to make changes in our worldviews.*

We now turn to some specific suggestions as to how we can make changes and escape from worldview captivity. The fact that such changes can be made opens up to us a whole new possibility—a Christianity lived with power.

EIGHT

Escaping from
Worldview Captivity

I SAW IT WITH MY OWN EYES! A leg that had been a full inch and a half short was now the same length as the other one! And about forty other people were gathered around and saw the same thing. Further, we had all gotten a good look at the leg before it was lengthened and had heard the scraping sound of leather against leather as I held Elsie's shoes against each other. All of us were visibly stunned. Many of us had our mouths hanging open in amazement—especially Elsie and I! God had grown her short leg! And we were left dumbfounded.

Medically speaking, "leg lengthening" of about a half an inch is more likely to be the result of the loosening of back muscles than the actual lengthening of the leg. But tight back muscles could not be the reason for a leg this short. And if the medical explanation of what we saw is different from what I think happened, so be it. The fact is that about forty people saw a sizable physical change as a result of my taking authority over the condition and commanding it to change in Jesus' name.

But from that time to this, there is something inside of me that keeps saying rather forcefully, "What happened was not supernatural. There has to be a natural explanation for it." And that voice has been with me from the time I first began ministering healing right up to the present. I thought it would disappear after a while, but it hasn't. I simply know better now than I used to how to ignore it!

That voice was there again recently when I heard that a woman with terminal cancer to whom I ministered didn't seem to have the cancer anymore. It is with me now as I pray for her daily and as I pray for a young man who apparently doesn't have a longstanding back problem anymore. It is there as I remember an older woman who no longer suffers from the severe back problem she endured for thirty years. God is alive and doing such things through me almost daily!

Yet sometimes I get so upset at my inability to completely squelch that voice that I'm tempted to join Paul in his frustration as he cried out for a different reason, "What an unhappy man I am! Who will rescue me ... ?" (Rom 7:24). I understand in my head that worldview conditioning is embedded very deeply within us. But it is still extremely frustrating to try to deal with the considerable residue of Western rationalism within me. It requires a high degree of resoluteness and mental and spiritual discipline just to keep me from dropping out of this kind of ministry.

Will I ever get over it? Aren't the hundreds of things I've seen happen as a result of authoritative "prayer" enough to drive away my doubts? Apparently not. Only God's abiding grace, a strong will, and my intense curiosity seem to help me fight the doubt, the weak faith, and the fear that plague me. Another comfort has been to hear those who have participated in thousands of healings confess a similar skepticism. I relaxed considerably one evening when John Wimber, my mentor, revealed that he too struggles to believe what God does through him. At least I'm in good company!

Can We Change Our Worldview Perspectives and Really Believe in God's Power?

Can we change our perspectives then? Or should we simply give up? Satan would, of course, be very happy if we gave up. But all is not hopeless. Change can happen. I know. It has happened to me. The keys are will, knowledge, experience, and the abiding grace and encouragement of God. Let's look at these factors.

1. **Will is undoubtedly the most important factor in a change of perspective.** There are at least three points in the process where the way we exercise our wills is crucial. a) We either will to be open to a change or to be closed to it. Then, even if we open up to the possibility, b) we either will to make the change or not. If we do decide to make the change, c) we either will to continue with our decision or eventually give up.

Though we have dealt with the place of the will in hindering openness to change, it is helpful to discuss some largely positive aspects of the will's place in the process of changing a perspective. As we've seen, social factors may work either for or against change in someone's life. Mostly, they tend to inhibit abrupt, major change of the kind we are here advocating. Opening up to a supernatural perspective simply goes strongly against the grain of the worldviews of most Western Christians. Surprisingly, many non-Christians— especially those affected by "New Age" thinking—are more open than most Christians. Here internal factors tend to be more crucial as "will enhancers" than might be true if the change were of a kind to which the group is more open.

Among these is the relative *satisfaction or dissatisfaction* a person feels with a present perspective in this area. Many Christians have the feeling, "There must be more to Christianity than this." They read the Scriptures and see all kinds of things happening that don't seem to happen in their experience today. They believe in their heads that Jesus is "the same yesterday, today, and forever" (Heb 13:8), but what he seems to be doing today doesn't come close to what they read about him doing in the past. So they feel let down by Christianity, even though they are frequently quite committed to it.

Such Christians may have an important, unmet *felt need* to investigate a brand of Christianity with power to see if there is indeed more to it than they have experienced so far. This need is heightened if they or a loved one is in need of physical healing. Desperation tends to make people more open to displays of God's power. Desperate people will often risk social disapproval to get the help they sense they need. People who feel personally secure are also more likely than others to be venturesome since they no longer fear that social missteps may deprive them of their prestige.

Among the will strengtheners is the knowledge that there are others whom you respect who are "in this with you." A *credible witness* was very important in my own change of perspective. We knew that John Wimber was not a "wild-eyed radical," a person we might term a "weird Pentecostal or charismatic." He was someone we knew and respected. And others around him were also credible. So there was a respectable community to fit into if our own rejected us.

In spite of this, it is hard to overestimate the importance of knowing and getting frequent support from *at least one other person* within one's own reference group who embarks on the same journey into uncharted territory. For me, the companionship of my colleague Peter Wagner on the same pilgrimage has been very important, as has been my involvement to him. We have had each other for support in all kinds of tangible and intangible ways as we have moved into an area not ordinarily thought of as academically "safe." Though we have had others who supported us at a distance, the fact that two— rather than one of us—have been taking approximately the same steps at approximately the same time has at every point strengthened our wills to continue.

The *openness of one's reference group* to the change is another important will strengthener. Many groups will exert extreme pressure to keep a person from "getting out of line." Even groups that seem open to new ideas—such as the academic community of which I am a part—will often turn negative when it comes to changing perspectives on spiritual power. They might be charitable if you simply change your belief, since religion is usually regarded as a private matter. The rub comes if you begin to practice ministering in power as Jesus did. Those among my academic colleagues who objected to our *Signs and Wonders* course, for example, made it clear that they would not complain much if we simply offered a course that discussed healing ministries. It is when we insist on practicing what we preach that they get upset. Westerners, especially academics, are typically a good bit more open to "talking about" something than to "doing the works."

2. If the will is there to move into supernatural Christianity, is the knowledge? Every shift of perspective requires, at the very least, that a person know a shift is possible and has enough understanding about what lies on the other side to have an inkling of what to expect. One of the biggest hindrances to change is the lack of knowledge that there is an alternative. There are, however, at least *three kinds of knowledge: intellectual, observational, and experiential.*

In Western societies, it is information at the purely *intellectual* level that we are most aware of when we think of knowledge. Such knowledge is valuable but seldom life-changing in and of itself. Unless a person goes on to observational and experiential knowledge, a change of perspective is not very likely. That is where the will needs to be involved.

There is a close interaction between knowledge and will. People often allow purely intellectual knowledge to keep them from deciding to investigate a new idea. For instance, what the Pharisees thought they knew intellectually they used to reinforce their willful rejection of Jesus (see chapter six). Yet one Pharisee came to Jesus by night to check out his claims because he had observed and come to "know that [Jesus is] a teacher sent by God" (Jn 3:2).

Even the intellectual knowledge that God is healing people somewhere can provide a powerful impetus for a person to open him or herself up to investigating spiritual power. As a missiologist, I became intellectually aware that Pentecostal and charismatic Christianity was and still is by far the most rapidly growing kind. When I came to understand that the major reason for this was that signs and wonders are a prominent dimension of charismatic Christianity, I began to open up to people from these traditions. However, I had very little idea of how one went about such a ministry. Earlier Peter Wagner had become intrigued by the same realization and had moved from intellectual to observational knowledge.

For me, it wasn't until I attended the class on signs and wonders, that my intellectual knowledge became *observational knowledge*. I began to "know" at quite a different level when I was able—like Nicodemus—to observe others ministering in supernatural power and then see tangible results. It was only at this point that my openness was transformed into a genuine shift in perspective.

Yet many are quite capable of observing and rejecting something. Because of a strong will or some lack of ability on their part, they may not be able to see in a new way. The young man I called Jim in chapter six who watched part of a deliverance session may be in such a bind. His intellectual "knowledge" that such things don't happen anymore may have kept him from even observing what was happening, since such knowledge affects imagination. And one's inability to imagine a new perspective can provide a powerful barrier to keep one from moving toward that perspective.

On the other hand, an ability to imagine something different can aid one greatly in an attempt to move into a new perspective. Indeed, I have heard it said that "the difference between a good scientist and a great one is imagination." Certainly the greatness of Einstein lay largely in his ability to imagine new possibilities. Can you imagine yourself ministering healing to the ill? If so, you will probably move more easily into such a ministry than one who cannot imagine him or herself in such a role. Personally, I was hindered in my movement by a weak ability to imagine myself as a healer.

3. The thing that really did it for me was experience. Though this might be treated as a kind of knowledge, its importance warrants, I think, separate treatment. If in a perspective shift, one needs to move out of head knowledge and into habit, one needs to practice, practice, practice. There is absolutely no substitute for experience to bring one into a new perspective. That's why Wimber felt it necessary for us to "do the stuff" if we were ever to really change. The importance of my "practice shift" to my new perspective is eloquent proof to me that he was right.

To help us continue practicing until it has the force of habit, it's helpful to have a goal in mind. I tell people that they should make an agreement with God to begin praying for healing and not to stop unless they have failed fifty times in a row! If they fail fifty times running, they may conclude that God doesn't want them in that kind of ministry. It must be fifty times in sequence, however. Failing twenty times and then succeeding once means one has to start counting all over again. I don't believe anyone who launches out in this way will find that he or she fails fifty times in a row. Nor will the person stop praying for the sick and injured. The new habit will be confirmed and the blessings received will be so great that the person will not want to go back to the old habit of not ministering in God's healing power.

The Steps to Take

In moving from largely rationalistic into what I like to call "kingdom Christianity," the following steps need to be taken:

1. First, make sure there is no will problem. Learn from our earlier discussion of the Pharisees (chapter six) to abandon the kinds of attitudes they were condemned for. Reject such things as vested interests, rebellion against God, unwillingness to risk prestige for truth, and fear of becoming odd. Exercise your will to discover and practice all that God has for you.

2. Open yourself up intellectually. Let your mind and your imagination accept, at least tentatively, that God is still doing marvelous things. Accept the possibility that God may be doing things in other contexts that you have not seen in yours. Don't adopt the attitude of a preacher who said something like, "If these gifts were for today, they would have come to us first." The fact is that sizable groups, even of sincere Evangelical Christians, can easily get insulated and miss important facets of life, whether it's understanding the plight of the poor or experiencing the reality of God's healing activity. So open up.

3. Expose yourself to experiences where God's power is being manifested. Expose your old perspective to new experiences. The "perspective-experience circle" at the right symbolizes the continuing process one goes through as perspective is tested by experience, and then experience is based on perspective. Obtain as much observational knowledge as possible. Go out of your way to be where demonstrations of God's power are

taking place. There is currently a constant stream of healing and spiritual gifts seminars being offered all over the U.S. In addition, many churches offer healing services. Go to a variety and be curious enough to get close to the action. Let that newfound observational knowledge challenge your previous knowledge and imagination.

4. Read the Gospels with the assumption that these things can happen today. There is nothing in Scripture that indicates that signs and wonders were meant to stop after the early days of Christianity. The theories about the termination of certain spiritual gifts all come from human interpreters under the influence of Western worldviews. They don't come from God's Word. Furthermore, one suspects self-interest among those who hold such theories, since the theories support their own lack of experience and participation in this area that was so central to Jesus' ministry.

Contrary to some of those theories, we are not to allow the Gospels to be relegated to a secondary place in the Scriptures behind the more rationalistically oriented Pauline Epistles. I have heard preachers say, "Mine is an Epistles' Christianity," as if the letters of Paul contain a revelation superior to the words and works of Jesus himself. Take seriously in both belief and practice the orthodox contention that both the Gospels and Epistles are still inspired and normative for God's people today.

Recognize that it is a particular worldview and limited experience, not a difference in the value of the inspired writings, that has led Western Christian leaders to focus on the Epistles—especially those written by Paul—at the expense of the Gospels. A major reason for this focus on the Epistles is that several of them were aimed at the Greek-speaking world, a world much more like ours than the Hebrew world. They seem from a Western point of view to be more relevant. But *all* of God's Word is to be taken seriously and followed.

5. Read books and listen to tapes on the subjects in focus here. There are many worthwhile materials, along with some that are of questionable value. Read and listen widely, though, for only then will you be able to distinguish between the best and the worst of what is available.

6. Be willing to reexamine and reconsider doctrinal understandings where Scripture allows for another possibility. Remember that most doctrinal statements are but interpretations springing from human experience and knowledge. They are not to be held to as if they were a part of Scripture itself or, worse yet, had replaced Scripture.

I don't mean to question the value of creeds and other doctrinal statements. It's just that all such statements—no matter how well and sincerely stated—usually reflect the limited experience of intellectuals. Such statements are seldom written by practitioners. They, therefore, tend to ignore the truth that only those who—like Jesus and Paul—are both effective practitioners and solid Christian thinkers adequately present what the Bible teaches. Don't let anyone else replace the Bible for you. It alone stands as God's inspired Word.

7. Practice what you learn. Feed every change of understanding into your experience. Be willing to experiment. You will not know whether you have any given gift until you experiment a lot. As mentioned earlier, I have found that any "gifting" I have in the area of healing has developed just as did my gift of teaching—through practice and experimentation. We learn only by practicing these things how to venture forth in faith, how to hear God, how to take authority, and how to counsel those who seem not to have received help. You can't learn to swim by simply swinging your arms on the beach! You need to jump in and swim!

Try the "fail fifty times in a row" experiment I've mentioned. Don't give up on ministering in the authority and power Jesus gave you without a fair trial. How else can you discover whether God wants you in such a ministry? And take seriously the possibility that ministering in this way is not a matter of "gifting," it is simply being obedient to God and his Word in Scripture. After all, isn't healing coupled with preaching in the commands to Jesus' disciples in Luke 9:2 and 10:9? I have come to believe that we are to minister in this way out of sheer faithfulness, even if God never brings the results we expect.

8. Don't let a sense of spiritual inadequacy keep you from ministering in authority and power. Like the disciples, you will never be spiritually, psychologically, or intellectually adequate for this task. But God chooses people like the disciples, like Gideon, and even like us (Jn 15:16) to do incredible things by using his power and his power alone—we have none of our own.

It is Satan who tells you that you shouldn't be doing such ministry because of your spiritual condition. God assures you that you are forgiven—assuming, of course, you have confessed and repented of all known sin. Further, he knows your motives—not just your weaknesses. When you try, stumble, and fall because you made a mistake, he will not treat you as if you had a rebellious heart. Instead, as he did with Peter (Jn 21:15-17), he simply lifts you up and gives you yet another chance.

9. Be patient with yourself and with God. Any learning process takes time. There may be a few people who are immediate experts. But most of us don't get there that quickly. We try something and fail. Then we pick ourselves up and try again. We can get discouraged and even consider quitting. But don't quit until, like Jacob (Gn 32:26), you receive the blessing from God that you sense he wants for you—the one God promises to those who are faithful.

10. Give God permission to do anything he wants with you, even to the point of allowing you to be embarrassed! Practice listening to him before, during, and after ministry times, as well as on other occasions. Give him permission to bring people to you for ministry and pray that he will. Then be content with whoever God brings. I like to ask him to bring someone each day. You may want to start with less. Learn to *focus on thanking him* for every good thing that happens. Ponder each event, whether you consider it a positive or a negative experience and learn from it. Don't dwell on the "failures." Don't let Satan rob you of the blessing God intends for you.

11. Don't worry about your doubts. Jesus honored the faith of the man who said, "I do have faith, but not enough. Help me have more!"

(Mk 9:24). He knows how hard it is for us and honors our attempts even though they are feeble. I once heard someone say, "Little faith is not necessarily weak faith." Thank God for that! Remember: the healing is not finally the result of our faith. It is God and God alone who does it. And he reads our motives and blesses the faithfulness and obedience we render to him as more important than the struggle we may have to believe as we think we ought.

Can We Escape?

Much of what I've been saying in previous chapters concerning the influence of worldview and the strength of our habits to keep us from changing could be quite discouraging. Hopefully, this chapter has been more encouraging. For the truth is *we can change* both our perspectives and our habits. I know because I've seen it happen in my own life. When I note how readily I now seek to pray with those in need, I know a perspective and the powerful habits that enforced it have been changed. A naturalistic habit has been replaced by a kingdom habit. If we work at it, asking God to help us and to bring us opportunities to practice a prayer ministry, it can happen.

Our ultimate goal is not, however, simply to minister healing to others. It is to be like Jesus. He came for several reasons, one of which was to provide a model for our belief and behavior. As a human, he had a worldview. Let's look at it.

NINE

Jesus Had a Worldview

I HAD BEEN ASKED TO WRITE an article on miracles for a Pentecostal publication. How would I approach it? As I sat before my computer screen pondering the subject and seeking for an "angle," I began to "feel" a vague distaste for the subject, especially for the word "miracle." At first, I couldn't quite put my finger on the reason for this feeling. Indeed, I argued with myself that I should be enthusiastic about these wonderful interventions of God that I had recently begun to experience quite frequently. After all, I reasoned, wasn't it this new experience of miracles that was responsible for the marvelous renewal going on in my own life?

Yes, these power demonstrations—evidence of God's concern and willingness to use his power to bless me and others—were changing my whole outlook on life. For the first time in my Christian experience, I was seeing the kind of things I had read about for so long in the New Testament. God had become closer, more real, and more credible to me. In short, he was more of everything than I had ever believed he was. So why was I so uneasy about this label that was commonly used to describe these interventions of God?

And then it dawned on me. *The concept of "miracle" implies interference, intervention, and the interruption of normalcy.* It is a term that fits quite nicely into a semi-deistic view of God. It implies that he is well outside the human sphere, only occasionally stepping in to break a "natural" law here, to speed up a "natural" process there, to bring about an event that seemed "statistically very unlikely" here, or to create a "puzzling circumstance" there. In sum, *the term miracle implies abnormality and the breaking of natural laws.*

101

But those definitions of "normalcy" and "natural law" need to be examined. For they come from our naturalistic worldview. It is normal, we say, for someone to fall if he or she trips over something. The "law of gravity" will see to that. It is also "normal" for people to fight to preserve their lives, we say. For there is a "law of self-preservation." We have many such "laws" and have quite a bit of confidence in them when they relate to the world of nature—our Western focus. We can have much less confidence in the validity of those "laws" that apply to the human world and still less in the dependability of those we may think apply to the spiritual world.

As Westerners, we label "natural" or "normal" those things that our assumptions concerning the universe lead us to define as such. Other things we call "supernatural," "abnormal," "mythical," "fanciful" and the like. We take the so-called "natural" things seriously and study them "scientifically." Reports of events in the other category tend to be regarded as "fairy tales" since they are "unscientific." All or most of religion fits into this category for a high percentage of Westerners, including many who regularly attend church! If, then, we see or experience something good that doesn't fit into the "natural" category, we often label it "miraculous." For Westerners, healing as a result of naturalistic, scientific procedures seems normal. Healing without the aid of such "normal" techniques, though, is called "miraculous" since it is unexplainable in terms of the limited worldview perspective that we have been taught.

But Jesus acted as if healings and other uses of spiritual power to overcome natural, human, or spiritual conditions ought to be normal occurrences! Not that every problem was to be automatically dealt with through what Westerners would call a "miracle." Jesus himself did not do that. But he seemed to expect the children of the kingdom, as a normal part of their lives, to be in constant contact with God and claiming his power in the living of life.

"Where is your faith?" (Lk 8:25), he asks after the disciples wakened him during the storm on the lake. It looks as though he expected the disciples to check with the Father and find out what he found out—that the storm was to be calmed through the use of God's power—and then to do it themselves without bothering him! Similarly, he says to the disciples, "You yourselves give them something to eat" (Lk 9:13), when the five thousand are hungry. They were to do what he considered the natural thing—to consult the Father and do whatever he said. Nor did he consider inability to cast out a demon normal. "How unbelieving you people are!" (Mk 9:19), he says to his followers when they failed at this task. To Jesus these were normal parts of life, to be dealt with normally—by turning to God.

Yet when the disciples were able to cast out demons and rejoiced over it, he put things in their true perspective by saying, "Don't be glad because the evil spirits obey you; rather be glad because your names are written in heaven" (Lk 10:20). The greatest wonder of all ("miracle") is the salvation of our souls, he seems to be saying. These other things are meant to be normal occurrences for kingdom people. It's not such a big deal to cast out demons! The big sign and wonder is that we have been admitted into God's family.

These and other passages from the Gospels came to mind as I asked myself the question, What did Jesus consider "normal"? And it began to dawn on me that Jesus had a worldview! As a human being he had a set of perspectives on life, most of which he shared with the rest of his society—including his enemies. But there were certain distinctives—certain perspectives—in Jesus' understandings that did not originate in the society in which he lived his earthly life. These came directly from God the Father and are normative for us, his followers.

Why Not Call This the Christian Worldview?

Many try to label these perspectives *a* or, worse, *the* "Biblical worldview." Such a term is, however, imprecise enough to be misleading, since *it confuses a set of perspectives revealed by God and integrated into one particular cultural worldview with the worldview as a whole.* Such a term could easily be misconstrued to imply either that there is only one cultural worldview in the Bible (which there isn't) or that God endorses one or another of those worldviews as normative for everyone (which he doesn't).

The use of the term "worldview" in this way easily misleads Western people into believing that God endorses Hebrew cultural perspectives on life. But there is nothing sacred about Hebrew perspectives, even though they are recorded in the Bible. They simply make up a human culture that God was pleased to work through to reveal something much more important.

The more important perspectives are those that God has advocated throughout Hebrew history and supremely in the life and ministry of Jesus Christ. These come to us embedded in the perspectives of the

Hebrew worldviews present in the Scriptures, none of which he endorsed. He merely uses, without endorsement, first the worldview of the pastoral Hebrews, then that of the time of the Judges, followed by those of the united and divided kingdoms and of the prophets. Only the perspective of Jesus is endorsed, "This is my Son, whom I have chosen—listen to him!" said God on the Mount of Transfiguration (Lk 9:35).

That's why I prefer to specifically speak of Jesus' perspectives or paradigms when referring to the biblical assumptions we should strive toward. Another label I like to use for them is "kingdom perspectives or paradigms," referring to the same content but focused on the central theme of Jesus' teaching. Recognizing that even most of Jesus' worldview had a cultural rather than a "supracultural" (from God) source, however, I am reticent to assert even that Jesus' *whole* worldview is normative for us. For he was a first-century Galilean Jew who learned the purely human part of his worldview in a Hebrew corner of the Greco-Roman world. A large number of his perspectives, then, would have been specific to that way of life and not necessarily applicable to ours.

Peter's Worldview in Contrast With Ours

Before going on to outline Jesus' kingdom perspectives, let's contrast certain features of a typical first-century Hebrew's worldview with that of a typical American. Such a contrast will provide a basis for better understanding both the changes required of first-century Palestinians and those required of us when we attempt to integrate kingdom perspectives into a human worldview.

We will attempt to imagine what the worldview of the apostle Peter looked like. To the extent that we are able to do this, we will get an idea of how Jesus' worldview would have looked had he not worked kingdom perspectives into it. It would have looked like Peter's. But it differed significantly from that of his contemporaries because of the divinely endorsed paradigms or perspectives that he held. Since these divinely endorsed perspectives are normative for contemporary Christians of any society, they are the perspectives to be incorporated into the worldviews of Christians of every society.

Peter, as a normal Hebrew, would have had a keen sense of the supernatural world. He would have believed in God, angels, demons, and Satan. Peter would have expected certain evil powers to be very active in everyday life. He also may have believed in such things as empowered fetishes and the power of the "evil eye." With Gideon, he probably believed that God had largely abandoned Israel. Yet as a faithful Hebrew, he would have believed in the efficacy of keeping of the Law—including many of the Pharisaic additions to it—in properly relating to God. Peter certainly believed that such tragedies as blindness were caused by individual sin (Jn 9:2). Indeed, he probably believed, as did the people of David's day, that God causes evil as well as good (see 1 Sm 18:10).

He would have believed a number of things that Jesus opposed such as: Jews have the right to treat Gentiles and Samaritans badly; material prosperity and social prestige (such as that of the Pharisees) are signs of divine blessing; those close to a powerful person have the right to prestigious positions (see Mk 10:35-45); the establishment of the kingdom would involve the military overthrow of the Romans (see Acts 1:6); and that family loyalty superceded loyalty to God. Peter went against this value when he followed Jesus, but he probably had a guilty conscience over it.

Peter would also have been event-oriented rather than time-oriented. (Imagine the time taken by the events in Acts 2!) He would have considered competition between people within the ingroup to be evil (see Acts 15:7-11). Peter would have considered the group—especially the family and tribe—to be more important than individuals and the real measure of social status. His logic would have been more like that of the Book of Hebrews, more "contextual" and cyclical than linear like ours.

On the other hand, our typical American Evangelical Christian—we'll call him Sam—has everything neatly packaged into "natural" and "supernatural" categories. The supernatural is regarded as vague and largely uninvolved in day-to-day matters. He attributes most of what goes on around him to chance, not to the activities of spiritual beings. Sam seeks to control his life more through science and technology than through prayer.

More time-oriented than event-oriented, Sam thinks linearly and is extremely individualistic. He believes people are equal—though he doesn't necessarily treat them that way—and considers competition a good thing. Sam measures himself and others in terms of money and material possessions. He regards change as good and considers it an indication of progress. Probably like Peter, he sees the things of biblical history as quite different from the things that go on in his day, since he reads the accounts in the Bible of people and events in which God seemed to be more involved than those he experiences.

The question becomes then: What will it take to incorporate Jesus' kingdom perspectives into each of these worldviews? It will require a considerable amount of change for both Peter and Sam. But in the area of spiritual power, the changes for Peter will be largely matters of refinement. For Sam, however, the changes in that area will be radical. With respect to valuing individual persons, the changes will be more radical for Peter than for Sam. In this area, though Sam's behavior may require some significant change, his belief in the equality of persons is probably closer to Jesus' ideal than was Peter's. And so the comparison would continue.

From Peter to Jesus

As we have seen, a worldview is a cultural phenomenon. As I have discussed at length in my book, *Christianity in Culture,* God works *through* culture; he does not oppose whole cultural systems. A position that sees it necessary for people to totally replace their cultural worldview with something called a Christian worldview does not really understand the Scriptures. God is not against culture in this way, though he has plenty to say in opposition to many sociocultural beliefs and practices.

On the other hand, we have said that Jesus had a worldview. That worldview, then, provides for us the clearest picture of how God's ideals are to be combined with the human perspectives of a typical worldview. And Jesus' example is intended to be imitated by his followers (see Philippians 2:5; 1 Corinthians 11:1). *In Jesus, then, we have God's ideals combined with both a human worldview and fully human surface-level behavior to provide the supreme example of how God wants to work in and through a person within the sociocultural matrix in which he lives.* We are called to follow that model and combine his ideals with our own worldview and behavior.

Though we must deny that there is a Christian culture or worldview, we can assert that we can learn from Jesus those perspectives and behavior that are to distinguish a person attempting to live the Christian life within a sociocultural setting.

We are, I believe, to be taught by Jesus in both word and deed. We are to believe what he believed and to behave as he behaved in the areas on which he focused. This does not mean that we are to eat and dress as he did, or to worship at a temple, or to classify life as first-century Palestinians did, or to use time and space as Jesus did. Most of our normal cultural beliefs and behavior are no worse or better than most of his. They needn't be abandoned.

Yet Jesus' example does give us perspectives or paradigms and behavior that are distinctively Christian. These are the things we are required to believe in and live out within our societies. These assumptions and behaviors are to be integrated with the human perspectives and behaviors that we have been taught. Just as Jesus had to modify and replace some of the perspectives and behaviors taught within his society, so we need to modify and replace some within our societies.

What we finally come up with, then, is not a Christian culture with a Christian worldview, but a modification of the human culture and worldview we have been taught. We are still distinctive as American Christians just like Sam—even if we learn and apply Jesus' perspectives perfectly within our society. Likewise, Africans, Asians, and Latin Americans are still distinctive culturally, even if they learn and apply Jesus' perspectives perfectly.

What, then, are the kingdom perspectives we all need to incorporate into our worldviews?

Jesus' Kingdom Perspectives

As we have seen, a worldview consists of thousands of semi-independent picturings called perspectives or paradigms. And people with essentially the same worldview will show differences within their worldview when these individual perspectives are compared. This means that when Western Christians differ as to whether God performs signs and wonders today, they are not differing at the total worldview level. Rather their differences involve competing perspectives *within* the same overall worldview. That is, they hold to different paradigms within the same worldview, not to different worldviews.

Likewise, the differences between Jesus and the Pharisees were differences *within* rather than *of* worldview. The vast majority of Jesus' and the Pharisees' assumptions remained the same. There were, of course, crucial contrasts between Jesus' perspectives and those of the Pharisees. But there were not as many differences between the way Jesus viewed things and the way other members of his society did as there are between Hebrew views and those of any of us within Western contexts. Their differences were between perspectives within a single worldview.

Our primary concern is to point to a selection of Jesus' assumptions that we believe transcend those parts of his particular worldview that he held in common with his own countrymen. These we hold to be normative whether or not they contrast with either our assumptions or those of his enemies.

Most of the assumptions of Jesus that challenge our perspectives center around two themes: power and love. The first falls into the worldview category, causality, the second into the person-group category, each of which is described in Appendix B. These are the worldview categories most frequently challenged by Christian perspectives.

1. Jesus assumed the existence of God. He also had very definite assumptions concerning the nature and activities of God. He saw God as:

a.) **A Father with absolute authority over his children** (remember: this was a Hebrew father, not an American one) **but who always remains favorably disposed toward them, though demanding obedience and faithfulness.** The Father's children are always welcome in his presence even though his power is awesome. He pines for those who turn away but welcomes them back with feasting when they return (Lk 15:11-32).

b.) **One who is actively involved in and with his creation** (Jn 5:17). The God and Father of Jesus is no absentee landlord. He is interested and active in all that goes on, constantly close and willing to help (Jn 15:16). He likes it when his children spend time with him as Jesus did frequently.

c.) **One who stands against oppressors** (such as the Pharisees) but who is tender and gentle toward victims (such as the woman caught in adultery, John 8:1-11), and even toward recalcitrant disciples (such as Peter, John 21:15-19).

d.) **One who values people with agape love.** This love, as William Barclay points out, is meant to be applied by humans to other humans. Barclay tells us that *agape* love:

> describes an active feeling of benevolence towards the other person; it means that no matter what that person does to us we will never allow ourselves to desire anything but his highest good; and

we will deliberately and of set purpose go out of our way to be good and kind to him.[1]

Jesus clearly saw God as one who stood primarily in favor of human beings, as a lover in contrast to the common view of God as one who was basically negative and judgmental toward human beings.

e.) **One who understands and relates to people on the basis of their motives rather than their surface-level behavior or condition.** To the Jewish leaders, those who were ill or poor were so because they were sinners. Those who, like themselves, were in positions of wealth and power, however, were considered to be in God's favor. Yet Jesus demonstrated God's true attitude which was often the opposite of the leaders' evaluations (for example, the paralytic, Luke 5:17-25; and the Pharisees, Matthew 23:1-36).

2. Jesus also assumed the existence of the spirit world. He assumed the existence of angels (Mt 4:11; 25:31), demons, and Satan. That world was probably more real to him than the physical world. It should also be more real to us.

3. Jesus believed in two kingdoms, the kingdom of God and the kingdom of Satan. As he makes plain in Matthew 12:22-29, these kingdoms are at war with each other. Further, the kingdom of God is now assured of victory (Col 2:15; 1 Jn 3:8) because of Jesus' death and resurrection. Yet Jesus doesn't dispute Satan's claim that he is in charge of the world when Satan says:

> I will give you all this power and all this wealth.... It has all been handed over to me, and I can give it to anyone I choose. All this will be yours, then, if you worship me. (Lk 4:6-7)

Jesus seems to have accepted the fact that the "kingdoms of the world" have "been handed over to [Satan]" and that now "the whole world is under the rule of the Evil One" (1 Jn 5:19). One view is that this handing over was done when Adam sinned. We do not know for sure. But Jesus' assumption seems to be that Satan actually had the control he boasted about and that it is the mission of Jesus and his followers to establish another kingdom behind enemy lines.

It is as if Jesus had parachuted into enemy territory, gathered followers, trained them, and then set them loose behind enemy lines with the intent of taking more and more territory from the other king. Taking that territory is done through freeing those who are captive to and oppressed by the enemy. Our mandate, then, is the same as he announced for himself:

> The Spirit of the Lord is upon me, because he has chosen me to bring good news to the poor. He has sent me to proclaim liberty to the captives and recovery of sight to the blind, to set free the oppressed and announce that the time has come when the Lord will save his people. (Lk 4:18-19)

Jesus' kingdom people are to receive the Spirit of the Lord as he did, through the infilling of the Holy Spirit (Lk 3:21-22). Then in the power and authority given by God, we are like Jesus to release poor, captive, blind, and oppressed people from the enemy because God values and loves his creatures. For "the time has come" when God will rescue those who have fallen under the evil influence of Satan. Jesus assumes conflict and enlists us in his war. Then we, like Jesus, are to use *God's power to demonstrate God's love.*

4. Jesus also seems to assume that this is a power confrontation. Though he says much about love in relation to the people we are to free, the assumption with regard to Satan is power versus power. Jesus exercised his authority and power continuously in opposition to satanic captivity both in teaching (Lk 4:32) and in healing (Lk 4:36, 39).

Then he sent his disciples out as the Father had sent him (Jn 20:21) with "power and authority" to oppose Satan by driving out demons, curing diseases, communicating the kingdom of God (Lk 9:1-2; 10:9; Mt 10:1, 7-8), and even forgiving sins (Jn 20:23). The power to bless is also assumed (Lk 6:28). Because Jesus himself has been given authority, he commissions us to go out to do the same things he did (Mt 28:18-20) and to do even more than he did (Jn 14:12). We are to receive power from the Holy Spirit just as Jesus did and to go out as witnesses (Acts 1:8). We are called ambassadors (2 Cor 5:20), representing Jesus' kingdom.

5. It is assumed, I believe, that both Jesus and his followers receive all their power from the Holy Spirit (Lk 3:21-22; 24:49; Acts 1:8; 10:38). Jesus apparently did no supernatural acts before "God poured out on him the Holy Spirit and power. [Then] he went everywhere, doing good and healing all who were under the power of the Devil, for God was with him" (Acts 10:38). To quote the famous early twentieth-century Bible teacher, R.A. Torrey, who wrote from a noncharismatic perspective,

> Jesus Christ obtained power for His divine works not by His inherent divinity, but by His anointing through the Holy Spirit. He was subject to the same conditions of power as other men.[2]

Neither can we do any of the works Jesus promised we would do (Jn 14:12) unless we are thus empowered.

6. Jesus only does God's works as he sees and does what the Father is doing (Jn 5:19). So too *we* can only do God's works as we see and do what the Father is doing. We are to maintain a close relationship with God as Jesus did, listening, watching, and doing what the Father shows us we should do. We are, like Jesus, to do nothing on our own authority, but to say only what the Father instructs us to say and to "always do what pleases him" (Jn 8:28-29).

It is crucial, therefore, that we learn to hear God. If Jesus had to spend lots of time in prayer to do this, we must also learn to do so:

> The Father and the Son were, as it were, continually in each other's presence, relating to each other—communicating. Jesus' prayer life was an integral part of this relationship. (Lk 5:16, etc.)[3]

7. To Jesus believing is seeing (Lk 8:9-10). The knowledge and wisdom of the kingdom are only available to those who first believe and trust the King. As noted, the Pharisees willfully refused to believe and thus blinded themselves to the real issues of the kingdom. To those who did believe, however, Jesus said things like, "Your faith has made you well" (Mt 9:22; Mk 10:52).

8. Obedience to God brings knowledge. "How does this man know so much when he has never been to school?" the Jewish authoriti·s asked (Jn 7:15). And Jesus answered:

> What I teach is not my own teaching, but it comes from God, who sent me. Whoever is willing to do what God wants will know whether what I teach comes from God or whether I speak on my own authority. (Jn 7:16-17)

9. Agape love is the appropriate human response both to God and to humans. When Jesus was asked what is the greatest commandment, he answered:

> Love the Lord your God with all your heart, with all your soul, and with all your mind. This is the greatest and the most important commandment. The second most important commandment is like it: Love your neighbor as you love yourself. The whole Law of Moses and the teachings of the prophets depend on these two commandments. (Mt 22:37-40)

But we are not only to love our neighbors, we are also to love our enemies and others who treat us badly, even to the extent that we use the spiritual power God gives us to "bless those who curse [us]" (Lk 6:27-36). That is, we are to "do for others just what [we] want them to do for [us]" (Lk 6:31). We are to "be merciful just as [our] Father is merciful" (Lk 6:36). We are to imitate Jesus by treating our fellow human beings as God treats human beings, including us.

10. Jesus assumed that forgiving others enables God to forgive us, while unforgiveness of others blocks God's forgiveness of us (Mt 6:12, 14-15). Because of our own propensities for sin, therefore, we are to refuse by an act of our will to judge and condemn others. Instead, we are called to be generous like God, for "the measure you use for others is the one that God will use for you" (Lk 6:38).

Human inclination and worldly "wisdom" pressure us to give others what we get from them or, worse, what we think they deserve. And the unforgiveness, judgment, and condemnation that result often make us ill. Such attitudes also block our relationship with God and the healing he would like to bring to us. There is no greater blockage to a person's receiving healing from God than that person's refusal to forgive others. Only adopting God's attitude toward others can free us to relate properly to God, others, and ourselves.

11. If we acknowledge our sin, God will forgive us (1 Jn 1:9). Though the direct statement of this principle comes from 1 John, Jesus' teaching on repentance (Mt 4:17) and his forgiveness of the sick who came to him acknowledging their need (Lk 5:17-25) show that it is his assumption.

It is a common worldview assumption that we should attempt to hide our sin either by denying it or by comparing it to that of others. "I'm not as bad as so-and-so," we say, trying to rationalize our own sin. But God's standard is the only one that counts. And by that standard we are all guilty but, through confessing our sin to him as he says to do, we will be forgiven.

12. **We are not to fight back** (Lk 6:29). Absorb whatever blows are leveled at you; don't resist them. This seems to be the principle. The real winners and losers will be determined by God at a later date, not by humans on the basis of what happens now.

We are never to take revenge, but instead to repay good for evil (Rom 12:17-21). God himself will take care of repaying those who deserve punishment, for he says, "I will repay, I will pay back," (Rom 12:19; Dt 32:35). Therefore, if we are to act like Jesus, we are to bless and "pray for those who mistreat" us. We are to allow them to hit us on both cheeks and to give them more than they attempt to take (Lk 6:28-29; Rom 12:14).

13. **Concern for the kingdom and faithfulness to God is the only worthwhile goal to aim at** (Mt 6:33). Contrary to what the world recommends, we are to forget ourselves. We are not to try to get ahead in the world's eyes but to unashamedly follow him by refusing to worry about material things (Lk 9:23-26; Mt 6:24-34).

14. **As God's stewards, we are to risk with God rather than to preserve for God.** The parable of the talents (Mt 25:14-30) is the key passage making this perspective explicit. Each of the servants started out with something with which he was to bring about an increase for the master. Those who were commended risked what they were given. They brought back to the master more than they had been given. The one who simply sought to preserve what he had been given was condemned, and his talent was taken away to be given to one who knew what to do with it.

In reflecting on this passage, I have asked myself, "What if those who risked had lost? What would the master's attitude have been to such a situation?" I believe he would have encouraged his servant and given him another set of talents to go out and risk again. Doing the right thing with what God gives us is, I believe, the key principle being taught. Whether or not there is "success," especially success as measured by human standards, is not the issue.

15. To be great in the kingdom, become like a child (Mt 18:1-5). Though we probably don't know all that Jesus intended by this analogy, he does specify humility. Perhaps we may also speak of the attitudes of dependence, trust, and innocence. Children are willing to experiment and even to fail, in spite of the chance they might be laughed at. They have an insatiable desire to learn through experience. Likewise, a child is tender. There is a willingness to express emotion and an inability to hide one's real motivation (a lack of guile, Jn 1:47). Whatever Jesus intended to imply here, we know that the kingdom requires us to shed many of our "adult" attitudes and behaviors to become childlike before God.

16. One who would lead should seek to serve (Mt 20:25-28). Both by word and by example, Jesus modeled what has been called "servant leadership" in contrast to the way the "rulers of the heathen" exercised their power. The way human worldviews lead us to expect to relate to power is not the perspective Jesus would have us take:

> If one of you wants to be great, he must be the servant of the rest; and if one of you wants to be first, he must be your slave—like the Son of Man, who did not come to be served, but to serve and to give his life to redeem many people. (Mt 20:26-28)

Kingdom Normalcy

These are at least some of the perspectives evident in Jesus' worldview that tend to contrast, often sharply, with those of human worldviews. In advocating these perspectives, Jesus was both opposing the normalcy of certain human paradigms and *advocating a new normalcy* for his followers. Kingdom people are to make whatever adjustments are required to move to kingdom normalcy from whatever patterns had been laid down for them by those who taught them their human worldview.

What Jesus advocates may be called kingdom principles, the principles that are to become a part of the worldview of everyone from any society who seeks to put Jesus' kingdom first. These principles provide a balanced approach to kingdom living. They relate to more than simply the area of spiritual power. And they challenge different societies in different ways.

But the focus on spiritual power figures very prominently in these perspectives. We from the West are challenged head on to incorporate that focus into our worldviews. What we call "miracles," then, are expected by Jesus to be normal occurrences in our part of the kingdom, as in all other parts. They are not, as we have been taught, to be regarded as interferences by God in a domain from which he ordinarily keeps his distance. As I pointed out in an article on miracles:

> Are there miracles in the kingdom? No. Only normal events such as people being saved and obeying God who then are involved in other normal events such as healings, deliverances, control of weather, angelic protection, leading and revelation via words of knowledge and wisdom, salvation, loving the unlovable, "important" people serving "unimportant" people, forgiving the guilty, refusing to worry or be bitter or to take revenge or to seek worldly prestige and honor. Such things are only miracles to those whose definition of *normalcy* is tied to the earth.
>
> In God's reality, the universe cannot be split up as Western worldviews do. Nor can the spiritual aspect be disposed of. Jesus came to earth in part to show us how to behave in relation to the universe as God understands it. The concept of miracle as we ordinarily understand it is not helpful to us as we strive to see and relate to things as Jesus taught us. May we learn to judge normalcy by Jesus' standards.[4]

Let's learn to define "normal" as Jesus defined it by integrating into our worldview Jesus' kingdom perspectives and by living our lives in accord with them. When we take that step, we will discover that the benefits are great as God gets close.

TEN

Things Become New When We Invite God to Get Close

I'LL CALL HER JEAN. She was a badly damaged woman. There had been sexual promiscuity, abortions, miscarriages, and a very rocky marriage. You name it, Jean had experienced it. As she looked back over her life, it seemed as though nothing had ever gone right. She was the product of a very conservative Christian home. But even when she had been faithful to him, God seemed far away most of the time, not really caring what happened to her—never showing any evidence that he heard her prayers. So she wandered. And by now Jean had wandered so far away that she was ashamed to come back. She had within the past few years begun attending a church with quite a different approach to Christianity than the one she had been brought up in. But while helping in some ways, going to church also made her feel hypocritical.

"I have no idea why I'm telling you all of this," she blurted out halfway through her story. But the desperation in her voice was all the explanation necessary. And my wife and I, with tears in our eyes, encouraged her to continue.

She knew all the Bible stories, including the first one I directed her to—that of the woman caught in the act of adultery (Jn 8). But that story and the next one I mentioned—that of Jesus reinstating Peter after his denials (Jn 21)—didn't seem to connect with her. For she saw herself as a Pharisee, one who had deliberately turned her back on Jesus. "So," she said, "whenever I picture Jesus, he always has a stick in his hand." And even if the good stories applied to people like her, they only happened long ago and far away. Jesus is never near when you really need him. Somewhere back in history he stopped doing wonderful things and rescuing unfortunate people. So all was hopeless for Jean.

"Let's pray and see if God will do anything," I said after awhile. And as we prayed, a spiritual transaction took place that was so tangible that each of us were forever changed by it. We asked Jesus to come and to minister to this victim, as he had ministered to so many victims during his earthly ministry—to gently but powerfully bring healing and the reality of his loving presence into the life of this desperate woman.

And he came. He came and inspired her imagination to be able to picture him quite differently than she had ever been able to previously. Jean was able to "see" Jesus taking her by the hand and gently leading her across a river, through the deep waters to the edge of the river, and then up a rocky bank. She paused and wept as she was able to picture Jesus putting his arms around her and embracing her![1]

Jean will never be the same. She was so moved, it was a day and a half before she could share that moment with her husband. And when it did come out, the breathless words were, "I saw Jesus!" Her husband had noticed the transformation in her, but he doubted that what he thought he was seeing could be true. Until that moment, he had no explanation for it except that she had spent a morning with some newfound friends.

Can such things happen? Is the power of God still available to bring about such a transformation? If so, why hadn't Jean experienced it before? And why wasn't I seeing it before in my ministry?

Jean was sure that the norm was for God not to be close. She actually thought that if he got close it would be bad news! Probably she felt like Peter after an unsuccessful night when he and some fellow fishermen had obeyed the command of a carpenter named Jesus to go back out onto the lake at a time when fish are not caught. But Peter obeyed, and he and his companions caught more fish than they could handle (Lk 5:1-11)!

Peter recognized that it was God who had come near and suspected that his being close was not a good idea. So he blurted out, "Go away from me, Lord! I am a sinful man!" (v. 8). Or Jean may have felt like Peter when, after he had denied Jesus three times, the Lord invited him for a little walk on the beach (Jn 21:15-19). Peter undoubtedly expected a severe reprimand and must have been quite anxious about the meeting.

But Peter learned that good, not bad things happen when God is near. And so did Jean. They got new insight into God's intentions, and it changed their perspective. They went through the kind of perspective or paradigm shift that I went through in 1982. And that centered around a whole new view of God.

A New View of God

The subject of this book is the influence of our worldview on our understanding and experience of spiritual power. But the influence of our worldview on our view of God is no less important. So in dealing with the changes we need to make, let's discuss what can and should happen to our view of God.

First of all, we need to face the question of *whether God is positively disposed toward humans.* As with Jean, it is all too easy to assume that God basically dislikes us. He may like others. He may have liked those whose stories we read in the Bible. They seem to have had the cards stacked in their favor. But we often see ourselves as so bad and unworthy that we assume God couldn't like us.

We may even make a distinction between God's loving us and the possibility that he likes us. We sort of accept the notion of God loving us. After all, he made us and is kind of obligated to love us. But we can't imagine God *liking* us. That's a wholly different thing. Where two or three are gathered in his name (Mt 18:20), does Jesus really show up? And if so, is it simply out of obligation? Or does he really like to be where we are?

As I gain more and more experience in power ministry, the conviction gets stronger and stronger that *God really does care,* especially for victims. He really comes when we ask him to. But God waits to be asked. And when he comes, he does so with genuine care, concern, and acceptance. *I've seen him come in this way over and over. And it has forced me to change both my view of God and my view of myself.*

Many of us are blocked in our view of God because we have such a low opinion of ourselves. We have been worn down in our self-concept by constantly being forced to recognize the disturbing distance between what we think we ought to be and what we actually seem to be. Even before we get to "mid-life crisis," many of us have become terribly discouraged over the realization that we are never going to come even close to our goals in life. And in keeping with the individualism that is so prominent in our worldview, we blame ourselves and, perhaps, God for our failure.

It usually doesn't occur to us that the expectations we have been taught as members of Western societies are unrealistic. We have been led to expect such things as, everyone can get to the top, everyone can have a beautiful, well-proportioned body, everyone can be healthy and live in comfort, everyone can be happily married, and the like. But somewhere along the line we begin to realize that we're not ever going to reach one or more of these ideals, and we blame ourselves for what we think is our failure, without recognizing the unrealistic nature of the promises made by society. Since we see ourselves as failures and blame ourselves for it, how then could a God who knows our inadequacy and failure possibly be positive toward us?

As a result of this kind of thinking, one woman candidly confessed to me, "I hate myself." Another confided that it was pure agony for her to look at herself in the mirror. They naturally felt that God's attitude toward them must be even more condemning than their own.

Our theology is, of course, pervasively affected by our personal experiences. And up to 1982, my impressions of God were largely like those of the women I just mentioned. I knew intellectually that God loved me. But I seldom felt it because I couldn't understand it. That God would love someone who failed as often and as badly as I just didn't make sense to me. And my commitment to rational thinking led me to feel that if I can't understand it, it can't be so.

But, in the process of discovering God's power, he also led me to discover his love in a new way. What happened was that God started to bless me at least as much as he blessed those to whom I ministered. That is, as he began to do incredible things through me, God also began to work on my insides. As I saw him work through me, I began to accept more of God's love toward me and his trust in me. As God allows me to lead others to experience his warm acceptance of them, I continue to experience in a new way his acceptance of me.

It hit me hard one day as I was reflecting on my low opinion of myself. My thoughts took me to the place where I remember saying to myself something like, "The fact that God sticks with me indicates either that he needs his head examined or that he knows something I don't know about myself—something that keeps him hanging in there with me!" Then I realized that continuing to focus on my own inadequacy and unworthiness constituted a questioning of God's judgment and thus some sort of rebellion against him.

So I began a process of exerting my will to believe—in spite of the fact that I don't understand it—that God really does accept me. And God's willingness to use me is as unlimited and as incomprehensible as his acceptance of me. If he is going to use me, then I'm going to "go for it" and not even try to understand it!

He's a different God to me now. He's a whole lot like Jesus! And I'm freer than I've ever been to love him, others, and even myself. Now I can accept and invite others to accept Jesus' invitation in Matthew 11:28-30:

> Come to me, all of you who are tired from carrying heavy loads, and I will give you rest. Take my yoke and put it on you, and learn from me, because I am gentle and humble in spirit; and you will find rest. For the yoke I will give you is easy, and the load I will put on you is light.

I could present this Jesus to Jean because I had myself been experiencing the freedom he brings to people like Jean and me. I could recommend to her the gentle forgiveness Jesus offered the woman of John 8 and Peter in John 21 because I have been experiencing Jesus' gentle use of his power to free me.

A New View of the Present Activity of God

Was it because nearly every sermon turned out to be a history lesson? Or because the language of the Bible was so out of date? Or because the church rituals seemed to connect us more with the past than with the present? Where did I get the idea that God was real in the past and would be real again in the future, but that he didn't really have much to offer us today?

We studied the Bible faithfully because we were taught that God speaks to us through his book. And we sought to get to know as much as possible about what God did in biblical times. We accepted Jesus as our personal Savior, defended his miracles, worked out the important biblical doctrines, prayed faithfully, and witnessed to others concerning their need for salvation from their sins. But all of the events of Scripture seemed awfully far off. And, though we often tried to pick out events in our lives that could be labeled "answers to prayer," most of what we pointed to would be quite unconvincing to a skeptic or even to us.

It was very good to know we were saved and headed for heaven. And it was good to be able to take our burdens to the Lord in prayer. Even the hymns and sermons were frequently good, though they were often couched in antique language and theological jargon. But it was really hard to convince a casual visitor to our church that something worthwhile would happen if he or she would continue to attend. I remember inviting a high school girl to whom I was attracted to an evangelistic rally once. I'll never forget the look of boredom on her otherwise pretty face.

But something deep inside me, something I tried to keep from surfacing, kept asking, "Isn't there more to Christianity than this? Isn't there something for the present? It's nice that God did all those wonderful things in the past. It's nice that he's redeemed us. And it's nice that we have so much to look forward to in the future. But where is God now?"

That's why when I began to see concrete evidence of God's action right in the very classroom in which I sat, it quite literally "blew my mind." Prayers were being offered and ailments were actually commanded to leave. Things were happening in the *Signs and Wonders* class that reminded us of New Testament days. God started to "show up" right where we were and to make it very clear that he was there by doing concrete things. We no longer had to pride ourselves in the blindness of our faith. We could actually see the results of his presence all over the place.

God really came to life again for me, first in observation, and then in participation. At last the gap was being filled. God became a God of the present as well as of the past and future. And I came to like it so much this way that I never want to go back to the old understanding.

A New View of Power in Love

A new view of God and his action in the present led naturally to a new view of the relationship between his love and his power. In the early days of my "breakthrough," I found myself saying to others, "I have long known God as a God of love. Now I also know him as a God of power." And that still seems like a true statement. But the more I pondered what I was saying, the more dissatisfied I became with the implicit dichotomy between love and power. For Jesus was not love one minute and power the next. He was both at all times.

How, then, should we think and talk about the relationship between the two? As I pondered this question, I began to ask myself about the place of power in Jesus' ministry. Was it peripheral to his real purpose, as some would lead us to believe? Was he simply proving his divinity or signaling a transition in God's plan for the ages? Was he merely accommodating to a situation in which medical techniques were not well-developed? Or was Jesus' use of spiritual power integral to his message of love? I came to the conclusion that *in Jesus love and power are inseparable. Put simply, that's what a loving God who is powerful is all about—especially when he is in battle with the enemy of our souls.*

Was Jesus not most loving when he was using his power to free a captive? Were not healing and deliverance by Jesus at least as impressive for what they show us about God as for what they accomplished in the life of the person healed? For Jesus never used his power either to show off or to serve his own ends. *Jesus' use of spiritual power was always a means, never an end. He used God's power always to demonstrate God's love.*

The purpose of spiritual power in Christianity is, then, to show love. And since—for reasons we can't understand—God has some sort of "love affair" with humans, his desire to use power to help the hurting springs from his very nature. It is "just like God" to use his power to free those he loves from captivity, to reduce the pain of those he cares for, to suffer with those who for his own reasons he allows to suffer, to bless those who are struggling.

But as with nearly all of God's workings in human affairs, he chooses not to exercise his power alone. *Just as he works through humans to communicate his love to other humans in words, so he works through humans to communicate that love via the use of spiritual power.* He works with and through humans in both word and deed.

As with Jesus so with us; God's power comes wrapped in God's love. Spiritual power is not a thing apart, to be used as an end in itself. God's purpose is to minister to his creatures, and it is for that purpose that he and we are to use his power. This is kingdom normalcy.

A New View of Prayer and Taking Authority

As Christians, we believe in being in contact with God through what we call "prayer." Well and good. Jesus believed in and frequently practiced prayer. But prayer was not his central activity when he was healing people or delivering them from demons! He certainly prayed before such events (Jn 11:41-42), to get his directions from the Father (Jn 5:19). But in his healing ministry, *Jesus did not ask God for help. He simply took the authority God had given him and acted on God's behalf.*

I'm afraid the way we usually refer to the part we are to play in God's healing ministry is very misleading. We usually speak of "praying for healing." But prayer is ordinarily understood as petition or asking. We would not label what Jesus did when he ministered to people as "prayer." He usually commanded the condition to be well (Lk 4:39; 5:13; 7:6-10 implied), or the spirit to leave (Lk 4:35), or the winds and waves to be still (Lk 8:24), or the person being healed to do something in faith (Lk 5:24; 6:10; 7:14). Sometimes he would touch the person (Lk 5:13). At other times people would touch him and be healed (Lk 8:44; Mt 14:36). *He prayed before he did his deeds, not during them.*

So I don't think "pray" is the right word for what we are expected to do. I believe we are to imitate Jesus and *take authority* as he did. "Whoever believes in me will do what I do" (Jn 14:12), Jesus said. I think he meant to include the way he did things in the "what" of that verse. Jesus didn't ask God to do the works for him. He simply (in prayer) lined his will up with God's will (doing only "what he sees his Father doing," Jn 5:19) and then spoke not *to* the Father but *on his behalf.*

Several years ago when my younger son, Rick, was in university, he talked me into adding his name to my Visa credit card. Though at first I was apprehensive about the arrangement, I finally consented. My name was listed first on the card as the one with ultimate responsibility. But Rick's name was immediately under it, giving him authority to spend whatever the company would allow me by way of credit. He said he would only use the card in an emergency, a purpose I approved of. And he stuck to his word. Though I laugh about the arrangement now, I was happy to give Rick that authority. For he is my son.

In a similar way, God gave Jesus a kind of credit card with the Father's name listed first and Jesus' name right under it. Jesus had full authority to spend whatever was in the Father's account as long as he spent it for purposes of which the Father approved. And Jesus sent his disciples into the world with the same kind of credit card, giving us the authority and power to spend whatever is in Jesus' account as long as it is for purposes of which he approves. "As the Father sent me, so I send you," credit card and all (Jn 20:21). And he says, "I will back up with my authority whatever you say and do that is in accord with my will and the Father's purposes" (Jn 14:13).

Our task, then, is to get our will lined up with Jesus' and the Father's will. On that basis, we then exercise the authority they have given us. We, like Jesus, are to spend time in prayer and fellowship with the Father to get instructions and to line up our wills with his. We then receive from God the necessary power and authority for the specific task(s) ahead of us. During this first step of ministry, prayer is crucial. And throughout any given ministry session, we are to pray continually for guidance. But *the ministry itself is a ministry of exercising authority which has already been given. We are to minister as Jesus did.*

If We Only Realized How Much Power We Carry

A friend of mine was chatting one day with a woman who had recently been converted to Christianity out of the occult. While in bondage to Satan, she had the gift of being able to "see" the amount of spiritual power different people carry with them. She told my friend that she had been able during that time to spot Christians "a mile off" because of the amount of power they carried! She remarked that she suspected that things might be quite different for a lot of Christians "if we only realized how much power we carry."

A similar story comes from the experience of a fourteen-year-old girl I'll call Lisa. While in rebellion against her parents and her Christian upbringing, Lisa became involved with a popular rock and roll group. Reportedly, she was invited by one of the stars of the group to join them after the concert for partying, drugs, and sex. As Lisa attempted to go backstage, however, she was stopped by a woman who forbade her to pass. The woman identified herself as a witch and told Lisa that no Christians were allowed in the gathering. When Lisa asked how the witch knew she was a Christian, she was told, "I saw it on you."

Such stories stretch the credulity of Western Christians. They seem like fairy tales. We have been carefully taught! But what if they are true? What if Jesus did really give us the "power and authority" he spoke of in Luke 9:1? How would we know?

As pointed out in chapter eight, experience is a great asset in the process of change. Not that we should—as some have—turn to experience as more authoritative than the Scriptures. *But when something is advocated in the Scriptures that we have not experienced, should we not take Scripture as the launching pad for new experience?* Given the ways in which humans restrict experience based on the limits of their worldviews, should we not be suspicious of areas that are advocated by Scripture but that are not emphasized by our society? So let's experiment with such things to see if they are for today.

Exercising the Authority We've Been Given

So far I have experimented in at least five areas: 1) physical healing, 2) inner healing, 3) deliverance, 4) blessing, and 5) forgiving. Yet I have no idea whether or not I have any of the gifts (1 Cor 12:9, 28, 30) of healing. All I know is that I was led to believe that praying for healing and taking authority is something we are to do as a matter of *obedience,* not because we think we have a gift in that area. And as I obeyed, more and more things started to happen that couldn't be explained simply as chance. Perhaps God has "gifted" me in this area. But my theory is that he has chosen to minister healing through me simply because I have started to be faithful to him in this area. In the process, I have grown in faith.

1. **Physical healing** is usually the easiest of the applications of spiritual power to verify. If a person is ill or has strained or broken something and the condition is no longer there after a time of ministry, we conclude that God has relieved the person of that problem. The healing of a physical problem is, however, often merely the start of what God wants to do with that person. I sometimes refer to physical healing as "surface-level" healing that—though real enough—often seems designed by God to function primarily as a gateway into something more important. The physical healing often provides a powerful "faith boost" toward the healing of something much deeper.

My experience to date has included hundreds of physical healings, most of them quite small. Yet all of them were used by God to bless the person receiving them, often to show to that person that God is really there and really cares for him or her. So far in my experience, no one has responded to such a blessing from God by saying to me, "I wish you hadn't ministered to me." They always say, "Thank you."

Since my aim is to minister and to faithfully mediate the love of God, it doesn't matter that most physical healings are small. Those who contend that because most modern "miracles" tend to be small, they must not be the result of God's empowering us are quibbling and missing the point. The point is that God likes to show his presence and concern by touching people at points of physical need.

Though most of the healings I've been involved in are small, I can claim to have been a part of a few large ones. After two years, a pastor's wife is still free of a serious 30-year back problem. After four years, Sharon (see chapter seven) is still free from any residue of the apparently serious injury she suffered to her neck or shoulder. I've also been involved in two medically verified apparent healings of cancer (one of whom died later of what seemed to be another form of cancer). And there are several others in the "biggie" category.

With respect to physical healing, I seem to see more happen when ministering to people with problems in various parts of the skeletal framework of the body. As I have taken the authority given by Jesus, God has often healed or alleviated the pain for many spinal, leg, shoulder, and knee problems—plus one finger! He has also let me participate in the "growing" of many legs—most of which from a medical standpoint were probably due to God enabling the person to relax certain back muscles. But he added about one-and-a-half inches to legs in two cases! These probably involved more than simply the relaxing of back muscles. And then there have been numerous stomach ailments and headaches that have been alleviated.

But the point is missed if we do not focus on the way God shows his gentle love and mercy through such touches whether large or small. *For the subject is ministry, not merely healing* (see chapter eleven). And even when the touch is small, it comes in response to a human being taking the authority he or she has been given in Jesus' name to claim God's blessing. Such a fact provides experiential evidence both for me and for the person receiving the healing that God still does the things Jesus did.

2. Inner healing is a name frequently given to healing at a deeper emotional or psychological level. I find most of those to whom I minister needing God's touch at this level, even if the problem that brings them appears to be purely physical. A woman, I'll call Irene, came asking prayer for her left arm that hung limp and had no strength. As is my custom, I asked if there was anything else in her life that was especially bothering her. Irene said she was having a problem with obsessive worrying. When we claimed Jesus' power over that obsession, God seemed to take it away. And the strength came back into her arm at the same time!

Similarly, an older woman, I'll call Katie, came complaining of severe pain in both upper and lower back. I asked when the pain started and whether there were any special circumstances attached to the start of the pain. Katie replied that the pain had started seven years earlier, when she married her present husband! Katie's first husband had died and so had the first wife of the man she is now married to. He, however, had been very pushy when they were courting, and she felt she had been forced into the marriage against her will. Katie was, therefore, very angry at both her husband and herself. She was also angry at God for letting the whole thing happen. When her anger, bitterness, and unforgiveness were dealt with, the pain in her back disappeared. And we never dealt specifically with her back! The pain has come back several times since but has always disappeared again when she commands it to leave.

Over and over again a physical problem—whether caused by the lodging of tension in some part of the body or by some more serious malady—becomes the occasion for claiming God's power to heal something much deeper. Often the person is unaware of what the underlying problem is. Frequently, though, the person is quite aware of what the "inner" problem is. Obsessive worry or fear or bitterness or unforgiveness or lust or guilt or inadequacy and unworthiness or rejection or depression come up over and over again. And in each case God gives us power and authority to minister his love and grace to his hurting children. If we only knew the power we carry and made use of it more boldly!

Frequently, God does not heal such deep-level problems all at once. Ministry to such people usually requires several sessions, plus all the psychological skill and insight one can muster. Not infrequently, such problems are reinforced by demonic beings that need to be banished. Such ministry provides great opportunity to demonstrate the caring and loving kindness of Jesus. There is power both in the authority we take and in the love we show.[2]

3. **Deliverance** is the term used for the ministry of freeing people from demons. This was an important part of Jesus' ministry. Freeing people who are under the enemy's domination, then, is to be a normal part of our seeking to do the works of Jesus.

Satan is very active with Christians as well as non-Christians and frequently needs to be confronted and defeated in his attempts to control part or all of a person's life. He apparently has no access to a person who does not allow him to take over some part of his or her life. But many give him the opportunity to influence them by hanging onto such emotions as bitterness, unforgiveness, desire for revenge, fear, and the like. Indeed, I believe that there is no problem a person has with an evil spirit that is not tied to some such inner problem. These people need deliverance and then also inner healing to deal with the purely human aspects of their problem.

It is helpful to avoid terms such as "possession" and "oppression" when talking about demonization. I find it more helpful to see demonic attachment on a scale from 1 to 10, with level one signifying the weakest "attachment" and ten the strongest. The Gospels show Jesus casting out demons with a strength of attachment at a level of 9 or 10. Most of those we regularly encounter are, however, in the 1, 2, or 3 category. They usually go quietly when commanded to in the name of Jesus.

For instance, I was sitting in a restaurant next to a pastor one evening when I perceived—through a hunch that turned out to be a word of knowledge—that he was being troubled by a spirit of fear. Without any fanfare, I commanded it to leave and it did. In amazement, he repeated several times, "The fear is gone!" The spirit was probably about a level 1 or 2, strong enough to keep him constantly battling fear, but not strong enough to put up much of a battle for the territory it was occupying. One command freed the person, and his own determination and dependence on God to keep him free has prevented the spirit's return.

In another case, I was sitting knee to knee with a woman whom I perceived to have a spirit of fear. When I commanded the spirit to leave, it "hit" her from behind so that her head landed in her lap. It then struggled to keep control of her for about five minutes, shaking her about as she remained in that position and frightening her husband who was sitting next to her. In response to my repeated commands, it finally released its hold on her. And as she wrote me later, she is now "a new creation." The attachment of that demon was probably at about a level 3 to 4.

Demons that are more strongly attached usually take longer and get more violent. I dealt with one at about a level 4 or 5 once that took about an hour to get out and one that probably was a 7 or 8 that we weren't able to get out during a five-hour session. On the other hand, we were able to relieve one lady of nineteen demons varying from about a 2 to about a 4 in two-and-a-half hours. But she was Spirit-filled and actively ministering in spiritual power. This fact, I believe, weakened the ability of the spirits to attach to her so that the strongest was only at level four, though it had been much stronger previously—I'd guess perhaps a 7 or 8. Don't ask me how a Spirit-filled Christian can be demonized. It doesn't completely make sense to me. But it is beyond doubt that Christians do become demonized. See C. Fred Dickason's book *Demon Possession and the Christian* (Chicago, Illinois: Moody Press, 1987) for a thorough treatment of this subject.

In such a ministry of deliverance, we are imitating Jesus by freeing his creatures from the enemy. This is a very loving thing to do and God gives us the power and authority to do it. We need, however, to prepare ourselves by prayer and often by fasting to gain the authority and power that is essential in challenging demons. We will not always succeed on the first try. Deliverance often takes several sessions. It also takes careful listening to God on behalf of the one who ministers and the full cooperation of the victim, both in claiming God's assistance and in willing to be rid of the demon.

4. Blessing is one of the most enjoyable things we have been given the authority to do. As with healing and deliverance, spiritual trans-actions take place when we bless people in Jesus' name. The Bible is full of blessing. Not only did an Old Testament father pronounce blessings on his sons as Jacob did (Gn 48-49), but Paul starts most of his letters with a blessing (Rom 1:7; 1 Cor 1:3; 2 Cor 1:2; Gal 1:3). Jesus was blessed before he was born (Lk 1:42) and shortly afterward at the presentation in the temple (Lk 2:34-35). Jesus blessed children (Mk 10:16), people who live kingdom values (Mt 5:3-11), his disciples after his resurrection (Jn 20:26), and those who were present at his ascension (Lk 24:50-51). Further, he commands us to bless those who curse us (Lk 6:28).

The custom would undoubtedly have been mentioned more in the Scriptures if it hadn't been so universally assumed by those with a Hebrew worldview. Invoking God's blessing on those you favor was almost as natural as breathing for Hebrews. The favorite Hebrew blessing was peace. In each of Paul's letters, then, he speaks peace on his readers. Since he is working in the Greek world, however, he adds a favorite Greek blessing, that of grace. Thus his usual opening blessing is grace and peace, plus mercy—another favorite Hebrew blessing—on two occasions (1 Tm 1:2; 2 Tm 1:2). In each case, these are not to be taken as mere words of favor but as the invoking of God's spiritual power for the benefit of those being addressed.

A blessing may either be general or specific. "I bless you in Jesus' name" is general. Blessing one another with peace, mercy, grace, patience, or joy is an example of a specific blessing. In fact, in the Beatitudes, Jesus may have intended that his statements confer specific blessings, not simply describe the blessings available to those with the qualities he mentions. That is, Jesus may have intended, "I bless you who are spiritually poor by giving you the kingdom of heaven," "I bless you who mourn with the comfort of God," and so on (Mt 5:3-4).

Material objects such as food and the communion elements may also be blessed. I believe it is the power of God conveyed through blessing that explains how Jesus' garment (Mt 9:20; 14:36), Paul's handkerchiefs and aprons (Acts 19:12), and Peter's shadow (Acts 5:15, if it worked) could bring healing. Jesus regularly blessed food. The disciples who walked to Emmaus with him recognized Jesus as he blessed and broke the bread (Lk 24:30). Before distributing the food to the five thousand, he lifted it in blessing as he thanked God for it (Lk 9:16). With regard to the communion elements, Paul speaks of blessing the cup used in the Lord's Supper (1 Cor 10:16). I have seen God minister healing to people during the Lord's Supper as the congregation ate and drank of the elements that had been blessed.

Over and over I have blessed a person with peace, and the person has immediately felt God's peace come over him or her. On one occasion a woman said it felt like electricity. Usually it is like a wave of relaxation, and sometimes the manifestation of it is visible to others. This happened dramatically once as I blessed a young man with peace at the start of a public ministry session. The Holy Spirit brought peace to his body so forcefully that he nearly fell off his chair! I once blessed a young woman with, "A greater experience of God's love than you've ever had before," and the Holy Spirit came on her with such strength that she nearly fell over backwards.

People blessed with joy often find their minds quickly filled with God's praises. Once I blessed a woman with joy, and a demon (of about a level 2) manifested itself! The demon couldn't stand the praise for God that welled up in the woman's heart. I try never to either start or conclude a ministry session without blessing the person with whatever the Lord shows me he or she needs. It is one of the most wonderful privileges we have as representatives of the supreme blesser.

Unfortunately, cursing is also real. As Christians, we are not, of course, to curse. But we will often find that persons we minister to have been cursed. I believe that this may even happen through a careless or an angry word uttered by someone. I recently ministered to a woman whose father repeatedly told her she'd be blind by the time she turned forty. At thirty-seven she was experiencing physical symptoms that led her to believe she was indeed going blind. We treated the matter as a curse. I don't know how that one came out, but I pray that we were able to break it! Some people seem to curse themselves by uttering negative wishes or predictions toward themselves. All such things, our gracious God wants to free people from. And we get to assist.

5. Jesus gives all believers the authority to **forgive** in John 20:23. Satan frequently uses guilt and a failure to forgive oneself to cripple Christians, even after they have supposedly repented and given their sins to God. Thus, in ministry, God frequently leads us to pronounce as forgiven those who either have already confessed their sins or who do so during the ministry session. The freedom this brings is often quite dramatic.

Recently, God led me to speak forgiveness to a woman who remarked, "I feel ten pounds lighter!" She had been experiencing a heaviness in the chest region that disappeared when I took the authority Jesus gives us and pronounced her forgiven. Often in such cases, there are tears of joy as a person who knows intellectually that God has forgiven him or her actually *feels* that forgiveness for the first time.

What Do We Aim At?

Jesus said, "As the Father sent me, so I send you" (Jn 20:21). We minister in his name, in his place, and under the guidance and empowerment of the same source he drew on, the Holy Spirit. We are to be as he was in the world. Like Jesus, we are to commune with God, listen to his leading, and then minister his love and power to those captive to the enemy. There is no higher calling.

But how can you begin to minister in love and power? How can you move into a ministry of signs and wonders?

ELEVEN

Learning to Minister in Love and Power

A LARGE PART OF WHAT I HAVE PRESENTED here is my own story. But that story is still in process. I am still very much on the way—learning, experimenting, replacing old understandings with new ones. But I am more than willing to recommend this process to you if you have not yet begun it.

For I'm having the time of my life! I've never known the presence of God to be so real and seen so much evidence that he is still alive and active—and very tender and loving, especially to those who have been victimized in one way or another. I never dreamed that even Christianity could be so good! I just love to see the smiles on the faces of people God frees from physical, spiritual, psychological, and relational problems.

By now you probably have a pretty good idea of how to start the process. But you may be wondering what things might look like six or seven years down the road. To help you picture where you might be heading, I will devote the final chapters of this book to discussing some of what I have been learning as I move more and more in God's power. Much of this will serve to recapitulate what has already been said. And for much of it I am greatly indebted to John Wimber and others who have passed on to me what God has given them. In keeping with their desire to "give away" what they've learned, I seek to pass on to you whatever God has given me in this area in hopes that you too will be able to enter that "more" that God has for all of us.

As I write, it is nearly seven years since the *Signs and Wonders* course started in January of 1982. By now I've experienced an incredible number of good things and have become thoroughly addicted to ministering in what I call "power wrapped in love." I have become so committed to this kind of ministry and so bold that I regularly ask God to bring me people to minister to. And he usually does. Though other duties press in, a few minutes praying either in person or over the telephone for someone who has been victimized is time well invested in "seeking first the kingdom."

What a change this is from my previous attitude and behavior! People say I've changed. They're right—and it feels great! I pray that the following sharing about what I've been learning will help you to change, too.

Learning to Minister, Not Just to Heal

Though it was the healing that originally attracted my attention, my focus has expanded considerably. For it is people, not miracles—and certainly not techniques—that God is concerned about. We are, therefore, to learn to minister to people, not simply to pray for healing. The following points, then, will focus on certain discoveries I've made in this area.

1. Perhaps the biggest surprise for me, once I got started, was the **need for learning and experimenting.** I had always assumed that people received the "gift" of healing all at once. But what I have experienced is a gradual learning process that comes along with constant practice and a lot of risk taking.

What I'm conscious of in teaching is a great deal of work, probably built on some natural ability. I think God has confirmed both my natural teaching ability and the work into what people now perceive as a "gift." On the basis of others' and my own experience, I have come to believe that this is also the way God leads many other people into a healing ministry.

It came as no small surprise to me that *even I could pray effectively for healing.* I was quite convinced before I got into this type of ministry that it was not one of my gifts. Then once I began and found that little or nothing happened quite frequently, there were voices from inside and outside of me that kept urging me to give up praying for healing altogether. I remember times when the discouragement was intense and the fear well-nigh irresistible. It has, however, been more than worth it to persevere.

Another surprise was the fact that *even "faithing" seems to grow through practice and learning.* It has become very clear that the more I practice and learn in the ministry of praying for healing, the stronger my faith gets. Do we learn to have "faith"? I think so. And we learn primarily by practicing. Apparently faith is one of those things that gets strong through exercise.

The learning has centered on at least three areas for me: a) ministering to people, b) listening to God, and c) developing greater faith and confidence to risk doing what one thinks one hears from God. The fear of being wrong is a powerful impediment, but God seems to bless more when we launch out in faith in spite of our fear. Then when we make mistakes, we pick ourselves up and try again.

a.) I will deal with **ministering to people** under point 3 below.

b.) **Learning to listen to God has been an enormous challenge.** Jesus said, "I do nothing on my own authority, but I say only what the Father has instructed me to say" (Jn 8:28; cf Jn 8:26 and 7:16). In John 5:19, Jesus speaks of his powerlessness and utter dependence on the Father. As the Son of God, he willingly laid aside his glory and divinity. We, too, are powerless except when we do what the Father approves of. He backs anything that is according to his will. But getting our signals straight so that our wills and actions line up with his is something I am working hard to learn.

Our praying for guidance has to be a two-way conversation with God. It shouldn't simply be like one end of a telephone conversation. Listening in private and listening in ministry are crucial to working effectively with God. I know no way to learn this except by practicing. I practice listening to and waiting for God at every available opportunity. I am still not very good at it. But I'm a lot better at it now than I used to be. So things are going in the right direction. I will speak more concretely about words of knowledge, which is an important aspect of this, in the next chapter.

c.) **Developing greater faith to risk with God is another area that I find simply takes practice.** Faith grows stronger through use. And, as Wimber says, faith is spelled R-I-S-K. If something is not risky, it is not of faith. The parable of the talents (Mt 25:14-30) teaches that if we are not willing to risk what the Master has given us, it will be taken away from us and given to someone who knows the Master well enough to realize that he expects *use, not preservation.*

Where this applies in the kind of ministry we are discussing is in the need to launch out and try to pray for the sick. It is scary. "What if it doesn't work?" we ask ourselves. We fear embarrassment. We'd like to protect both ourselves and God from being embarrassed. And we don't want to risk adding disappointment to the hurt the person who needs ministry is already feeling.

Our motives may be very admirable in this. But I'm afraid God looks at things differently. He seems to want his people to be out on a limb—trusting him for things we can't possibly do on our own. Note the lengths he went to with Gideon (Jgs 6-8) to make sure no one would make the mistake of thinking the defeat of the Midianites under Gideon could have been accomplished by human power alone. He requires risk as a prerequisite to blessing. I can't explain why he lets many of those go unhealed whom we minister to in the early experimenting period. But my experience and that of countless others with whom I have discussed this issue indicates that we need to launch out and risk such disappointment and failure. Otherwise, we will never be "successful" in ministering for him. So get out and risk with God if you ever expect to be used by him.

2. Second, I believe **Jesus wants everyone to minister to people by praying for their healing.** When Jesus sent the disciples out to minister, he empowered them and commanded them to "preach the kingdom of God and to heal the sick" (Lk 9:1, 2). Later he told the disciples to teach their disciples everything they had been taught (Mt 28:20). As his contemporary disciples, we are a part of what Jesus intended would be an unbroken line of disciples who are to be taught to practice such ministry. We are, therefore, to respond to such commands in obedience.

I'm not saying that I don't believe in "gifting." But as I see it, Jesus commanded us all to do two things: to communicate the gospel and to heal (Lk 9:2; 10:9; Mt 10:7, 8). Thus the point of "gifting" with regard to these two tasks is to discover just which aspects of evangelism and healing we are *most* gifted in. For there are many types of healing and many ways to communicate the gospel. We are meant to discover which of them God has given us through being faithful in ministry.

In obedience to his command, then, we are to launch out to discover first our "gifting" and then to use those gifts in the cause of Christ. It looks to me as if a person nearly always has some natural ability in the area he or she is "gifted" in. As we give ourselves to God, launching out in risk to work at what he has commanded us, he builds the kind of healing ministry he chooses in and through us. Healing ministries, however, differ from person to person. God gives "gifts of healings" (1 Cor 12:9), differing, I believe, largely according to the natural talents that he uses to work with the "gifting."

It is not, then, that some are gifted to heal while others are not. Rather, all are given this power and authority, and then commanded to minister in this area. But while we are all to pray for all kinds of healing, some will find greater effectiveness in relation to a certain type of physical problem, others to a certain type of inner healing or deliverance. Some will have greater success with one part of the body than with other parts, or with one kind of disease rather than others. Some will be especially blessed with the ability to deal with emotional problems and to cast out demons. Interestingly enough, often the problem areas a person is most "gifted" in are those that the person has been delivered of. This is especially true in emotional and spiritual areas (see 2 Corinthians 1:4).

3. The third thing I'd like to emphasize is that I believe we are to **minister, not simply to heal.** Further, **we are to minister to the whole person.** It is the *person* who is needy, not simply a body part, or even a soul or spirit.

Typically, we are asked to pray for some physical, psychological, or spiritual problem. But our calling is broader than simply dealing with a problem. *We are to be vehicles of God's ministry to the whole person.* And often God has something in mind that is quite different than what the person requesting prayer is focused on. In fact, I believe God often uses a physical or emotional problem that may be only minimally related to a person's root problem to bring that person to request ministry. Having learned this, I consider it crucial to ask God what it is he has in mind for the person. *We cannot take it for granted that the problem presented by the person is the main issue.*

Whatever the problem or need in focus, I find God often gives insight concerning a person's spiritual and psychological needs, either through words of knowledge or by leading the person to bring up a matter other than the obvious one. Over and over God gives insight that the root cause is psychological or spiritual when people seek help for what they assume to be a physical problem. Ministering in authority to the whole person, then, usually results in healing both internally and externally.

A woman, I'll call Elsie, came to me recently complaining that her extremities had been cold for years. After several prayer sessions, Elsie was able to forgive both herself and God. Then she was able to accept and love herself as God loves her. As this process continued, Elsie began to get warm all over, from the inside out. She will probably discover that as long as she has a positive, faith-filled attitude toward God and herself, she will remain warm. If she allows herself to revert to negative attitudes and distrust of or anger toward God, however, the coldness will probably return.

In another case, a pastor's wife came who had had a troublesome lump in her throat for about a year. When God led me to ask if she was holding anything against someone who had hurt her, she burst into tears. When she gave up to God her right to be bitter toward a particular person, the lump disappeared.

On several occasions I have been addressing myself to a physical problem only to note that the person has been reduced to tears by God as he deals with something deeper and more important in the person's life. I was once praying for my friend Dale who had a serious problem with a leg that had been broken and wasn't healing properly and God spoke to him about his bitterness.

I prayed that God would release a young woman, I'll call Christine, from her crippled condition, and God began (in her words) to "clean me up inside." I prayed over the crippled legs of a woman, I'll call Rachel, who had been a victim of polio early in her life, and God seemed to do nothing. But Rachel considers that time of ministry to be a "high point in her spiritual life."

Since we are to minister to people, not problems, it is important to take time. Perhaps God calls some to "assembly line" types of prayer for healing. But I don't think such an approach does justice to one's personhood. I believe a person needs to be ministered to as a person, as one needing to be listened to, as one needing love, concern, and personal attention. So I take time with people.

4. A fourth important lesson to learn is that **God's purpose in ministering in power is always to show love.** Our purpose should be the same. If ministry is not done in love, it is not done God's way. He is the epitome of love, even when he uses power. He wraps his power in love when dealing with victims. He also uses his power to judge those who victimize. But that aspect of God's use of power is not in focus when we are discussing ministry to those who are hurting.

Unfortunately, it is easy for us to get sidetracked into focusing on spiritual power for its own sake. We may mistake our strong desire for healing for the power to bring it about. It is even easy to be so impressed with the fact that God's power is flowing through us that we become careless of the feelings of the person we are ministering to. Such abuses are unworthy of our Lord who steadfastly refused to use his power either to show off or to rescue himself from trouble. But our own insecurities or our fascination with the power at our disposal may easily lead us into misusing the authority God has given us. Such pitfalls are easy to fall into in at least three types of commonly occurring situations:

a) The first is right at the start of ministering to a person. It is easy **to allow the person to believe you have promised that God will heal him or her.** Often we don't realize what the prayee is assuming. We may have shared with the person exciting stories of our past "accomplishments" and unwittingly given him or her the impression that God will certainly honor our prayer this time. Those of us who minister are all too aware that many do not receive what we ask for from God. But this may be the prayee's first time to be ministered to in this way. So the loving thing to do is to say a few words to the person concerning the possibility God will not do exactly what we ask.

I often let a person know that God doesn't always do what we ask, though he almost always makes his presence manifest in some way. Then, as we are about to begin the ministry time, I like to say, "Let's see what God will do."

b) The second problem is **how to deal lovingly with a person who does not receive the healing he or she seeks.** Even if we have been careful not to promise too much, a person can be very disappointed if healing doesn't seem to happen. It is bad enough not to be healed. It is tragic when a person goes away with both the original problem and the additional burden of disappointment.

When praying for a person who does not get healed, it is tempting to promise him or her that the healing will come "soon" or "by tomorrow." Sometimes God does bring healing in such a delayed fashion. But the blow can be devastating if the person who received such a promise wakes up still experiencing the problem. It is unloving to raise a person's hopes in that way, even if we think we have a word of knowledge to that effect. Though I feel free to mention that God sometimes delays a healing, I try never to promise that he will heal. Rather, I suggest we wait a few days and then schedule a further prayer session if nothing happens.

The personal nature of this kind of ministry would seem to me to indicate that if little or nothing seems to happen during the first session, we should schedule another. Often it takes several sessions for God to do what he wants to do in a person's life. Thus, if he did it all the first session, the process might well get short-circuited.

In recognition of the fact that what God seeks to do often differs from what we are focused on, it is my habit to ask a series of other questions as well in order to get as much insight as possible into the overall picture. Often this process uncovers areas that God seeks to deal with other than the one in focus. If God ministers in one of these other areas, frequently the person goes away quite satisfied, even though what he or she came for may not be healed. Treating whole persons, rather than simply a few symptoms, requires that we get more than the minimum amount of information and look for God's help in more than just a single area.

As I minister, I try to bring the power of God to bear on as much of the person's experience as I feel led to. This often means that whatever God does will in one sense be more than was originally asked for, but in another sense it sometimes turns out to be less. For example, person after person has come to me with a physical problem and gone away with that problem resolved, plus a number of deeper problems either healed or on their way toward healing. Sometimes, though, God deals with inner problems but chooses to leave the physical problem intact.

Though many I pray for don't receive what they came for, probably most receive more than they asked for. When I first started praying regularly for people, it seemed as though many went away without anything. Now it seems as if nearly everyone receives some significant blessing, even when what they receive is not what our primary focus has been. I honestly don't know, though, whether what I am now observing is the result of greater "effectiveness" in being used by God, or if I am simply better now at observing what God is doing than I was at first.

c) Another serious and unloving mistake often made is to **overemphasize the importance of the hurting person's faith to the healing process.** If the person's faith level is high, well and good. From the Scriptures we learn that a person's faith is an important component of the healing process. A bit of experience in praying for people, however, leaves one puzzled concerning just what part faith plays in the process. For a disturbing number of people with apparently very little faith seem to get immediately healed, while some with an apparently high faith level have not been healed! Recently, a friend prayed for a man who agreed only reluctantly, stating, "Nothing will happen." He was healed but didn't even notice it until two days later. Yet his wife who seemed to have a lot of faith was left with her condition unhealed. People to whom I minister several times, however, seem to develop greater faith as time goes on.

Given this kind of experience, I believe it is unkind in the extreme to give the impression that whether or not a person will be healed is dependent on the amount and quality of the person's faith. If after prayer they are not healed, they then go away blaming themselves. If we really don't know what the rules are, we should not risk misleading and disappointing people by placing the emphasis too strongly on human faith, rather than on the will and power of God.

It is not loving and, I believe, not of God to give a person the impression that "If you only had enough faith, God would heal you." God is not coerced by faith. He responds to faith. But he does *his* will and not ours. The fact that God heals through us does not give us the right to lay a guilt trip on those who are not healed. It only gives us the right to keep ministering to them as lovingly as possible.

Those who minister to large groups are particularly susceptible to giving misimpressions. The problem I have with "assembly-line" healing is that it treats people as machines that simply need a screw turned or a nut tightened to fix them. Though such a "quick-fix" approach to healing may be necessary in large meetings, I believe we should avoid it or get beyond it as often as possible in order to show love. Ministering in love takes time and involves treating the entire person.

God is gracious and does bless a certain amount of such impersonal ministry. But there may be great damage to those who are not healed. Some have experienced God's grace and perhaps a bit of his love has come across. But others have felt disappointed and rejected. Sometimes the speaker has been so enthusiastic about the truth that God heals that he or she gives the impression God will heal everyone who simply meets certain requirements.

I saw this happen in a very large healing meeting in which God did heal several blind, deaf, and lame people. The picture that sticks in my mind, however, is that of a much larger number of people with those and other problems who went away disappointed. The speaker unrealistically and unlovingly had implied that God would heal everyone and he didn't. Their disappointment was painfully obvious.

How much more loving it would have been for that speaker to be more realistic and less triumphalistic. The speaker probably felt that by being so optimistic, he was building people's faith. My guess is, however, that God would have healed just as many if he had honestly admitted that God is unlikely to heal everyone. For God is sovereign, and we cannot coerce him. The speaker could then have invited those God didn't touch this time to keep seeking ministry by coming to him and his servants. That would have been loving.

5. One of the most exciting things about this kind of ministry is that **when the prayee gets blessed, so does the one who ministers.** In fact, I would find ministering in this way worth it just for the blessing I receive! There seems to be a kind of "splash" or "spill over" effect received by anyone nearby as God pours out his love and mercy on the person being ministered to.

Frequently, I feel I am on holy ground as I watch God ministering to someone. I felt this way recently as I sat listening to a young woman I'll call Judy, who had experienced deep emotional damage in her early years, recount what seemed like an hour-long moving picture of her life. There was, however, one major difference between how she felt as she reexperienced these events and how she had felt when they originally happened. In response to my request, Jesus gently showed himself to Judy in each of the events. He led her through and healed her pain in each of these difficult periods as her guide and protector. She was radiant when it was finished! And all those present were all in tears as we shared her joy!

Over and over I have found myself crying tears of joy with a person whom God has healed or brought into a new experience of emotional and spiritual freedom. One woman exuberantly exclaimed, "For the first time in my life I am looking *up* rather than down." Another wrote following a time of ministry, "As I looked in the mirror, I laughed and laughed, knowing that I am a completely new creature!" Several others have just hugged me and cried tears of relief and release.

6. **Often the prayee needs to go through a learning process** if he or she is to effectively receive what God wants to give. People who come for prayer usually are nervous and uptight. They may never have been prayed over before. This is why I usually start by blessing the person with peace and counseling him or her to relax as completely as possible. If people start praying or trying to utter other "sacred"

words, I counsel them to stop and to keep their mind, body, and emotions as relaxed as possible.

High emotion is especially to be avoided on the part of the prayee. It is also to be avoided on the part of the one doing the ministering. We work on the assumption that neither God nor Satan are hard of hearing. Though we take authority, we do not think it is necessary to state that authority loudly. One important reason for working without high emotion is that when the prayee's emotions are high, the person often doesn't seem to be as receptive to God. Thus, the Holy Spirit doesn't seem to be able to work as freely as he would like to.

It is too easy to mistake emotion for faith or to depend on emotion to surely and magically bring the results we seek. So we exhibit as little emotion as possible in ministering, and we counsel prayees to reduce their emotional level as much as possible. They cannot heal themselves by getting emotional. Nor can we heal them by getting emotional. Neither kind of emotion seems to impress God. The best results seem to happen when both the one praying and the prayee are as relaxed and open to the working of God as possible.

Learning to accept blessings from God is a problem for many, especially those who are "givers." One dramatic healing of a serious 30-year back problem came as a pastor's wife learned to let God take from her the burdens she had lifted from other people! The process took several sessions, however. This marvelous woman had the gift of compassion but—though she could readily give help to others—she had great difficulty receiving the same kind of help from the Lord.

Often the thing that keeps a person from accepting healing from God is a deep sense of unworthiness. Another block is a kind of passivity in which the person won't make the effort to exercise faith or to deal with internal problems that may be blocking God's desire to grant healing. These and other blockages can often be done away with—if one spends several sessions with a person during which the prayee is helped to overcome the problem and open up both to the one ministering and to the blessing of God.

Learning to "faith" is, I believe, a big problem for many. As Westerners, our individualism often conflicts with God's desire that we depend solely on him. Many of us cannot seem to release ourselves from our drive to be totally independent of the assistance of any others. Women, however, often seem to have less of a problem in this area than men. That's one reason why this book contains more illustrations of women being healed than of men.

Though I won't claim to have this problem solved, I've found that often a person's faith level seems to rise over the course of several ministry sessions. It also seems to rise in proportion to the trust the person feels toward the one praying with him or her. I have noted also that God frequently provides what I call "faith boosts" during the course of ministry. These are typically small, sometimes trivial tokens of his healing power given to the prayee during the course of ministry.

Often God lets a person feel a blessing. Those mentioned above who felt something like electricity course through their bodies received a faith boost from that experience. This made them more ready for whatever God wanted to do. Often God will apparently lengthen a leg to give a person a faith boost. As mentioned above, when a leg appears to be lengthened up to about a half inch, the reason is often that certain back muscles have relaxed. When they are relaxed by God, however, and the results can be seen in the "lengthening" of a leg, the faith boost can be powerful. After that, the person is ready for anything else God chooses to do.

7. The question is often asked, **"Should we pray for everyone in need?"** The answer, based on Jesus' example, would seem to be "No." He must have walked right by large numbers of those who needed healing in his own day. In John 5, he went to a place where many were seeking healing and ministered to only one man as far as we know.

The key is listening to God. We should minister to everyone God tells us to minister to. The question is, "How does God show us those we should pray for?" Some speak of hearing God speak audibly to let them know who he wants them to minister to. One friend of mine is usually able to visualize Jesus sitting on his throne. When in doubt, he simply looks up at Jesus and asks him. Jesus will then either nod or shake his head to let my friend know what he wants him to do! I envy people like him!

Usually when I ask for such specific guidance, I seem to get nothing. Maybe someday I will find a way of discerning his guidance more clearly. I do, however, keep asking him. And to date, I have usually felt peaceful about ministering to the person I asked about. So I go ahead. My tentative conclusion is that either he has wanted me to minister to each of those I have asked about or that I am not hearing him clearly.

I am quite puzzled in this regard about one situation I experienced on a plane. The man who sat next to me came in on crutches with a broken hip. After praying about whether God wanted me to minister to this man, I felt the answer was "yes." So I offered to pray over the man's hip. He accepted, so I did. Nothing at all seemed to happen, and I felt quite embarrassed. Should I have prayed for him? I think so, but I am not sure. I am determined, however, not to allow such embarrassment to keep me from ministering to the needy, even if I am not sure God wanted me to minister. *I would ten thousand times rather make the mistake of praying for somebody not according to God's will than to miss praying for somebody he wants me to minister to.*

With regard to the question of whether or not to pray for someone, I believe it is very important for a person to be *willing to be prayed for*. God seems to require a willing spirit, plus willingness of mind and emotions, as prerequisites to his working effectively with a person. My rule of thumb is that I gladly minister to anyone who comes to me asking for ministry. In addition, I let it be known that I am available to pray for anyone who asks. So people constantly ask me to pray for them. On occasion, I will first ask God and then, if I seem to get a positive response, ask a person if he or she would appreciate a time of ministry. Only once have I been turned down when I asked to pray for someone.

8. In ministering to people as whole persons, **it is helpful to minister as a part of a ministry team** whenever possible. Though often we will need to minister one on one, it is usually best to work with others, unless the person being ministered to is sensitive about revealing confidential information to more than one person. People are complex. With several ministering, God is able to make use of different sensitivities and gifts to reveal and deal with whatever needs are present. When ministering in teams, however, it is important for one person to take the lead to avoid confusion. This also enables the prayee to focus his or her confidence more easily.

Ministering in a team is particularly important when demonization is involved. The combination of gifts present is particularly important at such times. In one case, I was so involved in commanding the demon to come out that one of the other team members had to tell me that it had already happened! I hadn't noticed the child's movement when the demon left him. The need for the greater amount of authority and power that a group of people brings is important in these situations. It is also good for such a group to fast and to pray before the ministry session in order to increase their authority and power over the demonic intruder.

With these points in mind, let's take a closer look at the elements in a ministry of signs and wonders to see how they all work together to make up such a ministry. What exactly does such a ministry look like?

TWELVE

Elements of Ministry

A S I HAVE INDICATED, MY FIRST STEPS into ministering in power were quite scary for me. And the fear has never completely gone. There is something fearful about each ministry situation, something that raises apprehension. Will the Holy Spirit "show up" this time? Or will he take me at my word when I rashly promised that I would continue in this ministry, even if he chose to allow me to be embarrassed?

Several weeks ago, though, I began to reflect on the level of my fear. It was clear to me that there is usually still fear in me when I begin to minister to someone. But the fear seldom is powerful enough now to make me seriously consider not ministering. Indeed, it used to be that because of my fear, I would choose what looked like "easy" cases if I had a choice. Now, though, I am quite likely to choose cases that others shy away from.

As I have pondered what has happened to me, I've come to what I believe is the key to my present boldness. It is *curiosity*. I find that my curiosity rises to a very high level whenever I begin to minister to someone. It is *curiosity concerning what God is going to do next*. As I have grown both in confidence and in the ability to see what God is doing, I have learned to expect something to happen in every situation. And the situations are very few when we can't point to something fairly obvious that has happened.

The variety of what God does is really fascinating. I have already recounted several of the most interesting. Add to those the man who recently received a healing of his back accompanied with what he described as a "feeling that 220 volts of electricity just went through

147

me." On another occasion, I asked a woman if she could remember any time she had been abused. She couldn't. But within about five minutes of the time we started praying, God brought to her mind a picture of herself as the victim of an attempted rape. Though she had not consciously been able to recall that event, she was convinced that it had actually happened. This picture that God gave her, then, proved to be the key to the freedom we were able to lead her into.

Then there was the time when I simply blessed my audience of about thirty-five people with peace and found that the Holy Spirit came on five or six of them in such a tangible, though pleasant way that they seemed asleep—resting and enjoying his presence. Later with that same group, the Lord healed a man's leg while gently bouncing him up and down on his chair.

Here's another fascinating example. Betty came to me for prayer for a hearing problem. She had originally been hard of hearing in both ears but had been prayed for by my colleague Peter Wagner. As he prayed, God healed the hearing in her left ear. Later in private prayer, Betty asked God why he had not restored the hearing in both ears. She thought she heard God say, "The right ear is Kraft's ear!" So she came to me; and, after she had received a bit of inner healing, God graciously restored the hearing in that ear, too!

When Bill—the man mentioned earlier who had a very painful ankle injury—came, we first prayed for the ankle but nothing happened. So I asked God what else might need to be dealt with and got an impression he was feeling guilty. As I began to pray for that, Bill began sweating profusely. His shirt literally turned as wet as a dishrag! I discerned that we were onto something and continued ministering in that direction. His guilt, a poor self-concept, and some other related problems surfaced and were dealt with. Afterwards Bill looked up in amazement and said, "My ankle doesn't hurt anymore!" Yet after our first unsuccessful attempts, we hadn't prayed again for the ankle injury!

Perhaps the strangest experience I've had was the time when I was asked to pray for a pastor who had just taken charge of a liberal church. As I was about to pray, a song from a Broadway musical came into my mind and I couldn't shake it. After pleading with God to take it away, I finally confessed to the pastor and his wife the problem I was having. As soon as I told them what the song was, they both concluded that the song was God's message for them! The song was "How To Handle a Woman" from the musical *Camelot*.

That turned out to be their favorite musical! We concluded that God's message was that their posture toward the people in their new church should be to behave as the song recommends: "To love them, simply love them. Merely love them, love them, love them."

God is full of surprises. Seldom is any ministry situation routine. The best antidote I've found to fear is the intense curiosity I feel concerning what he's going to do next. I pray that you'll develop the same kind of curiosity. It is a powerful stimulus to ministry.

Let's now turn to a more systematic presentation of some of the details of a power ministry.

Taking Authority

As I've indicated earlier, I see an important *difference between praying and taking authority*. Though we often use terms like "pray for" or "pray over" to label what we do when we minister, in actual ministry I find myself more likely to *command* the condition to leave than to ask God to relieve it. In Luke 9:1, we read that Jesus gave the disciples "power and authority to drive out all demons and to cure diseases." I believe it is the taking of authority over the condition on behalf of Jesus, rather than the need to ask Jesus to heal, that is our primary function in this kind of ministry.

There is an important place for prayer, of course. Nothing gets done without it. But the prayer comes primarily in preparation for the ministry. Before we ever attempt to minister healing, we need in prayer to assure both God and ourselves that what we desire is his will and not ours. In prayer we attempt to line up our will with his and to ask God to minister to the person who seeks his help. In prayer we confess our sin and unworthiness and ask for his power to defeat the enemy in the coming encounter. Without such preparatory prayer, we have no authority and power. Then, at the start of the ministry session, we pray to request God's presence, power, and insight.

In the encounter itself, however—whether we seek healing or deliverance—we take the authority we have been given and command the condition to be gone. We have no authority or power in and of ourselves. We go into every situation with empty hands and no ability at all to fix people. But he has given us his power and agrees to do whatever we command if it squares with his will (1 Jn 5:14-15). The big challenge, then, is to be so close to him that we "read" his will accurately. When we do this, what we command is a certainty.

Taking authority in this way is most obvious in deliverance. We are not to beg or even to pray for demons to leave. We are to command them. But we are also to command physical and emotional problems to leave. We have been given authority over diseases, affected body parts, damaged emotions, curses, bondages, and whatever other things the enemy uses to enslave people. So we command them to be well, even as Jesus did when "he ordered the fever to leave her," (Lk 4:39) or when he said to the leper "be clean" (Lk 5:13).

The Ministry Sequence

The *process I have learned to follow in ministry* is essentially that outlined by Wimber in *Power Healing.*[1] Wimber lists five steps. I list seven and use some different names. There is a step that he deals with throughout the book but does not include in his list—the step of inviting the Holy Spirit to come and take over. It is the most important step in my opinion. I list it first. I also add blessing as a step.

Prior to taking any of these steps, of course, we need to have settled several things with ourselves and with God. Among these are a number of the matters we have been discussing here, such as our relationship with God and self, our spiritual condition, our faith, and a variety of worldview issues. If these are in relatively good shape and our heart attitude is one of wanting to do God's will, we are ready to proceed in ministry.

1. Step one must be to invite the Spirit of God to come, to reveal his will, and to lead the time of ministry. This is both the first step and a continuing prayer throughout the ministry session. I often try to make it obvious to the prayee that I am inviting the Holy Spirit to come. I find, though, that I am so in the habit of inviting the Holy Spirit to come that I do it unconsciously, even when it doesn't seem appropriate to make the prayee conscious of it. Without this step, there can be nothing more than human ministry. With it, even human words, wisdom, and action are empowered by God to accomplish much more than would be true if our human abilities were unaided.

It is this step that makes the difference between what can be done in this type of ministry and what can be done by a psychologist, counselor, pastor, or other helper who does not invite the Holy Spirit to take charge. It is a sad thing that many Christians who counsel and even pray for people have not learned to start with this step. If they did, their valuable insights would be empowered by God to a greater extent than they now experience.

The step consists simply of inviting the Holy Spirit to come and take charge for the specific purpose at hand. I believe Jesus did this regularly. One indication of this is recorded in Luke 5:17 where we are told, "The power of the Lord was present for Jesus to heal the sick." It is usually good to pray audibly in the presence of the one being ministered to. This helps to increase his or her awareness that it is God who is doing the work. Here is one way you could phrase your prayer, "Holy Spirit, please come and take charge of this session. Show us what you want us to do and help us to cooperate with you in accomplishing your purposes here."

After inviting the Holy Spirit, we either wait or move cautiously ahead until he manifests his presence. If the person is open and ready for ministry, often the Spirit will make his presence obvious as soon as we ask him to come. Often though, the prayee needs to get rid of certain attitudes—such as unforgiveness, fear, anger, unconfessed sin, and so on—before the Holy Spirit is really free to minister. In such a case, it is likely that God will lead us in helping the person deal with these and related areas first. In that process, we usually discover that the Holy Spirit has come in power whether or not we can feel his presence.

Though it is true that the Holy Spirit is always with and in us, he comes with special power and "gifting" when asked (see Luke 5:17). He lets us know he has come in a special way by doing such things as letting us feel his presence, or by causing the prayee to sweat, shake, or have a particularly serene look on his or her face. These kinds of things may occur throughout the time of ministry.

2. My second step is usually to bless the person. I will usually bless him or her first with peace. Often it is at this point that the Holy Spirit makes his presence felt. Over and over again I have seen God bring relaxation, comfort, faith, trust in me, and whatever else he knew the person needed to prepare for ministry in response to such a blessing.

I love to bless people! And on several occasions God's Spirit has come in very tangible ways as the blessing was pronounced. One woman exclaimed, "What was that?" as an impression of warm, pleasant electricity coursed through her in response to a blessing of peace. Another was visibly jolted and burst into tears as I blessed her in response to a word of knowledge with "a greater impression of

God's love" than she had ever experienced before.

Following the examples of Jesus and Paul, my favorite blessing is peace. "Peace be with you" was Jesus' favorite blessing, especially after his resurrection (Mt 28:9; Lk 24:36; Jn 20:19, 21, 26). This was probably the blessing he pronounced as he ascended (Lk 24:50-51). Paul started all of his epistles with a blessing of "grace and peace" (Rom 1:7; 1 Cor 1:3; 2 Cor 1:2; Gal 1:3; Eph 1:2, and so on) to which he added "mercy" in 1 and 2 Timothy. But even general blessings, such as "I bless you in Jesus' name," are fun to use and effectively minister God's blessing to those who are receptive. Yet I prefer to use more specific blessings as often as possible. One formula I use often is, "In Jesus' name I bless you with peace, forgiveness, and confidence, and release from worry, fear, or guilt." I amend it as appropriate for specific cases.

Something akin to blessing is often an important step in ministry. In John 20:23 we are told, "If you forgive people's sins, they are forgiven." Several recent ministry sessions were turned from "so-so" to spectacular after I—in response to a word of knowledge— pronounced the person forgiven. As an Evangelical Christian, I believe that Christ has given all believers this authority. Through exercising it, I find that the person, who usually knows intellectually that he or she is forgiven, will often experience a tangible sense of forgiveness at that time. I mentioned one such instance of this earlier on. But whether they experience anything or not, transactions take place in the spiritual realm when we claim the authority Jesus has given us.

Often I feel led to further bless the person, either at the start or at various other points during a ministry session. I will often bless with such things as a deeper experience of the presence of God, joy, greater trust in God, patience with self and with God, an ability to give up trying to rationally understand what God is doing, an ability to love oneself more, an ability to forgive someone, protection from Satan and his forces, and so on.

If the person is relieved of some sin, hurt, compulsion, or a demon, it is often a good idea to "fill the void" with a blessing. If, for example, the person is released from some worry or fear, I like to bless him or her with freedom from the return of that problem and protection from any attempt by the enemy to reassert his power over the person in that area. I like to end each session with a "flurry" of blessings to seal what God has done during the ministry time.

3. Next comes the interview. Though we can count on God

revealing many things through words of knowledge, he usually expects us to gain insight through interviewing the person as well. From the Scriptures, we note that Jesus himself didn't always get his information totally through words of knowledge. Frequently he also asked the person for information. So we ask questions such as, "What would you like us to pray for?" or "When did the condition start?," and "What else was going on in your life when this condition started?"

Often we need to take a good deal of time in the interview. For in addition to the information it provides, it helps the prayee to feel more comfortable and confident in the ministry session. Avoid being so anxious to get to prayer that you cut the interview too short and thereby miss important information or fail to make the prayee feel comfortable. We do, however, need to be careful that we don't spend too much time in the interview, especially if that subtracts from the time available to spend in prayer.

In the early stages of your ministry, you may find yourself fearful of getting into prayer too soon, lest it not work. You may stall by spending too much time interviewing. The prayee may also be fearful and stall by going into more detail than is necessary. Or you may find the person's story so fascinating that you let the interview get more detailed than it should. As you practice, you will probably make all of these and other mistakes. But keep working at it. God is very patient.

4. The next step is a decision that we may call "the tentative diagnosis." This may largely happen as we listen both to the prayee and to God during the interview. As the person states his or her problems and we constantly ask God what approach we should take, we come to a tentative understanding about the problem. Note that this decision is tentative. Quite often it will turn out to be only a partial understanding. Sometimes it will be wrong.

5. The tentative diagnosis is followed by coming to "a tentative prayer strategy." This step may take place, to a certain extent, simultaneously with the previous two. It includes listening to God and drawing from experience. It is also tentative. It will likely result in decisions to: a) ask God for certain things such as guidance, receptivity on the part of the prayee, and the power and authority to deal with the issues; and b) to take authority over and command certain things to leave, such as whatever physical or emotional conditions have come up, and any interference by Satan or evil spirits.

6. Next comes taking the situation before the Lord. This step should not be delayed too long since movement into prayer does not mean we cannot go back to the other steps when necessary. One of the things about this type of ministry that I find most different from my previous experience in prayer is the way we go about this part of the process. As a friend of mine named Dan said after I had ministered to him, "I've never been prayed for like that before!"

For one thing, when praying, *we need to keep our eyes open to be able to make use of insights gained through seeing the Spirit work.* It is usually best for the prayee to keep his or her eyes closed, however. On several occasions in my ministry, it seemed as though nothing was happening until I was led to mention a particular problem in the person's life like guilt, unforgiveness, or fear. When God strikes home by raising such an issue, the person may begin to sweat, grimace, weep, or show other visible signs that what has been mentioned is indeed the problem. With my eyes open, I am able to notice that God is at work in the person and to pursue ministry in that direction. Had my eyes been closed in these situations, I would not have received that important clue. I have found it difficult to learn to pray with my eyes open. With a lot of practice, though, I have gotten used to it.

It is also important to know that there is *nothing wrong with interrupting a prayer* to ask for more information or to change the direction of the ministry in some other way. Praying is not to be seen as a magical thing in which the power is broken if the process is interrupted. We have invited God to be present in the whole process of ministry. The part when we are talking directly to him—rather than to each other or against the enemy—takes place no more or less in his presence than the other parts of the time of ministry.

It is often appropriate during this part of your time of ministry to lay hands on the person. In the case of a physical problem, the practice is usually to place one's hand over the place where it hurts, unless that is a "private part." In that case, it is my practice to ask the person to place his or her hand over the place. I may then place my hand over the person's hand or simply place it on the upper back or shoulder. For emotional problems, I often place my hand on a man's chest or over a woman's hands on her chest. Frequently, when hands are laid on a person during prayer, he or she will feel heat in the place where the injury is located. Sometimes such heat will course through the whole body. On occasion either the one praying or the prayee will experience tingling; sometimes both will experience it.

In practice, what usually happens during this part of the ministry time is a free and easy movement into and out of talking to God, into and out of interviewing the person, into and out of blessing the person, into and out of taking authority over physical and emotional problems, into and out of the laying on of hands, into and out of commanding the enemy to release any hold he has on the person, and into and out of rejoicing over what God is doing.

7. **The final step is post-prayer counseling.** This is a very important step since there are quite a number of things that can happen after the ministry session. Counsel concerning them is, therefore, at least as necessary as any of the other steps.

One of the things that frequently happens is that the problem prayed for comes back. I recently talked on the phone to the woman named Katie, whom I had prayed with concerning a back problem. She said it had recurred several times after our session, but that— following my advice—she had rebuked it and it had always gone away. Another woman named Mary seemed to have "lost" her healing due to strong doubts about whether she was really worthy of being healed. In discussing this with her over the phone, I felt led to ask her to visualize Jesus. She was able to see him but she said, "He is not looking at me." When she was able to accept the fact that Jesus considered her worthy of healing, she was able to picture him looking directly at her and her healing came back.

We need to counsel the prayee about such problems that may occur after the ministry session. Prayees need to know how they themselves can take authority in case the symptoms return. We should also commit ourselves to be available to help should they need it. Such counsel is especially important after a person has experienced some "deep-level" healing. Healing in the emotional area often involves an extended process, some of which is done in ministry sessions, some of which is done by the person later. It is often appropriate to give the person "homework" to do between sessions.

During a ministry session with a woman, whom I'll call Brenda, we were able to identify the deep roots of emotional and physical problems she was experiencing in her early life. Brenda revealed that the most difficult years in her early life were from age 12 to 17. Together we invited Jesus, through visualization, to take her through the year she was twelve. He did this gently, but Brenda was so exhausted by the experience that we called off the session with only that one year completed. During the next week, however, she was able to follow the process she had learned on her own. Thus Jesus led her through the rest of those troubled years before our next session together.

Counsel is particularly important for those who have been released from demons. A demon attaches itself to a weakness in a person. That vulnerable area is usually an emotional weakness. If the weakness is not remedied, the demon will almost surely return. The person needs counsel to remain strong in will, in prayer, and in taking authority so he or she can remain free. We were able to free up a woman, whom I'll call Marla, from a demon that made her fear being outside and in particular driving a car. We told her what to do if the demon came back. She resisted it for a few days but then allowed it to come back. A month or more later Marla finally got tired of it; and following our instructions, she sent it away again on her own! Marla had the same Holy Spirit within her that we have within us and the same authority we do to send the demon away. She just needed to exercise her authority over the demon.

Counsel also needs to be given to those who are not healed. They need encouragement, love, and the promise that we are available for further ministry whenever they need it. I find it easy to shy away from people who get prayed for over and over but never seem to get better. Yet recently I have started to push myself to seek out such people for both friendship and ministry. They especially need to feel God's love and care. I have been greatly encouraged recently in continuing to pray with those who never seem to get better, because one such person seems to have finally started improving after several years with little apparently happening. Our job is to be faithful by ministering to those in need, not to pick and choose among them.

Both those who have not been healed and those who have received healing need to be a part of small groups of caring, concerned Christians. Our Western individualism tends to work against making that kind of a commitment. God made us to need others. And those who have been healed are probably still weak in the area in which they received healing. Satan knows of such weaknesses and is quick to take advantage of them if we don't really work at strengthening the weak ones. Concerned groups help strengthen people who struggle with emotional and spiritual problems.

Such things as good nutrition, regular exercise, and other kinds of care for a person's physical body are important as means of retaining physical healing. Spiritual and emotional disciplines may serve the same function for soul and spirit. I have learned from a pastor friend of mine to use the beeper on my watch to remind me to pray and praise God frequently throughout the day. Memorizing helpful Scriptures and songs of praise can also be of great help. The counsel we give should include whatever common sense area is appropriate to maintaining that part of our life God has touched.

Words of Knowledge

What I have been learning about words of knowledge is particularly fascinating. As noted several times, this aspect of ministering in power has "blown my mind" more than any other. And to this day nothing amazes me more than the stunning fact that God actually puts his thoughts and plans into our minds as we minister. I have always prayed for guidance, but to experience it so immediately and so often is exhilarating. Yet it has its dangers as well. I would like to focus on three aspects of this important topic: 1) patience; 2) recognition; and 3) right and wrong ways to use words of knowledge.

1. **The first thing I experienced with regard to words of knowledge—once I got used to hearing others report them—was the frustration of not feeling I received them.** I found myself becoming envious of those obviously gifted persons who could stand up in front and reel off very specific words of knowledge. "When is that ever going to happen to me?" I would ask God. And it never seemed to. In fact, to this day, though I have often led meetings focused on healing, I am not aware of more than two or three words of knowledge coming to me while I have been up front. And seldom—either in public or private—do I get words concerning physical problems. This continues to be a frustration to me.

As I launched out in a healing ministry, however, I began to notice that *as I prayed for a person* I would get impressions concerning what to pray for that usually turned out to be right. At first I hesitated to mention things in prayer that the person had not indicated to be problems. But I began to take more and more risks in this area. Frequently, the person would ask after the prayer, "How did you know those things about me?" My answer is usually, "I didn't."

Having gotten over the hump and recognized that such messages can come from God, there is further need for patience. Hearing from God requires waiting for God before we start the ministry session. My habit down through the years had been to pray about something ahead of time. Then I would simply dive into ministry according to whatever plan I came up with. Yet in this kind of ministry, it is important to learn to wait for God to initiate the process. The first step needs to be a prayer inviting the Holy Spirit to come. The next is to ask God for insight into the problems that need to be addressed. Then we wait for some manifestation of his presence before going on. Waiting in this way is a great struggle for me. I often forget. But God in his graciousness usually meets me anyway.

When I have remembered to wait, what has usually happened is that both I and the one that I seek to minister to begin to feel the presence of God in a very tangible way before we start to deal with the problem. Such an experience facilitates the ministry incredibly.

Sometimes, though, God starts his work before we even ask. In a ministry session previously mentioned, Elsie, whose emotional problem was causing her extremities to be cold, experienced a tremendous feeling of warmth even before we began to pray about the problem. On another occasion, God took away a lifelong throat infection from a woman who was merely listening to my lecture on inner healing. On still another occasion, God began delivering one of my students of a demon during a class devotional!

It is important to be ready for any eventuality when we are serving God in power ministry. Frequently, the need is for patience and the ability to wait for God to initiate the time of ministry. Sometimes, however, it seems God is ready to start before we are!

2. Words of knowledge usually come to me feeling like hunches or guesses. Other people get them in a variety of other ways. Sometimes they feel a pain somewhere in their body indicating that someone needs to be prayed over for a physical problem in that part of the body. I think I've only gotten one "word" like that. Sometimes a word will come as a picture, often as a picture of some part of a person's body that needs to be prayed over. I have received a few insights in this way, but only once so far as I can remember for physical problems. I have sometimes received a picture of the person I am ministering to being involved in some relational difficulty—perhaps with a spouse, a parent, a child, or a friend. Sometimes I have been able to visualize Jesus ministering to the person in a tender, loving way.

The insights I get usually concern internal emotional and spiritual problems. For example, in a large meeting one time I walked up behind a woman and—without even being able to see her face—

prayed according to my "hunch" against disappointment. It was exactly what God had for her. On another occasion, my "guess" was to ask God to give a woman "the desire of her heart." Though on that occasion God didn't show me what the difficulty was, he healed her of a long-standing neck problem. Usually God shows me things like a sense of inadequacy—interestingly, one of the problems I myself struggle with—fearfulness, bitterness, worry, the need to forgive, and the like.

Often the word of knowledge is closely related to some problem easily discerned at the natural level. When a person is conscious of a physical or emotional problem, I usually ask, "When did this problem start?" On at least three occasions recently the person has told me the problem started when he or she got married. This clue easily led me to God-given insights about one person's relationship with his spouse and feelings of guilt and doubt concerning the marriage itself. In two of these cases, dealing with guilt and doubt and then calling on the forgiveness of Jesus resulted in relief from serious neck and back pain.

Apparently God individualizes his revelations to humans. I have learned to look for such insights in the ways they come to me, not to expect them according to someone else's patterns. It is, however, risky to go on something that feels as vague as most of my God-given insights. But though I make quite a few mistakes, the vast majority of these "hunches" turn out to be from God. He doesn't very often give them to me ahead of time, though. They nearly always come during the interview and the prayer—after I have launched out with God and taken the risk to minister to a hurting person. But he always gives something. I am amazed but very pleased.

Look for God to individualize his way of giving you such insight. It is unlikely that he will lead you in the same ways he leads me. But he will show you what you need to know if you ask him to. Ask the Lord to show you and ask him for eyes to recognize what he brings your way.

3. Words of knowledge, like all other aspects of power ministry, can be and frequently are misused. One of the most troublesome misuses of God's power is the way we sometimes hear words of knowledge and prophecies stated. The fact that we cannot always be sure we hear God clearly should keep us from using formulas such as, "God says you have done such and such," or, "God has told me you are to do such and such." If a word is not really from God, it can be very hurtful and definitely not loving. The person can then go away hurting more than when he or she came.

I find it far more loving to understate my certainty than to risk overstating it. Even when I am quite sure I have heard from God, I try to ask a question or state the word as an impression. Fortunately, I had learned this before I ministered to an older woman in New Zealand. I had the *strong* impression that she needed ministry in the area of her relationships with her grandchildren. So I asked her, "Are you a grandmother?" She simply said, "No!" I have seldom been more sure of a word of knowledge than I was at that time. But it turned out to be wrong! I would have looked even more foolish than I did if I had said, "God has showed me that you need to get things straightened out between yourself and your grandchildren."

Asking a question or stating something tentatively, however, is usually quite acceptable, very considerate, and loving. Often one can say something like, "I'm getting an impression that . . . ," or, "Is . . . a problem to you?" Presenting what may be God-given insight tentatively is especially important if the insight is in a sensitive area. It is both kind and protects one from looking bad if the impression turns out to be wrong. Further, such a gentle approach subtracts nothing from the effectiveness of the ministry.

In the case of Dan—a young man who had a problem with his knees and a short leg that would not respond to my ministering—I simply asked him, "Do you have a problem with anxiety?" At first he said, "I don't think so." After a few minutes, however, Dan realized that he was indeed feeling anxious. When he was able to cast that care upon the Lord, both his knees and his short leg responded to the healing power of Jesus.

Sometimes a correct word of knowledge is not acknowledged by the person it applies to. The person may feel embarrassed or shy, or for some other reason he or she may not want to deal with what has been pointed out. That's okay—though we may find it embarrassing to suggest something and appear not to be right. But attempting to be Christlike means attempting to be loving, even at the risk of being embarrassed. Ministering in love, however, means giving the person the option of hiding the problem. Yet that person will know God is knocking at the door and wants the problem resolved. Often the person will come back another time and admit that the word was right but that he or she was not ready to own up to it at the time. At such times ministry can be very effective. God is gentle.

One type of situation that can be troublesome is when you receive a word from God that you can't figure out how to present lovingly. On a few occasions, God has shown me that the person did not really want to be healed. How does one present this kind of word lovingly? I have decided that such a word is not to be shared with the one being ministered to. It is for my information only. My task then becomes ministering in such a way that the person is brought to a point of wanting to be healed. And this did, in fact, happen in one case after many ministry sessions.

Empowerment of Words and Objects

One surprising thing I've been learning is that *cultural forms such as words and objects can be empowered by God or Satan.* I had come from an anti-Catholic and anti-liturgical background. Any mention of things like shrines, holy water, the sacredness of the communion elements, or even anointing oil conjured up images of pagan magical practices that had corrupted Christianity.

Yet, as I moved into power ministry, I learned that God can use human speech to convey his mighty power. As I learned to take authority in Jesus' name, I found my words empowered in a way far beyond my own ability. The empowerment of words is not automatic, though. There are no magic words or phrases. We need to invite the Holy Spirit to come and take charge. We need to agree to let him use us and what we say and do.

I also learned that God can use other forms—such as the laying on of hands—to convey his power. We saw our teachers in the *Signs and Wonders* course use this form regularly. As we began to practice it, we frequently felt God using our hands in some way to minister his power. On one occasion, I was ministering to a friend by holding my hand on his shoulder when he asked me if I could move it because "It is too hot!" Either I or the person I've been praying for—or both of us—have experienced such heat on many occasions. At other times one or both of us have experienced something like electricity flowing through my hands. Such a phenomenon, though psychologically comforting, carries no supernatural power in and of itself. But as we minister, God empowers both words and actions that would otherwise be simply human vehicles.

I believe that he also empowers acts such as anointing with oil when it is done with his blessing. Again, there is no special power in oil. But when the oil is empowered through blessing it in Jesus' name, God uses it in exciting ways. The difference between just plain oil and blessed oil is brought into focus in the following true story. A pastor and his assistant were struggling to cast out a demon. In frustration, the pastor asked his assistant to go get some oil with which to anoint the demonized person. The oil was brought and they were about to use it when the demon said, "That oil won't work. It hasn't been blessed!" So the pastor blessed the oil, used it, and out came the demon!

I believe that satanic power can also reside in cultural forms such as words and objects. Satan can empower curses and other uses of words, physical objects, buildings, and probably other human structures as well. On one occasion I was asked to deal with a house where a demonized boy lived. There was a peculiar odor in the house and several other strange things going on there. We took authority over the house in Jesus' name as we walked through it, speaking against Satan and his demons. As we went through room by room, we also anointed the doorways with oil. The smell disappeared and most of the strange things stopped happening after the first "house-cleaning." The rest of it stopped after we took authority, prayed, and anointed the house a second time. We were also able to cast the demon out of the boy.

On another occasion, I was invited to a home in which a boarder had awakened one morning totally paralyzed for no reason that doctors could determine. As we went into the boarder's room, three out of the four of us could feel an oppressive atmosphere. As we took authority over the room and spoke against the enemy, that oppressiveness seemed to diminish. It did not leave the room entirely, however, until I had picked up a rug that had been bought by the boarder in Pakistan, and removed it. Several rooms of the house of a colleague of mine were similarly affected through the presence of several satanically empowered objects he had brought back from the mission field. Since the house has been "cleansed" and those objects destroyed, there has been no further problem.

When the communion elements are empowered by God through the blessing of the person administering them, God's power for blessing can flow through them in a marvelous way. Many are healed or otherwise blessed during communion services because of such empowerment. I have even received God's peace in a remarkable way myself through personally blessing the communion elements just before partaking of them.

In Scripture, we have such things happening through anointing oil (Jas 5:14), Paul's handkerchiefs and aprons (Acts 19:12), Peter's shadow (Acts 5:15), and Jesus' garment (Lk 8:44). I know of instances of God working through empowered water and even empowered salt to cast out demons. And I have come to believe that God has empowered certain places through his servants' use of their power to bless. This is why those who are receptive to God often receive blessing and even healing at such locations. I have on several occasions experienced a notable difference in freedom to preach and minister in rooms that have been "cleansed" before they were used for ministry. Such things are not the result of magic but of the grace of God who willingly empowers both humans and cultural forms—including words, material objects, and places.

This chapter has focused on how to use all the elements of ministry, so you can get a sense of how they all work together in a ministry of signs and wonders. Now we turn to what I have been learning about the personal life of the one who seeks to minister in spiritual power. What do we need to keep in mind about our life with the Lord when we begin to minister to others?

THIRTEEN

The Life of the One Who Ministers

WE'LL CALL HER DONNA. She was one of a team of people I had taken on a ministry trip to help demonstrate how to pray for healing. She had been used wonderfully by the Lord while on the trip. God had been giving her words of knowledge regularly, healing people through her ministry, and helping just about everyone she came in contact with. Donna had been functioning as a very important part of our team and had been an obvious conveyer of blessing to everyone.

Toward the end of the seminar, however, she came to me saying, "I shouldn't be here. My life isn't what it should be." I didn't know the details, but I had heard something about her struggles and failures. As I asked God how to handle the situation, though, the impression came strongly to say to Donna, "In Jesus' name, I pronounce you forgiven." I then pointed her to two of my favorite forgiveness stories: the woman caught in the act of adultery in John 8, and that of Jesus and Peter on the beach in John 21 when Peter was reinstated by the Lord after having denied him three times. I focused on the tender spot Jesus has in his heart for victims, even when on occasion they sin or make bad choices.

Of course, we cannot properly conclude from John 8 that Jesus was soft on adultery or from John 21 that he did not take seriously Peter's unfaithfulness. I believe, though, that we are justified in recognizing that Jesus bases his judgment of us on our heart attitude more than on our outward behavior. Jesus simply asked Peter, "Do you love me?" And when Peter answered in the affirmative, the Lord commissioned him to go minister on his behalf. I think Jesus was asking, "Peter, where is your heart?" And being assured three times by Peter that his heart attitude was to be faithful, the Master put his stamp of approval on him and trusted Peter to do the ministry to which he had called him. It was this same attitude that led Jesus to say to the adulterous woman, "I do not condemn you either. Go, but do not sin again" (Jn 8:11).

Donna was comforted, accepted God's forgiveness, and determined to straighten things out when she got home. And, though she still struggles, God continues to bless her as he patiently awaits the day when she will—with his help and encouragement—completely win out over the enemy in this matter.

In his wonderful mercy, God is entrusting Donna, in spite of the sinfulness she is so ashamed of, to minister in his name. Further, he is showering her and whoever she ministers to with blessings as signs of his love. Through all this, I believe he is saying to Donna, "What are you going to do about your life in response to my love and mercy?"

It is an interesting thing about God that he seems to bless us first and then invites us to respond. He doesn't make his blessings or his willingness to use us conditional on our being good first. But there are levels of ministry that he wants us to move into through spiritual discipline. For we are at war. There is a real enemy out there. And we serve a real Lord and Master who has enlisted us in a battle that will ultimately be won by our side. What then should the life of the one who ministers look like?

The Life of the One Who Ministers

1. **The one who would minister in power needs to start where Jesus started—with the filling of the Holy Spirit** (Lk 3:22). As pointed out earlier, Jesus did no signs and wonders before that point in his life. When Jesus ascended to heaven, he told his disciples to wait until the Holy Spirit would come upon them and empower them before they went out to minister for him (Lk 24:49; Acts 1:8). They, like Jesus, were not to do signs and wonders or witness to God's loving concern for humans *until* they were working under the complete control of the Holy Spirit.

The filling or baptism of the Holy Spirit has been a troublesome doctrine for Western Christians. Evangelicals have often steered clear of the doctrine, feeling that it is often abused. We have seen it connected too closely with emotionalism, tongues, sanctification, spiritual gifts, and new revelations in the form of prophecies, or sure words from God concerning other people's business. People who claim to be filled with the Spirit sometimes appear arrogant and intolerant of other Christians. Some of them claim that they alone have the "full gospel."

But the fact that a doctrine has been abused is no excuse to ignore or deny it. All doctrines have been and still are abused. Since this one has been connected with emotionalism and nonrational approaches to understanding and representing God, our worldview makes it especially easy to ignore or deny it and, of course, much more difficult to accept. Indeed, we often find it very easy to remember whatever excesses we have heard concerning this doctrine. We then easily develop entrenched stereotypes of the kind of people who endorse it, based on the exaggerated behavior of some. Our imaginations are crippled so that we cannot even picture what a sober, balanced understanding and practice of the doctrine might be.

I believe in the filling of the Holy Spirit. As an Evangelical who affirms the whole of Scripture, I am committed to believing the doctrine and to seeking to appropriate the reality of this filling in my own life. I would, though, like to disassociate myself from all unbalanced, unscriptural forms of belief and practice associated with it. Any arrogant, unloving behavior—even if in the name of being Spirit filled—certainly is not the "full gospel." Being Spirit filled does not make us any more perfect than we were before or assure that what we sense as prophetic utterances or words of knowledge will always be right. And it certainly does not give us any right to boast or act haughtily. Indeed, it should make us more humble, loving, and in every other way more Christlike.

Nor does being Spirit filled require that we become more emotional, though many Westerners who have been emotionally crippled through cultural conditioning find they grow in this dimension of their personalities as the Holy Spirit enables them to be released from such crippling. Our humanness is still very much intact, however, so that people who were emotional before being filled tend to be at least as emotional after, while those who were not emotional before may or may not be more emotional after. As for tongues, though often in Scripture those who were filled with the Spirit began to speak in tongues (see Acts 19:6), Paul says not everyone has this gift (1 Cor 12:30). In fact, in 1 Corinthians 14, he seems to suggest that it is the least of all the gifts. So why make a big deal about it?

What the fullness of the Holy Spirit brings is power (Acts 1:8)— *the power to be like Jesus and to minister like him.* And it is our privilege to receive this fullness of the Holy Spirit simply by asking for it (Lk 11:13). We receive the Holy Spirit when we accept Jesus as Savior and Lord (Rom 8:2,4,16). At that time we have the potential of being filled with him. We can, however, hinder the Spirit's full release within us. Most people, therefore, need at some later time to ask him to take over in his fullness, as the disciples did on the Day of Pentecost (Acts 2:1-4). *I believe such a filling is more like the release of the Spirit who already resides in us than like the pouring into us of someone who is outside of us.* Such release can and should take place many times as we live and minister with and for our Lord. This total release or filling may or may not be the same as what many call "a special anointing." Whether by anointing or filling, though, we can ask and expect the Spirit to come in special ways for his own purposes as he did in Jesus' ministry (Lk 5:17).

Though sometimes the full release of the Spirit with power happens with a lot of emotion, often it is quite unspectacular. Like a conversion experience, the filling of the Spirit is for some quite remarkable, while for others it is very gentle and unemotional. Some begin speaking in tongues, others don't. I didn't. Nor did I experience any kind of emotional "high." The whole experience was quite matter-of-fact. But the power was evident in my ministry and in a marvelous newness in my relationship to God. For instance, I had a constant urge to worship him. It was at least three or four years after receiving this release of the Holy Spirit that I began speaking in tongues. And again, this was unemotional.

For some the release of the Spirit comes with the laying on of hands. Though I believe it is good to seek it this way, this is not the only option. For to others the gift is given privately, in God's quiet response to our request for his filling. It is important, however, to recognize that with this gift from God, as with all others, we are not qualified for it by our righteousness, goodness, or achievements but by our openness and yieldedness to God. This, too, is an expression of his mercy and grace totally apart from our merit.

Another important thing to realize is that one does not receive the fullness and empowering of the Holy Spirit by being spiritual. Unfortunately, there are many spiritual people who do not seem to have been filled with the Holy Spirit. One receives this fullness *by asking for it, not by being spiritual.* Being spiritual is always meant to be an outflow of our relationship with God, never a condition for it.

2. It is important to deal with the matter of the spiritual condition of the one who ministers. For many people firmly believe, like Donna, that God cannot use them in a healing ministry because they are so sinful. For most, such a belief is the result of Satan's deceit. For he induces many to keep feeling guilty over sins for which they have already received forgiveness. But like Donna, some discover that the empowering of the Holy Spirit—received when one is filled with him—remains even though one's intimacy with God is not what it should be due to sinfulness. This is a fact that I frankly do not understand. But it has been well documented over and over again in the lives of prominent faith healers who have fallen into sin. Often they are still allowed by God to minister in power.

I have recently heard of a pastor who was so upset over having once again committed his besetting sin that he went to his church and literally crawled down the aisle on his hands and knees, begging forgiveness from God. The voice of God then came asking him what he was talking about. This shook the pastor into recognizing and accepting in a new way the ability of God to forgive and forget something that had already been paid for and confessed. As bad as the pastor felt about his failure, it was no big deal to God. All he asks is that we own up to our failure and do the same with it that we are called to do with all of our problems—give them all to him (1 Pt 5:7).

We do not kick little children if they fall down while learning to walk. Even if they know better than to fall, we are patient with them, reaching down a hand to help them up, knowing that eventually—if we are patient—they will learn. So it is with God. He never kicks his people when they fall (Is 42:3; Mt 12:20). He reads our hearts and makes a clear distinction between the mistakes we make, even sometimes willfully, and whether what we do is the result of confirmed rebellion on our part. *God knows what to do with those who have confirmed their wills in rebellion. But he is very merciful to those of his children who fall frequently while learning to walk.*

3. Our aim in our relationship with God should be nothing short of total intimacy. Again, Jesus is our model. He received his power from being filled with the Holy Spirit. His authority, however, seems to spring from his intimacy with the Father. He spent hours and hours in prayer, keeping in close contact with the Father. In this way, he kept his will lined up with the Father's, seeing to it that he never did anything except on the Father's authority (Jn 5:19; 7:16-18).

The same power is there for us through the filling of the Holy Spirit. But keeping our wills lined up with God's can be another matter. This comes for us, as with Jesus, from spending time with God in private and listening to him as we seek to represent him in ministry and in all other facets of our lives. When seeking to heal or to release people from demons, there is no doubt that through our filling we have enough power to accomplish whatever is desired. But we must ask ourselves, "Does what we want line up with God's will?"

Jesus' *success rate* in ministry was 100 percent since he always lined his will up with that of the Father. Our record is usually considerably less than his. The difference is, I believe, in our ability to hear and follow the Father's will. For us, the biggest challenge in a healing ministry is not in the area of power, but in the area of the intimacy of our relationship with the Father—a relationship that is essential to coordinate our wills with his.

Learning what the Father wants is one important aspect of our ministry. In general, he wants people to be blessed, to be free from satanic captivity (Lk 4:18), to be joyful, to experience love, and the like. To bring such release to any given person is likely to be in line with God's purpose. So we can confidently minister in such a way as to expect God to work at least in these key areas. Whether God desires to relieve any given person of a physical disability at any given time is, however, not always so easy to determine.

4. The fact is that we are at war. Satan and his forces are at war with God and his forces. And according to 1 John 5:19, "The whole world is under the rule of the Evil One." We are God's shock troops fighting on his behalf *behind enemy lines.* As soldiers we are to be obedient to our leader and disciplined in our personal life.

But as usual with God, we have a choice. We can enter the war actively, risking the possibility of defeats but also the possibility of victories. Or we can hide, assuring defeat at the hands of the enemy and also risking the wrath of our leader. It is no fun to be defeated. But if war it is, far better to be defeated in battle than in hiding.

I thought of this after not winning a five-hour battle with a demon. The situation was such that we only had a limited amount of time and would not have another opportunity to try to free this woman from a fairly powerful emissary of Satan. And we didn't succeed. I was and still am extremely disappointed about this defeat. I knew we had the power to lick him. But we couldn't do it. We were bested in that battle. Yet as I reflected on that experience, the thought came to me, "At least we were defeated in battle!" I wondered how many times during the previous forty-odd years of my Christian life God had wanted me to fight the enemy in just this way, but I was unprepared and hiding! For years I barely knew there was even a war being waged. I was probably more of a hindrance than a help to the war effort.

So how should we act in the war? First, we are to recognize the fact that there is a war going on. The New Testament seems fairly clear on this point. From Satan's attempt to kill the baby Jesus through to the temptations of Jesus (Lk 4) and the satanic attack leading to Christ's death, it is clear in the Gospels that there is always an enemy to defeat. We also have the experience and writings of the apostles, particularly Paul's classic call to do battle in Ephesians 6.

Second, we are to recognize that the war is taking place in the enemy's territory. Jesus calls Satan "the ruler of this world" (Jn 14:30; 16:11). John says, "We know that the whole world is under the rule of the Evil One" (1 Jn 5:19). Apparently something happened in the Garden of Eden that transferred authority over this world from Adam to Satan. The world around us is not neutral to the Lord we serve. People, and perhaps even weather and other forces, are at least some of the time under the control of Satan.

Third, we need to recognize that we—the followers of Christ—are automatically enlisted in his army. He puts uniforms on us. So we are not to behave like civilians. We are to:

> build up [our] strength in union with the Lord and by means of his mighty power. Put on all the armor that God gives [us], so that [we] will be able to stand up against the Devil's evil tricks. For we are not fighting against human beings, but against the wicked spiritual forces in the heavenly world, the rulers, authorities, and cosmic powers of this dark age. So put on God's armor now! Then when the evil day comes, you will be able to resist the enemy's attacks; and after fighting to the end, you will still hold your ground. (Eph 6:10-13)

We are to live, then, under the kind of discipline required of military personnel. As Paul says to Timothy, we are even to:

> take [our] part in suffering, as a loyal soldier of Christ Jesus. A soldier on active duty wants to please his commanding officer and so does not get mixed up in the affairs of civilian life. (2 Tm 2:3-4)

We are not being loyal to our Master if, in time of war, we act like civilians. To use another of Paul's analogies, we must behave like athletes—constantly either in training or in the race itself. We are to keep ourselves constantly fit—body, soul, and spirit. We are always to be on the alert and conscious of what our foe is up to. We need to learn what his tricks are and how to counter them. With that insight and the power we have been given, we are to alertly take every bit of territory we possibly can from him. And we are to carefully protect the territory that is already ours.

Fourth, *we know for sure who is going to win the war.* As Bob Mumford has said, "We have looked in the back of the Book. We know who will win!" Therefore, we can fight with gladness and confidence, rather than with fear. Indeed, we know that any fear of this sort comes from the enemy, not from God (2 Tm 1:7). We can rejoice and be joyful, for victory is assured. And whenever someone is converted, healed, freed from some kind of physical, emotional, or spiritual bondage, released from demonic control, or blessed in any other way, the enemy is defeated and territory is taken for the Lord.

I was dismayed to hear that a theology professor once advised his class, "If you see a demon, run!" He does not understand our mandate or the power at our disposal to fight even that kind of enemy. Another dismaying attitude was expressed to me by a pastor who was obviously "freaked out" by a discussion we were having about demons. I asked him, "If there are demons, would you rather know or not know?" He replied, "I'd rather not know!"

Someone has helpfully likened our present situation to that between D-Day—when the Allied forces began their invasion of Europe—and Victory-in-Europe Day when the Germans surrendered. During those eleven months there was no doubt who would win World War II. Yet there were reportedly more casualties during that period than during the rest of the war in the European theater. So it is in our day that Satan is behaving like a wounded and dying beast, ferociously attacking anyone who leaves him or herself vulnerable. As Peter has said, "Be alert, be on watch! Your enemy, the Devil, roams around like a roaring lion, looking for someone to devour" (1 Pt 5:8). So we need to be well prepared and always on guard, even though we can be confident and fearless. We need to wear our armor and attack fearlessly, recognizing that the Lord has given us no armor for our backs. There can be no retreat from this enemy!

A major part of our discipline is prayer, sometimes with fasting.

All of the attention to armor spoken of in Ephesians 6 is to be done in prayer, "asking for God's help. Pray on every occasion, as the Spirit leads. . . . *pray always* . . ." (Eph 6:18).

We are also to fast, but not ostentatiously as the "hypocrites" of Jesus' day did (Mt 6:16-18). Jesus said fasting would be appropriate for his disciples after the Bridegroom has left the scene (Mt 9:15). In Acts, we see the disciples putting this prediction into practice by fasting and praying whenever faced with a major decision (Acts 13:2, 3; 14:23). Those knowledgeable about fasting today suggest that it is helpful whenever we seek more of something such as guidance or greater anointing to do the work of the Master. Or it can be helpful as an act of devotion when seeking greater closeness to God.

I am just learning to fast. The first time I tried it was when I was seeking greater anointing in order to release a four-year-old boy from a demon. We had ministered to the boy on three occasions and had met with no success. So I denied myself solid food for a day and went to minister to the boy in the evening. By that time I had a headache and generally felt weak and powerless. But it was during that session that we were able to get the demon to leave the boy! Was it by chance? Or was there a relationship between the "price" I paid and the way God was able to use me? I think the latter. Since then I have fasted for one day on a few other occasions. It has been easier than it was on that first attempt.

5. **To minister effectively, we need to know just who we are. We are children of the King!** Royal blood flows in our veins. Children of kings have special rules when they come into the throne room. That's why we can come boldly and confidently into his presence (Heb 4:16). That's why we can call God "Abba," our "Dad." That's why we don't have to fear him as Isaiah did (Is 6:5). We never have to hang our heads in shame over our family relationship.

Further, we know *we are loved by God because of who we are, not because of anything we may accomplish.* As John says, "See how much the Father has loved us! His love is so great that we are called God's children—and so, in fact, we are" (1 Jn 3:1). It is by grace we are saved (Eph 2:8). It is also by grace that we are empowered.

But equally mind blowing is that by grace *God actually trusts us.* When Jesus forgave the adulteress and reinstated Peter, he trusted them. When he gave his disciples authority and power and sent them out to minister, he trusted them. (Would you have trusted the disciples with anything, especially with authority and power?)When Jesus left the earth, he entrusted us with the Holy Spirit and predicted that with him we "will do what [he did]—yes, [we] will do even greater things" than he himself did (Jn 14:12). Jesus trusted the disciples and us so much that he calls us his *friends, not slaves,* because he has entrusted us with "everything I heard from the Father" (Jn 15:15). It is, therefore, our kingdom as well as his (Lk 12:32; 22:29-30).

6. **So we are to imitate our Master.** What he did we are to do, and even more (Jn 14:12). Many Christians think they have no right to make this kind of assertion. After all, they say, "He was God and we are not. He had the power and authority of God; we are merely human."

But it is clear from Scripture that he laid aside his divine prerogatives to become human (Phil 2:6-7). Though in some mysterious way Jesus continued to be fully God, he became human in such a way that he expects us to be able to imitate his works (Jn 14:12). He, like us, lived in a powerless state until his baptism. And even after that he claimed to have no power of his own—only the power to do what he saw the Father doing (Jn 5:19). Though in his sinlessness his humanity differed inherently from ours, we are not to despair of being able to follow in his steps.

Scripture seems to allow a much greater possibility of imitating Jesus than Evangelicalism has ever before allowed. As we obey Jesus' command to imitate him by being filled with the Holy Spirit (Lk 24:49; Acts 1:4, 5, 8), we can be launched into a ministry like his and actually do what he did (Jn 14:12). What a privilege!

7. **It is important for anyone engaging in spiritual warfare to be supported by as much prayer as possible.** In spite of the individualism of our society, we are not expected to fight all by ourselves. We are to enlist others, especially those with the gift of intercession, to keep our ministry constantly before the Lord. We are parts of a body and can only function adequately when we are supported, encouraged, and equipped by other members of the body.

How much of this kind of support we need, I have no idea. Personally, I try to get on as many prayer lists as possible. Especially on ministry trips, the way God works frequently makes it very obvious that the people back home are supporting us in our part of the battle.

8. **Another important support for those who minister is to have a spiritual mentor.** It is unfortunate that our worldview assumptions lead us to believe that those in positions of ministry are spiritually strong enough to be independent. As we enter this kind of ministry, we are often unconsciously trapped into assuming that we can go it alone. On the contrary, it is especially important for those most likely to be attacked by Satan to have a person from whom they can receive ministry. Many of the Christian leaders who have recently fallen from high positions might still be effective for Christ if they had been accountable to someone.

Even though we are in active ministry, we often carry wounds that need to be dealt with. We are "wounded healers" at best. It is good for us to be constantly working toward greater health for ourselves. We also need to receive the kind of encouragement and blessing we seek to give to others.

Moreover, working with a spiritual mentor provides valuable learning. The person I go to is greatly gifted in ministering inner healing. This helps me both in probing into areas where I need inner healing and in helping me to develop my own gifts in this area.

9. **A further personal matter is dealing with our level of skepticism.** As I've indicated, my skepticism has never completely disappeared. I am not nearly as skeptical now as I was at first. But my mind still frequently asks, "Was that really God's doing? Or was it by chance?"

I suppose we just have to live with some skepticism. We have been carefully taught to be skeptical, especially about spiritual matters. And though we probably do right to be concerned about our skepticism, it may be that we can use it to some advantage. Some who have gotten into a ministry of spiritual power have become credulous and uncritical to a disturbing extent. To them, any healing, almost any ecstasy, any speaking in tongues, or any prophesying is to be applauded.

Yet Satan is a master counterfeiter. He cleverly imitates each of the things God does, even performing great signs and wonders "in order to deceive even God's chosen people, if possible" (Mt 24:24). Unless we retain some critical faculty, we can easily be led astray. It is to encourage discernment in this area that we are commanded to test those who claim to have the Spirit, "to find out if the spirit they have comes from God" (1 Jn 4:1). For not all of what is done ostensibly in

Jesus' name is from God. For he says,

> Not everyone who calls me "Lord, Lord" will enter the Kingdom
> of heaven, but only those who do what my Father in heaven wants
> them to do. When the Judgment Day comes, many will say to me,
> "Lord, Lord! In your name we spoke God's message, by your
> name we drove out many demons and performed many miracles!"
> Then I will say to them, "I never knew you. Get away from me, you
> wicked people!" (Mt 7:21-23)

I believe we should seek the gift of discernment to avoid this pitfall.
Perhaps, when that gift comes, God will use at least some aspects of
our culturally inculcated skepticism to strengthen it.

Research into the ways in which God moves in power also requires
critical faculties that may be enhanced by a certain amount of
skepticism. Researchers need to "check things out," no matter how
plausible the stories sound. And from a Western perspective, many of
the stories seem quite implausible. Those that are implausible do
need to be regarded with a certain amount of skepticism until they are
proven. There are, however, enough solidly verifiable signs and
wonders that we need not be concerned if some of the accounts are
disproven. Better to be honest and cautious—even at the expense of
some of the data—than to believe and teach inaccurate stories just
because we know God could do it that way if he chose to.

But let our skepticism be that of Thomas who, though doubtful
before he saw, gladly accepted the truth when he saw it. Let us not
imitate the skepticism of the Pharisees who steadfastly refused to
believe even though they saw the work of Jesus (Jn 9).

10. As pointed out throughout this volume, I am still learning.
**Moving into a healing ministry is an incredibly interesting and
exciting adventure.** And virtually every event holds within it something new to learn. I have learned much. But there is undoubtedly still
much God wants to teach me. The same will be true for each of us. We
can always look forward to more growth in the Lord in this area and
others.

The biggest challenge is to learn to listen to God. And the greatest
learning happens when we hear from him and follow what we hear. It
will probably take eternity to learn it all.

Conclusion

WHAT I'VE BEEN TALKING ABOUT in this book has only just begun. As you can tell, I'm enthusiastic about what's been happening—about what I've been seeing. But there are still many areas of some uncertainty for me.

I doubt that all my questions will ever be answered. The same will probably be true for you. But I strongly recommend that you get involved anyway. Christianity seems now much more like what it was intended to be than it used to. So does God. So do I.

Let me conclude, then, with seven blessings intended to assist you to enter and continue on a pilgrimage similar to my own. I bless you in Jesus' name with:

1. A strong desire and determination to discover and practice all that Christianity was meant to be;
2. The ability to make whatever paradigm and practice shifts are necessary to move into a ministry in spiritual power;
3. A strong sense of daring to take whatever risks may be necessary and to launch forth into this unfamiliar territory;
4. Great authority and power in ministry;
5. Patience with yourself and with God as you experiment and learn;
6. Great renewal and growth in your relationship with and commitment to our wonderful Lord and Savior Jesus Christ;
7. An ever-increasing manifestation of the fruits of the Spirit in your life, especially love.

May his kingdom come, may his will be done in your life as it is in heaven.

Appendices

Worldview and Its Functions

This appendix provides a more detailed and technical discussion of worldview and its functions than was possible in the body of this book. After a brief introduction to the comparative approach that led anthropologists to the kind of comparisons and contrasts underlying the study of worldview, we discuss the functions of worldview. In Appendix B, then, we go on to explore what we call "worldview universals"—the areas of life covered by all worldviews.

A Comparative or Crosscultural Approach

From the earliest days of formal anthropological study in the latter third of the nineteenth century, it has been the habit of anthropologists to compare cultures. It was by then obvious that different peoples approach the problems of life in quite different ways. Why the differences? it was asked, And which approaches are best?

So the customs of various peoples were compared. The first assumption made by those who made the comparisons was that our Western customs are clearly "superior" to those of other peoples. So they used their data to try to discover how we got to be this way. Comparisons were made between Western and non-Western cultures with the assumption that what we were seeing in other cultures were the stages Western cultures had gone through on their way to our present position. Their customs and beliefs were assumed to show us what our ancestors once practiced but then grew out of.

After awhile, though, it became apparent that our approaches to life are not necessarily better than those of non-Western peoples. Nor are the practices of other peoples indicative of the stages our ancestors went through. Rather, different cultures represent different creative approaches to life—each with areas of strength and areas of weakness. So anthropologists turned more to comparing cultures without assuming ours is superior to theirs. In the process it became clear that the ways of life of the various peoples of the world are each quite respectable. They are also very complex.

The complexity of cultures lies in at least two areas. First there is the complex structuring of each of the vast array of components of which life is made up. People need to communicate, so there is language. And language is always complex. People need to be regulated, so there are rules and enforcers of rules, concepts of propriety, and social pressure to keep people in line. And all of the social customs going to make up these patterns are complex. People need food, clothing, shelter, and techniques for obtaining and maintaining these necessities. So there are complex cultural patterns to govern those aspects of life. Likewise, this is true with the patterns governing family relationships, economics, religion, art, education, and all the rest. All such cultural patterns are complex. They are also interrelated with each other.

Secondly, though, it has become clear that each of these areas of cultural patterning consists of surface-level behavior and deep-level assumptions. The latter—the assumptions—we call worldview. This is beneath the surface of culture, usually below the level of a people's awareness and often difficult for outsiders to discover.

So as we attempt to compare cultures, we need to compare them at two levels. The early anthropologists and most contemporary travelers tend to compare largely at the surface level. The diversity of different cultures on the surface is very interesting. If, however, we are to really understand the significance of those surface-level differences, we need to understand the deep-level assumptions and values on the basis of which people generate that surface-level behavior.

It is at this point that the comparative study of worldview helps us. When we look at other people's assumptions and compare them with ours, we become aware of at least two things:

1. There is a great variety of underlying assumptions and values held by the various peoples of the world;

2. And our own worldview assumptions aren't the only ones that make sense.

We can, therefore, perhaps learn something more about REALITY as God sees it by taking seriously the insights of those of other societies.

True, we all see dimly. Yet through looking at cultural (worldview) data concerning how other peoples see, we can learn to see more than the limited perspectives of our own worldview allow us to see. In this way, we can get insight into both the strengths and weaknesses of our own perspectives. One thing that becomes clear is that the area under consideration in this book is of great importance to most of the peoples of the world, including biblical peoples.

Another type of insight that such study has yielded is the fact that there are certain things common to all worldviews. Two of these areas will be highlighted here. *In Appendix A we will focus on a series of functions served by all worldviews. In Appendix B we will focus on worldview universals.* What follows is an overview of those two areas.

Overview of Worldview Functions and Universals

1. **All worldviews seem to serve certain functions for the members of the society of which they are a part. We call these worldview functions** and will deal with them in this Appendix. The worldview provides patterns in terms of which people do the following kinds of things:

a. **Explain** aspects of life according to socially approved ways of seeing REALITY;

b. **Evaluate** all aspects of life in socially approved ways;

c. **Validate** common perceptions and behavior;

d. **Assign commitment priorities** that help people identify what people and other aspects of life to pledge allegiance to;

e. **Interpret** things in ways that are consistent with those of the rest of the society;

f. Pursue life in a reasonably **integrated** fashion;

g. **Adapt** to internal and external pressure for change.

2. In addition, **all worldviews also seem to enable people to deal with at least five basic areas of life. These we call worldview universals.** They will be treated in detail in Appendix B. Each worldview provides a structured approach to a society's perceptions of reality in each of these areas. The areas are:

a. **Categorization**—all people classify, categorize, and think according to the logic of their worldview;

b. **Person-Group**—all people relate to the various persons and groups in their lives on the basis of their worldview assumptions concerning how they should relate to them;

c. **Causality**—all people explain and relate to the various things in life that cause other things on the basis of their worldview assumptions;

d. **Time-Event**—all people structure the time and event aspects of their lives on the basis of their worldview assumptions; and

e. **Space-Material**—all people conceive of and arrange their relationships with space and material objects on the basis of their worldview assumptions.

When we begin comparing the worldviews of other societies with those of Western peoples, we find quite a number of important contrasts. For example, such comparisons show marked similarities between the worldviews of the Hebrews and those of many contemporary non-Western peoples. We will chart some of these differences at the end of Appendix B.

This fact is of obvious benefit to those of us involved in communicating the gospel crossculturally. It is also of immense importance to biblical Christians in understanding both Old and New Testaments, since all of the authors of Scripture, except Luke, were Hebrews. They wrote, therefore, in terms of Hebrew perceptions of REALITY—that is, out of Hebrew worldview perspectives.

Since our special focus in this volume lies in the area of causality (number three above), we will give more detailed treatment to that area than to the others in Appendix B.

Worldview Functions

There are many functions served by a worldview. In this appendix, I highlight several of the most important.

1. **Explaining.** A large number of the assumptions making up a peoples' worldview underlie the explanations they give concerning how things got to be the way they are and what keeps them that way. In terms of these explanatory assumptions we develop our picture of what REALITY looks like. Assumptions underlying explanations cover the whole territory of life and answer questions such as Who?, What?, When?, Where?, How?, and Why?

The explanations people give in any area of life relate strongly to what they assume concerning the basic nature of the universe.

Though people may be able to express explicitly their beliefs concerning how the universe came into existence, most of the assumptions in this area are likely to be unconsciously held. A common contrast is between those who believe the universe to be mechanistic, impersonal, and controllable by humans, and those who picture the universe as capricious and spirit-controlled.

If the worldview assumption is that the world is mechanistic as in Western societies, explanations of how and why things happen will focus on the place of impersonal cause and effect in the process without reference to any involvement of personal spiritual beings. For many peoples, however, their worldview assumptions lead them to explain as the activity of personal spirits most of the same phenomena that Westerners attribute to impersonal causes.

A Christian commitment, of course, leads most Westerners to replace purely natural explanations about the origins and the continuance of the universe with those that assert God has created and is sustaining it. But we may not know just how much God depends on impersonal forces (cause and effect, "laws of nature," for instance) for the day-to-day operation of things and how much control he assigns to humans and spiritual beings. Not knowing this may lead us to wonder whether mechanistic, humanistic, or spiritual worldview explanations are more accurate. We might even wonder whether one explanation might be more accurate in certain situations and another in other situations.

In any event, the worldview of one's society leads one to attempt to explain all such phenomena in terms of the culturally prescribed assumptions. The confusion we may experience at this point comes from the fact that, as Christians, we have committed ourselves to a perspective other than that of our society—a perspective that at least partially contradicts the assumptions of Western societies in areas such as this.

In addition to explanations concerning the origin and nature of the universe, we look to our worldview to provide the assumptions on the basis of which we explain such things as how people, animals, plants, and other phenomena got here and what we should expect of them. Areas covered by science, history, philosophy, myth, legend, and the like fit under this category. It is by means of these approaches or techniques that certain worldview assumptions and understandings are made explicit. Whether such explanations can be proven or not is irrelevant. If they are assumed by a people, they are a part of their worldview.

2. **Evaluating and Validating.** A second function that these assumptions that we call worldview serve is to enable people to evaluate what goes on around and inside of them. In the learning of a worldview, people are taught to evaluate as well as to picture reality. This provides an approved structuring of the emotive or affective dimension of human life. We evaluate on the basis of how we understand that the pictures of REALITY "ought to appear." Such evaluation results both in the feeling that what we are doing is valid or invalid, right or wrong, good or bad. People then commit themselves to what they highly value.

These value assumptions provide the bases for judgments concerning what is good and what is not good, what is valid and what is not valid. Here are some typical areas in which these assumptions are applied: esthetics, including judgments as to what is visually or aurally pleasing; ethics, including judgments as to what is moral and what immoral; economics, including judgments as to what ought to be more or less expensive; human character, including judgments about proper versus improper, or admirable conduct and/or character traits versus conduct and/or character that ought to be criticized.

A broader cultural concern would be the way both individuals and groups relate. Most societies seem to assume that it is good for persons and groups within the society to strongly value a cooperative relationship with each other. Working together, then, would be seen as good and competing with each other as bad. In American society, however, we assume that competition between many individuals and groups within our society is a good thing. We particularly encourage boys and men to compete against their same sex peers and increasingly against women as well. The same holds for girls and women in competing against each other and increasingly with boys and men. We also consciously or unconsciously encourage competition between young people and adults, one business and another, labor and management, and even church and church. "If we don't compete," we say, "how will we get anywhere?" We value and continue to encourage such competition in spite of the fact that there is ample evidence to indicate that it has gotten out of control and that our society is suffering for it.

Like all other aspects of worldview, values are both structured and taught as unchallenged assumptions. People ordinarily accept without question the patterns for evaluation and commitment as they are being taught them. But they may later choose to change certain ones of them and to pay whatever social penalty is assigned by the society for those who deviate from its norms. Such a change of evaluation and allegiance often paves the way for conversion to another perspective. Since allegiance involves emotional attachment, those paradigms or perspectives that are highly valued will be less easily changed than those less highly valued.

Since, for example, such values as individualism, privacy, and a materialistic evaluation of our worth to society are high on an American's value scale, we are likely to experience great difficulty if we try to make changes in these areas. What is most highly valued becomes easily apparent when one value comes into conflict with another. American males, for example, though they may highly value family, religion, and friends, tend to value their jobs above almost any of these. They often, therefore, sacrifice family, church, or friendship concerns for job concerns—such as when a man is asked by his company to move to another part of the country to receive a promotion.

Things that are valued at the lower end of the hierarchy of values, however, are easily changed, even when not in competition with other values. Americans readily change clothing styles, toothpaste and soap, and adopt new gadgets to replace old ones. We will even change ideas fairly readily if we are not too attached to them and the new idea comes from a prestigious source.

By definition, the evaluative assumptions people hold sanction and validate the basic institutions, values, and goals of a society, giving people the impression that their approach is the right one. That means any other approach is at least inferior and probably wrong. We value certain things positively because we have learned to assume that they are good. We evaluate other things as negative because we have been taught to consider them bad.

Thus American ways are sanctioned by our American worldviews, and visitors to our country may rightly be concerned about the way we Americans assume that our approach to life, our politics, our economics, and our religion are all endorsed by God. Some of us realize that this system is not endorsed by God. Yet the naive perspective held by many American Christians simply asserts: *since it is our way and we are a "Christian society," it must be the best way, God's way.* So many people assume that God himself is in favor of our kind of democracy and capitalism. They may even believe in the doctrine of "manifest destiny"—that God himself gave us the right to take the land away from the Indians, so we could establish this kind of government and develop the ability in technology and in warfare to achieve our present place of power and prominence in the world.

But a look at the distance between American values and Jesus' teachings should lead us as Christians to ask serious questions about how God evaluates things. For as Christians we are pledged to try to see things from his perspective, to value what he values, to stand against what he stands against. Because of this we may be required by our commitment to a Christian perspective to reevaluate and to modify, perhaps even to replace, some of the paradigms provided by our American worldview.

3. Assigning and Prioritizing Commitments. A third function that worldview serves is to enable us to sort out, arrange, and make different commitments, allegiances, or loyalties to the things we assume, value, and do. That is, we don't simply assume, believe, value, or relate to everything in the same way. The degree of emotional attachment—allegiance, loyalty, or commitment—to any given assumption will differ at least initially in accord with what we have been taught. And we are taught to relate to each aspect of life with some degree of intensity, committing ourselves quite strongly to certain beliefs, values, and behaviors—but weakly or even indifferently to others.

Commitments may be strong or weak. In most societies, for example, a man's allegiance to his wife and mother are likely to both be strong. So are a mother's commitment to her children. Other strong commitments include a person's allegiance to self, his or her social group, a career, God, family, and so on. Allegiances to such things as a particular type of soap or toothpaste, a make of automobile, a type of clothing, and the like tend to be at the other end of the scale for most people. Loyalty or allegiance to any given idea or institution may also be strong or weak.

Allegiances are prioritized—but often differently from society to society. This becomes most obvious when we compare how people of different societies choose when confronted *with a difficult choice between conflicting loyalties.* An interesting thing happens in this regard when people of different societies are asked what they would do in the following situation. A man, his mother, and his wife are crossing a river in a canoe when the canoe capsizes. Neither of the women can swim, the man is a weak swimmer, and the river is flowing swiftly. This means he can only rescue one of the women. If you were that man, which one would you rescue?

In response, Anglo-Americans and northern Europeans tend to opt for rescuing the wife. Non-Westerners, southern Europeans, and Latin Americans, on the other hand, usually claim (often without hesitation) that they would rescue the mother. "You can always get another wife," they often reason, "but you can never replace a mother." In discussing this conundrum in class once, a Japanese student provided us with another option. He said, "I would just have to drown without rescuing either. I could neither make such a choice nor face my community afterwards if I allowed either of them to die."

Americans frequently have to prioritize allegiances in choosing between job and family, between self-interest and the best interests of loved ones, between self and community. For Christians, it also comes down to choosing between God and any of these. For non-Westerners the need to choose between allegiance to God and to community is often excruciatingly difficult. Our real commitments are often most obvious when such choices are made unconsciously. A good example is when during wartime most Christian citizens of a nation unconsciously agree to put allegiance to nation above an allegiance to their Christian brothers who are fighting for the enemy nation.

Most of our allegiances are, however, much less spectacular. Yet they, too, are likely to come into conflict with competing interests in certain social situations. We are committed via our worldview to the values, structures, and practices of our society. The degree to which we believe in the primacy of these values, structures, and practices is a measure of the intensity of our commitment to them. Note how strongly we Westerners are committed to our technology, social customs (including courtship and marriage, the "equality" of women), political beliefs (including our notion of democracy), and educational practices (including the right to go to college and receive a "quality" education), not only for ourselves but for the other peoples of the world as well. In general, the more intense the commitment of groups or individuals is to an assumption, value, or practice the less likely they are to change it. But if they become dissatisfied with the custom or discover an attractive alternative, the strength of their allegiance is likely to weaken. And they become more open to change.

In Western societies, for example, the allegiance of many is strong to their religious beliefs and the institutions that support them. Thus, religion in Western societies is considered to be one of the most conservative aspects of those cultures, stimulating high allegiance on the part of many people. In many of the societies of the world, however, the kind of loyalty we in the West have learned to expect to one's religious system is simply not there. For many peoples the crucial consideration seems to be not their allegiance to their religion but their quest for greater spiritual power. They are only conservative religiously when they are not convinced of the power claims of the new allegiance. One might say, then, that the greater allegiance for these peoples is to obtain power rather than to preserve the religious institution.

Since the Western quest for power takes place more in the realms of science and technology than in religion, this motivation to seek more power through religious techniques is not as prominent in the West. We are more likely to seek solutions involving spiritual power only after we have exhausted natural means of solving our problems. This fact somewhat dampens the desire of many Western Christians to move into the spiritual power area that Jesus promised would be a normal part of Christian experience and witness.

It is likely that all peoples are provided by their worldviews with a prescribed, or at least strongly recommended, ultimate allegiance. For Americans this is likely to be one's self. Allegiance to career for men, to family especially for mothers, to reputation, to wealth, and the like are high enough on the list to sometimes vie for first place. For members of other societies the culturally prescribed first allegiance is often to family, to clan, or to some other kinship grouping. Ultimate allegiance to one or another of the above areas of life may, however, replace family in the lives of at least certain people in non-Western societies.

For Christians, of course, it is expected that our primary allegiance be to God with other commitments falling into line behind that supreme one. The requirement that God be first, however, means that we make a change within our worldview that is difficult both to initiate and to maintain. We see throughout the Scriptures and experience constantly in our own lives the tendency for those who have once put God first to replace him with someone or something else. Such replacement is labeled idolatry in the Scriptures and thoroughly condemned.

4. Interpreting. All of this prioritizing, then, provides people with the structuring they need to interpret and assign meaning to life. As I have made clear elsewhere,[1] *meanings lie in people,* not in the external world nor in language, gestures, writing, or any of the other symbols we use to describe and discuss our perceptions of that world. Neither the external world nor the elements of life interpret themselves. *People interpret and assign meaning to the world in which they are involved.* They are, however, guided in this process by the "tracks" of the worldviews they are taught.

People ordinarily follow these tracks in assigning meaning, but they may choose to interpret differently—either occasionally or habitually. It is my impression that *new habits of interpretation are usually the result of new allegiances and perspectives.* When a person pledges allegiance to Jesus Christ, for example, at least one major component of his or her view of REALITY is changed. With that change at least some of the guidelines the person uses to interpret REALITY will also change. From a passage such as 2 Corinthians 5:14-17, we conclude that this change of allegiance results in a person replacing his or her human interpretation of people— including Jesus—with that of the new perspective that results from being "in Christ." Paul writes:

> We are ruled by the love of Christ, now that we recognize that one man died for everyone, which means that they all share in his death. He died for all, so that those who live should no longer live for themselves, but only for him who died and was raised to life for their sake.
>
> No longer, then, do we judge anyone by human standards. Even if at one time we judged Christ according to human standards, we no longer do so. When anyone is joined to Christ, he is a new being; the old is gone, the new has come. (2 Cor 5:14-17)

Interpreting is a complex process. But we do it automatically, without thinking. It is clear, however, that there is a direct and close relationship between the interpretive conclusions we draw and the assumptions we start with. As Christians it is important that the basic assumptions to which our interpretations are tied be truly Christian, so that we will automatically interpret and behave as God wants us to.

5. **Integrating.** A fifth function served by a worldview is to relate each aspect of culture to all others. Though no culture is perfectly integrated, all are integrated well enough that anything that is changed in one part of the culture automatically has ramifications for

the rest of the culture. This is because the whole of the culture is centered in the same worldview assumptions. The worldview then functions as the nerve center of a culture—anything that happens gets fed into it. In turn, the new input results in influences being sent out from the worldview to the rest of the culture.

Because they underlie all aspects of a culture, worldview assumptions function as the "glue" that holds things together. People with a common worldview tend to apply the same principles and values in all areas of life. If their worldview value in one area of life is individualism, they are likely to be individualistic in virtually all areas of life. Their life and culture are integrated around such a guiding principle.

If, their guiding worldview principle is to function as a community in one area of life, they are likely to practice such cooperation in virtually all areas of life. The same is true of other core (worldview) values in life such as freedom, hierarchy, male or female dominance, materialism, supernaturalism versus naturalism, a past, present, or future time orientation, conformity, and so on.

6. **Adapting.** A people's worldview does not always provide categories around which a person can interpret new ideas and experiences. So built into a culture we find worldview assumptions that provide guidance when we perceive that things are not as we believe they ought to be. When this happens, the most frequent initial response is defensiveness—we try to interpret what we see in such a way that it either conforms to our worldview or dismiss it as unreal.

But when there is a certain amount of openness, or when the perception persists and we are unable to deny it, then we may choose to make a change in some aspect of our worldview. A noncharismatic Western Christian who has learned to assume that God no longer heals people like he did in biblical times may, for example, choose to make such a change in worldview when he or she actually sees one or more healings. Or such a person may attempt to preserve the old perspective by explaining away the healings through purely psychological and physical explanations. Likewise, non-Westerners, under constant pressure from the teaching of Western naturalistic interpretations of reality, may choose to replace part or all of their supernaturalistic assumptions in certain areas with naturalistic ones.

Under these kinds of pressure, persons and groups may even attempt to retain two sets of mutually contradictory assumptions. They then live in a kind of "worldview schizophrenia"—sometimes basing their behavior on one set of assumptions, sometimes on the other. Many non-Westerners who have been to Western schools live constantly in such a state. So do many Christians even within Western societies as they try to choose in any given situation between their naturalistic Western assumptions and those they have committed themselves to as Christians.

Whatever the result, it is worldview assumptions that guide us in what to do when other assumptions are challenged and we are forced to modify our perspectives in a given area of life. Of course, sometimes the challenges are too great, or for some other reason people are unable to handle the pressures for modification. Then there can be breakdown at the worldview level possibly resulting in demoralization—manifest in symptoms such as psychological, social, and moral breakdown. If left unchecked and not reversed, such demoralization can eventually result in cultural disintegration.

Worldview Universals

Study of a sizable sampling of the worldviews of the various peoples of the world leads to the conclusion that there are several areas of life for which each one provides basic assumptions.[1] Though there may be more, at least the five following categories of assumptions seem to be found in every worldview. Thus we refer to them as "worldview universals."

Here we will go through a general discussion of each of the universals, and then present in chart form certain contrasts in each of these areas between Western and Hebrew worldviews.

1. Every worldview provides a structure or pattern for the way people categorize or classify their perceptions of reality. People classify plants, animals, people, things, material objects, social categories, natural and supernatural entities, the visible and the invisible. All are labeled and lumped into categories together with other items and entities believed to be similar to them.

Not only are the classifications themselves a part of a worldview, the very assumptions used to classify the items or aspects of reality are themselves worldview assumptions. That is, we divide things up according to the logic we have been taught. And that logic itself is a worldview phenomenon and differs from people to people. A people's language provides the most obvious clue to its system of categorization, though not infrequently the linguistic classification and the logic of a people will not correspond exactly.

To understand this aspect of worldview, consider the following: English and many other languages classify most items as either singular or plural. Many languages mark nouns as masculine or feminine. Many sort nouns into even more categories than that. The Bantu languages of Africa, for example, may show as many as fifteen or more "genders" called noun classes. In the West we ordinarily divide time into past, present, and future. In contrast, many Melanesian peoples divide time into "now time" and "myth time." Many peoples regard the life of plants, animals, people, and spiritual beings as qualitatively different, while others regard all life as of the same nature and quality. In Western societies we speak of animate and inanimate objects, though many peoples regard all objects as possessing life.

In these and a myriad of other ways, people divide up and compartmentalize the reality around them. Humans seem to have an inherent drive to categorize in their desire to understand reality. And the way we categorize and the values we put on the various categories affect every aspect of how we perceive, think, and behave. Westerners, for example, tend to categorize the spirit world along with fairies, elves, and other mythical beings that we do not take seriously. This evaluation affects our attitudes toward spirit beings and tends to block our attempts to take angels and demons seriously, even though as Christians we claim to accept anything we find in the Bible.

2. A second area that all worldviews treat is what I'll label the **person-group. This is the way the human universe is perceived in both its internal and external relationships, so that it can be understood in the same way by all the members of a society.** So a worldview provides perspectives by means of which people can portray this understanding. We are taught whether to see people primarily as individuals, as in America, or primarily as groups, as in many other societies.

Further, we are taught who is a part of our ingroup and who is outside of it. We base our treatment of other people on this understanding. Those in our ingroup are treated well. Those in our outgroup, however, are not treated with the same kind of respect and are often exploited. On the basis of such definitions of ingroup and outgroup, then, moral and social behavior such as that taught in the Ten Commandments is interpreted. The commandments say, don't steal, don't commit adultery, don't murder, don't covet, and so on. Each of the terms proscribes an activity against members of the ingroup.

For example, in spite of the mistranslation in the standard versions of Scripture, the commandment is against "murder," not "killing." Murder is the unwarranted killing of one of the ingroup. Other kinds of killing are not proscribed until later when Jesus presents a higher ideal. Likewise, stealing is defined as taking property from one of the ingroup. Yet taking things from enemies is seldom considered stealing, being viewed, rather, as the right of the victor.

In addition, a worldview will provide assumptions concerning how a human being is to be defined and how one ought to behave in the various contexts of which he or she is a part. Concepts of the ideal person, concepts of status and role, concepts of the proper relationships between people of different social classes, age groups, sexes, ethnic groups, and the like are thus defined by one's worldview. How one is to relate to the physical environment is also specified. As Westerners we learn to assume that we are to dominate the physical environment. In many non-Western societies, however, people learn that it is proper for them to submit to it.

All of this has important ramifications for Christians, because a serious Christian commitment often brings us into conflict with the way our society teaches us to treat other human beings. Westerners are taught, for example, to be quite competitive in relation to others. Yet the Bible commands us to love and to seek the best for all others, even those who threaten us or misuse us. The Bible sets higher ideals for us than those advocated by our worldview. We need power greater than merely human power to follow these ideals. It is God's power that provides us with the means to transform human attitudes and behavior, so we can live close to biblical ideals and standards.

3. A third area addressed by every worldview is the matter of causality. I'm speaking here of matters surrounding such questions as, What causes things? What power lies behind such causation? What forces are at work in the universe? What results do they bring about? Are the forces personal, impersonal, or both? The answers provided by the world's religious systems have names like God, gods, spirits, demons, luck, fate, karma, chance. In addition, there are cause and effect, political and economic structures, the power of persons, and so on.

There are at least three major spheres or domains within which questions of causality need to be treated. They are:

a) **Natural world causality**, including such things as weather, physical laws such as the law of gravity, heat, cold, electricity, water power, leverage, speed, and the like. All of these things impinge on human life to cause a variety of things, many evaluated as good, many evaluated as bad.

b) The area of **human causality** treats the power exercised by humans over the natural world, over other humans, and over spirit beings and forces. Under this heading come the political, social, and economic dynamics that seem to allow certain humans to pressure others in certain directions. Differences in status and role figure prominently in this area. It is important to learn about the place of human will in interpersonal relationships between those of unequal power. Can a human being be forced to do things against his or her will? Any power that humans seem to have over supernatural beings and forces also comes under this heading.

c) The area of **supernatural causality** is of particular concern in this volume. We are advocating greater understanding of the dynamics of the relationships between spiritual and human beings. Among the questions to deal with under this heading are, Is there a Supreme Cause? If so, is he all powerful or subject to limitations? Is there a hierarchy of spirit beings? What power do spirit beings have over humans? Are they limited by human will in the exercise of power in the human realm? And what power do spirit beings have over each other? Is weather purely a natural phenomenon? Or are spirit beings in charge of the weather? And can humans exert any control over spirit beings? If so, under what conditions?

As indicated at various points throughout this volume, different societies pay differing amounts of attention to these three areas of life. We have seen that Western peoples pay great attention to the natural world and little if any attention to the spirit world. In many non-Western societies the proportions seem to be reversed. Biblical societies were much more like contemporary non-Western peoples than like Western societies in this regard.

It may be helpful to diagram the approximate proportions of attention given by these three types of societies to each of the three areas or spheres of causality outlined above. Though any chart such as this is greatly oversimplified, my intent is to portray the fact that biblical societies and approximately two-thirds of today's societies give about the same amount of attention to each of the three areas of causality, while Western peoples give much less attention to the spirit sphere and much more attention to the nature sphere than either of the other sets of societies.

BIBLICAL SOCIETIES	2/3 WORLD SOCIETIES	WESTERN SOCIETIES
Spirit Sphere	**Spirit Sphere**	Spirit/God Sphere
(God the primary focus. Spirits a lesser focus)	(Spirits the primary focus. God a lesser focus)	Human Sphere
Human Sphere	Human Sphere	Nature Sphere
Nature Sphere	Nature Sphere	

That the contrast between our society is so great suggests at least two interesting facts:

a) The lack of development in the sphere within our Western worldview in which spirit beings and powers, including God, would be treated makes it very **difficult for us to understand either the Bible or the concerns of non-Western peoples in this area;** and

b) It is usually **easier for non-Western peoples both to understand and to receive God's message directly from the biblical accounts than from Westerners.** The Bible is more on their wavelength than we are for worldview reasons.

Note, however, that there is one major difference between the understanding of biblical peoples and that of contemporary non-Westerners with respect to the spirit realm. In the Bible, the focus is squarely on God while in two-thirds of the world's societies, the focus is usually much more on spirits than on God. This fact points to an important area needing change for many non-Westerners who turn to Christ. This is, however, often less of a problem than that caused by a secularized presentation of the gospel by Westerners to people who are much more aware of spiritual reality than their Western missionaries.

The area of causality and power is the part of worldview most likely to undergo change for those who accept the gospel message. For Christians, of course, the power above all powers is God. And he requires of us both knowledge of and commitment to himself. Acceptance of him, then, entails a radical change in one's view of and relation to supreme power in the universe. The communication of the gospel has as its aim the bringing about of belief in and total allegiance to the one true God—a belief and allegiance that replaces all competing beliefs and allegiances.

Further, most of the world's peoples are seeking greater spiritual power to cope with the exigencies of life. That is why following Jesus' example, we are to use spiritual power as a primary method of blessing and communicating to those whom God loves. An approach to presenting the gospel that focuses on power demonstrations and power encounters would seem then to be warranted by both Scripture and common sense.

4. The kind of focus a people will have in the area of **time/event** is another part of life structured by worldview. **All worldviews provide guidelines for people in this area.** What is considered appropriate organization is provided for daily, weekly, monthly, yearly, seasonally, and through other recurring events. The passage of time is also noted—though seldom quantified as precisely into seconds, minutes, and hours as in the West. Something is done to remember important events, to understand present events, and to anticipate future events. But the worldview assumptions underlying the way such events are treated vary considerably from society to society.

Not infrequently the worldview focus is on the quality of an event rather than on the quantity of time "consumed" by that event. People who seem to Westerners to "have no sense of time" are often basing their attitude on greater concern for the quality of an interaction—be that a conversation or a public meeting—than for the amount of time it takes. From their point of view, it may not be appropriate for a meeting to start until the right people are there. Nor should it end if something significant is happening. We often refer to such a focus as an "event orientation" as opposed to our own "time orientation." Such a concern is frequently mirrored in the language by means of constructions that highlight the nature of the action—continuing, punctiliar, habitual, rather than the time of the action—past, present, future.

Assumptions concerning time may be revealed in the pictures people conceive of in their minds when they deal with time. Americans, for example, seem to visualize time as a river in which we are swimming upstream toward the future. On the other hand, the ancient Greeks saw time as a stream in which a person was standing looking downstream toward the water that had already passed by. For them, therefore, it was the past that lay ahead of them when they "looked" at time; whereas, for us we "look ahead" to the future. At least certain New Guineans seem to see time as a small circle ("memory time") surrounded by a larger circle (mythological time) that encompasses all that is beyond memory, whether past or future. We have much to learn in this area.

Western Christianity has often short-circuited the possibility of Christians genuinely relating to God in corporate worship by structuring church meetings more as timed happenings than as events. Like other types of lovemaking, worship takes time. It is intended to be an event in which the quality of the relationship experienced is to take precedence over the time expended in the activity. Unfortunately, we Evangelicals have tended to lessen the quality of our worship in the interests of keeping the time of our meetings short. Evangelicals have a lot to learn from Pentecostals and charismatics in the area of spending quality time in worship. And there is often a direct relationship between the quality of worship and the effective exercise of spiritual power in a community of believers.

5. All worldviews provide people with assumptions concerning **space and the material world;** whether it is a matter of how to structure a building or how to arrange the space within a building; or whether it is a concern over how to conceive of and relate to certain features of the universe, or what value a society puts on material objects. The point is a people's worldview provides the rules.

Though the matter of space and concern for the material world may seem less important than some of the other categories, there are a few considerations that are relevant to our topic. The lure of materialism is certainly one. It certainly skews our American perspective. We are a people of things! Another is that our church buildings are seldom set up to facilitate times of ministry. They tend to be arranged as lecture halls in which everything significant is expected to happen in the front with the audience watching rather than participating. When the kind of changes I am advocating occur, however, people need space to minister to each other. We need flexibility in architecture, and movable furniture. And we need leaders who will come down from the pulpit and minister to their people, along with others in the congregation who are called to minister.

Another space consideration is that spiritual power is often conveyed through material objects. The use of oil that has been blessed (Jas 5:14), healing through the use of personal objects like Paul's handkerchiefs (Acts 19:12), and Jesus' garment (Mt 9:20) are cases in point. Contemporary experience among Christians adds the dimension that demons can inhabit objects and buildings. It even seems likely that certain demons have dominion over geographical areas. To minister effectively in those areas, therefore, the power of the evil spirit in charge must be broken. See Daniel 10:1-14 for what seems to be a scriptural example of this phenomenon.

The following diagram attempts to combine both the material on worldview universals and that on the functions of worldview presented in Appendix A. A worldview may be seen as a:

PERSON/ GROUP →	MAKING ASSUMPTIONS →	CONCERNING REALITY	PERSPECTIVES on
	1. Explaining,	and	1. Categoriztion
	2. Evaluating,	Organizing	2. Person/Group
	3. Defining	His/Their	3. Causality
	Allegiances,	Perceptions	4. Time/Event
	4. Interpreting,	into	5. Space/Material
	5. Integrating,		
	6. Adapting		

Western and Hebrew Paradigms

To illustrate the above presentation in a concrete way, I present the following chart of contrasts between certain Western and Hebrew worldview paradigms. Keep in mind the fact that all of the scriptural authors, except for possibly Luke, were thinking in terms of Hebrew assumptions as they wrote what God revealed to them. Jesus also was taught Hebrew assumptions as he grew up.

To pick out of the Scriptures what is normative for us, then, we need to be able to distinguish between Jesus' kingdom paradigms, which are normative for us, and those of the Hebrews, which are not. For those kingdom perspectives presented to us by God in the Scriptures are couched in Hebrew thought forms. If we are to effectively disentangle those paradigms from their Hebrew cultural context, we need to understand the differences between the two.

This is quite a challenge to us since our Western perspectives are so different from Hebrew paradigms. It is not so great a problem for millions whose native paradigms are those of non-Western worldviews. Interestingly enough, this fact makes it easier for missionaries to lead such people directly from their native paradigms into those of Scripture than to lead them first into Western understandings.

Let's take a look at some of these paradigms or perspectives and compare them with Western ones.

Western Paradigms	Hebrew Paradigms
1. Categorization, Classification, Logic	
a) Life is analyzed in neat categories.	a) Everything blurs into everything else.
b) Natural and supernatural dichotomy.	b) Supernatural affects everything.
c) Clear difference between human, animal, and plant life.	c) Similar assumption.
d) Linear logic.	d) Contextual logic.
2. Person/Group	
a) Individualism. Group interests usually subservient to individual concerns. Important decisions are made by individuals of almost any age or status.	a) The group is the reality. Individual interests are usually subservient to group concerns. Important decisions are made as a group.
b) Equality of persons.	b) Different persons are of different value, according to their status in the hierarchy.

2. Person/Group (continued)	
c) Oriented toward freedom. Society is to provide as much freedom as possible for individuals.	c) Oriented toward security. Society is to provide as much security as possible for individuals.
d) Competition is good (need to "get ahead").	d) Competition is evil (need to "work together").
e) The majority rules in a democracy.	e) Certain people are "born to rule."
f) Human-centered universe.	f) God and tribe/family-centered universe.
g) Money and material possession are the measure of human value.	g) Family relationships are the measure of human value.
h) Biological life is sacred.	h) Social life is supremely important.
3. Cause, Power	
a) Incredible faith is shown in "chance." Cause and effect relationships are key and limit what can happen.	a) God causes everything.
b) Humans are in charge of nature through science.	b) God is in charge of everything.
c) Scientific strategy and technique will give humans total power over all things.	c) Strategy and technique in the spiritual realm is the source of whatever control we may achieve. Learning control via spiritual techniques is crucial.
d) Power over others achieved via business, politics, and other organizations.	d) Power over others structured by social patterns ordained by God.
e) There are no invisible beings in the universe.	e) The universe is full of invisible beings who are very powerful.

4. Time/Event	
a) Linear time is divided into neat segments. Each event in life a new one.	a) Cyclical or spiraling time. Very similar events constantly recurring.
b) Oriented toward the near future.	b) Oriented toward the past.
c) "Time orientation." Events are scheduled according to the clock and calendar. We arrive at appointments at pre-arranged clock time.	c) "Event orientation." Quality (not time) of event is crucial. The event starts when the proper people are present (not according to clock time).
d) History is an attempt to record "facts" from past objectively.	d) History is an attempt to preserve significant truths in a way meaningful today whether or not all details are objective facts.
e) Change is good. It is called "progress."	e) Change is bad. It means destruction of traditions.
5. Space, the Material Sphere	
a) The universe evolved by chance.	a) The universe was created by God.
b) The universe can be dominated and controlled via science and technology.	b) The universe is to be responsibly managed by us as stewards of God.
c) The universe is like a machine.	c) The universe is more personal.
d) Material goods are a measure of personal achievement.	d) Material goods are a measure of God's blessing.

Though oversimplified, the above chart can be both illustrative of the material presented earlier in this appendix and instructive concerning some of the basic assumptions of those who wrote Scripture.

Bibliography

Barbour, Ian G., *Myths, Models and Paradigms* (New York, New York: Harper & Row, 1974).

Barclay, William, *The Gospel of Luke*, 2nd ed. (Philadelphia, Pennsylvania: Westminster Press, 1956).

Berger, Peter & Thomas Luckman, *The Social Construction of Reality* (Garden City, New York: Doubleday & Co., 1966).

Brown, Colin, "The Enlightenment" in *Evangelical Dictionary of Theology*, pp. 304-5.

Dickason, C. Fred, *Demon Possession and the Christian* (Chicago, Illinois: Moody Press, 1987).

Elwell, Walter A. ed., *Evangelical Dictionary of Theology* (Grand Rapids, Michigan: Baker Book House, 1984).

Hiebert, Paul G., "Epistemological Foundations for Science and Theology" in *Theological Students Fellowship Bulletin*, March-April 1985, vol 8, no 4, pp. 5-10.

"The Flaw of the Excluded Middle," *Missiology*, vol 10, 1982, pp. 35-47.

"The Missiological Implications of an Epistemological Shift" in *Theological Students Fellowship Bulletin*, May-June 1985, vol 8, no 5, pp. 12-18.

Hunt, David and T.A. McMahon, *The Seduction of Christianity* (Eugene, Oregon: Harvest House, 1985).

Kearney, Michael, *World View* (Novato, California: Chandler & Sharp, 1984).

Kluckhohn, Clyde, *Mirror for Man* (New York, New York: McGraw-Hill, 1949). Quotes from Fawcett edition, 1957.

Kraft, Charles H., *Christianity in Culture* (Maryknoll, New York: Orbis, 1979).

Communication Theory for Christian Witness (Nashville, Tennessee: Abingdon Press, 1983).

"The Question of Miracles," in *The Pentecostal Minister*, Winter 1986, pp. 24-27.

Kuhn, Thomas S., *The Structure of Scientific Revolutions* (Chicago, Illinois: University of Chicago Press, 1970).

Laudan, Larry, *Progress and Its Problems* (Berkeley, California: University of California Press, 1977).

MacDonald, Michael H., "Deism" in *Evangelical Dictionary of Theology*, pp. 304-5.

Newbigin, Lesslie, *Foolishness to the Greeks* (Grand Rapids, Michigan: Eerdmans, 1986).

Pytches, David, *Come, Holy Spirit* (London, England: Hodder & Stoughton, 1985).

Sandford, John & Paula, *The Transformation of the Inner Man* (South Plainfield, New Jersey: Logos [Bridge Publishing], 1982).

Schaeffer, Francis, *How Shall We Then Live?* (Old Tappan, New Jersey: Revell, 1976).

Seamands, David A., *Healing for Damaged Emotions* (Wheaton, Illinois: Victor Books [Scripture Press Publications], 1981).
    Healing of Memories (Wheaton, Illinois: Victor Books [Scripture Press Publications], 1985).

Sire, James W., *The Universe Next Door* (Downers Grove, Illinois: InterVarsity, 1976).

Skinner, B. F., *Beyond Freedom and Dignity* (New York, New York: Knopf, 1971).

Smart, Ninian, *Worldviews* (New York, New York: Charles Scribner's & Sons, 1983).

Springer, Kevin ed., *Power Encounters* (New York, New York: Harper & Row, 1988).

Stendahl, Krister, *Paul Among Jews and Gentiles and Other Essays* (Philadelphia, Pennsylvania: Fortress, 1976).

Torrey, R. A., *What the Bible Teaches* (Old Tappan, New Jersey: Revell, 1898).

Wagner, C. Peter, *How to Have a Healing Ministry* (Ventura, California: Regal Books, 1988).
    The Third Wave of the Holy Spirit (Ann Arbor, Michigan: Vine Books [Servant Publications], 1988).

Williams, Don, "Exorcising the Ghost of Newton," in Springer, Kevin, ed., *Power Encounters* 1988, pp. 116-127.

Wimber, John, "Introduction," in *Power Encounters*, pp. xix-xxxiv.
    Power Evangelism (New York, New York: Harper & Row, 1986).
    Power Healing (New York, New York: Harper & Row, 1987).

Wise, Robert ed., *The Church Divided: the Holy Spirit and a Spirit of Seduction* (South Plainfield, New Jersey: Bridge Publishing, 1986).

Chapter and Appendix Notes

Introduction

1. Wagner, C. Peter, *The Third Wave of the Holy Spirit* (Ann Arbor, Michigan: Servant Publications, 1988); and *How to Have a Healing Ministry Without Making Your Church Sick!* (Ventura, California: Regal, 1988).

Chapter Two
Puzzling Reflections in a Mirror

1. Do not be misled by the fact that David Hunt uses this illustration in his book *The Seduction of Christianity* and thereby associate me with "New Age" thinking. Any given illustration is capable of many legitimate uses. I, like Hunt, am unalterably opposed to "New Age" thinking.
2. Barbour, Ian, *Myths, Models and Paradigms* (New York, New York: Harper & Row, 1974).
3. Berger, Peter and Luckman, Thomas, *The Social Construction of Reality* (Garden City, New York: Doubleday & Co., 1966).
4. See Barbour, *Myths, Models and Paradigms*. For an excellent discussion of these positions from an Evangelical Christian point of view, see Paul G. Hiebert's articles on epistemology listed in the bibliography.

Chapter Three
How Do Westerners Picture the World?

1. Brown, Colin, "The Enlightenment" in *Evangelical Dictionary of Theology*, Elwell, Walter A. ed., (Grand Rapids, Michigan: Baker Book House, 1984), p. 355.
2. Brown in *Evangelical Dictionary of Theology*, p. 355.
3. Brown in *Evangelical Dictionary of Theology*, p. 356.
4. Kluckhohn, Clyde, *Mirror for Man* (New York, New York: McGraw-Hill, 1949). Quotes from Fawcett edition, 1957, p. 189.
5. Kluckhohn, *Mirror for Man*, pp. 185-6.

Chapter Four
Enlightenment Christianity Is Powerless

1. *Insight for Living* radio program, October 10, 1988.
2. MacDonald, Michael, "Deism" in *Evangelical Dictionary of Theology,* Elwell, Walter A. ed., (Grand Rapids, Michigan: Baker Book House, 1984), pp. 304-5.
3. Williams, Don, "Exorcising the Ghost of Newton," in Springer, Kevin ed., *Power Encounters* (New York, New York: Harper & Row, 1988), p.s. 116 and 118.
4. For excellent technical presentations of the influence of Western worldview perspectives on Evangelical theological thinking, see Paul G. Hiebert's articles listed in the bibliography.
5. I am grateful to my good friend Brent Rue, pastor of Desert Vineyard in Lancaster, California for this helpful analogy.

Chapter Five
What Empowers Culture?

1. See Skinner, B.F., *Beyond Freedom and Dignity* (New York, New York: Knopf, 1971).

Chapter Six
The "What We Think We Know" Problem

1. Stendahl, Krister, *Paul Among Jews and Gentiles and Other Essays* (Philadelphia, Pennsylvania: Fortress Press, 1976), p. 7.

Chapter Seven
From a Change in Perspective to a Change in Practice

1. See Schaeffer, Francis, *How Shall We Then Live?* (Old Tappan, New Jersey: Revell, 1976).
2. See Sire, James, *The Universe Next Door* (Downers Grove, Illinois: Inter-Varsity Press, 1976); and Smart, Ninian, *Worldviews* (New York, New York: Charles Scribner's & Sons, 1983).

Chapter Nine
Jesus Had a Worldview

1. Barclay, William, *The Gospel of Luke* (Philadelphia, Pennsylvania: The Westminster Press, 1956), p. 76.
2. Torrey, R.A., *What the Bible Teaches* (Old Tappan, New Jersey: Revell, 1898), p. 94.
3. Pytches, David, *Come, Holy Spirit* (London, England: Hodder & Stoughton, 1985), p. 55.
4. Kraft, Charles H., "The Question of Miracles" in *The Pentecostal Minister,* 1986, p. 27.

Chapter Ten
Things Become New When We Invite God to Get Close

1. A comment is in order here concerning the contrast between my positive attitude toward the use of visualization in ministry and the negative stance taken by David Hunt in *The Seduction of Christianity*. Though there are many interesting and disturbing facets to Hunt's opposition to just about everyone engaged in fruitful power ministry, let me focus on two.

   In the first place, though Hunt has correctly identified many of the areas where we need to be concerned that Christians not be taken in by those who serve the enemy, he has misidentified the problem. The problem, as he sees it, is that Christians are being seduced into using ministry techniques that belong to the enemy. This means that they are unconsciously serving the enemy. With respect to the use of visualization, his argument is that since "New Age" people and other servants of Satan use such a technique, *the technique is wrong*. Christians, therefore, should not use such a technique.

   His mistake is that he has associated the evil with the technique rather than with the power behind the technique. And this is a very serious mistake, leading Hunt to question and condemn both techniques and people that God is using mightily. While it is undeniable that servants of Satan use visualization, it is also true that they use every other technique employed by God and his people. For Satan is a master counterfeiter. For example, Satan's servants use books, miracles, money, sermons, church buildings, even the Bible. Must we regard all of these vehicles as evil? Or should we recognize that when such vehicles are used by the counterfeiter Satan, they are being misused because the power behind them is wrong. But when they are used correctly under the leading and power of God, they are helpful in a Christian sense because the power is coming from the right source.

   Indeed, since Satan is clever enough not to counterfeit things that won't be accepted (a three-dollar bill, for example), we can assume that something he uses might be worth taking seriously as a potential instrument of God. See Luke 16:8 for Jesus' advice that we learn from the "people of this world" to use techniques we may not have thought of ourselves. Though, like any useful technique, there are those who abuse it, those servants of God who use visualization, under God's guidance as a vehicle of his healing power, have found it to be greatly blessed.

   Second, note the influence of rationalism on Hunt. Under the influence of the kind of Enlightenment-influenced worldview we have been discussing, he fears anything that doesn't seem reasonable to him and the rigidly rationalistic tradition in which he was nurtured.

   For a valuable critique of Hunt's positions, see Robert Wise's book listed in the bibliography.

2. For excellent treatments of inner healing see the books by David A. Seamands and John and Paula Sandford listed in the bibliography.

Chapter Twelve
Elements of Ministry

1. Wimber, John, *Power Healing* (New York, New York: Harper & Row, 1987), pp. 199-235.

Appendix A
Worldview and Its Functions

1. See Kraft, Charles H., *Communication Theory for Christian Witness* (Nashville, Tennessee: Abingdon, 1983).

Appendix B
Worldview Universals

1. Kearney, Michael, *World View* (Novato, California: Chandler & Sharp, 1984).

Scriptural Index

Old Testament

Genesis
1:28, 28
32:26, 99
48-49, 130

Exodus
17:1-6, 47

Numbers
20:11, 47

Deuteronomy
32:35, 113

Judges
6-8, 136
6:11-12, 75
7:2, 76

1 Samuel
18:10, 105

Proverbs
3:5, 66

Isaiah
6:5, 83, 173
6:9-10, 71
42:3, 169
55:8-9, 44
55:9, 48
55:11, 45

Daniel
10:1-14, 202

New Testament

Matthew
4:11, 109
4:17, 112
5:3-11, 130
5:3-4, 131
6:12, 14-15, 112
6:16-18, 173
6:24-34, 113
6:33, 113
7:21-23, 176
9:14, 73
9:15, 173
9:20, 131, 202
9:22, 111
10:1, 7-8, 110
10:7-8, 136
11:28-30, 121
12:20, 169
12:22-29, 109
12:25, 73
13:13, 71
13:14-15, 71
14:36, 124, 131
18:1-5, 114
18:20, 119
20:25-28, 114
22:37-40, 112
23:1-36, 109
24:24, 175
25:14-30, 113, 135
25:31, 109
28:9, 152
28:18-20, 110
28:19-20, 87
28:20, 8, 73, 136

General Index

Japanese, 189
Jefferson, Thomas, 25
Jesus, viii, ix, 5, 8, 16, 38, 52, 67, 71, 74, 93, 95, 98, 100, 102, 103, 108, 109, 110, 111, 112, 113, 114, 115, 118, 119, 123, 168, 169, 170, 171, 197
    blessing, 131, 152
    demonstrating God, 46 (see also demonstration)
    divine, 17, 73, 135
    example of, 107, 114, 174, 200
    garment of, empowered, 131, 163, 202
    gentleness of, 74, 108, 121, 142
    humanity of, 73, 114, 174
    intimacy with God, 73, 132, 169, 170
    power of, 5, 123
    teaching method, 42, 43, 46
    under authority, 135
Jesus people, 34
John, the apostle, 49
joy, 131, 132, 142, 152, 170, 172

Kant, Immanuel, 25, 31
kingdom, vii, viii, ix, 71, 102, 105, 111, 113, 114, 130
    normalcy, 114, 123
    ours, 174
    of God, 29, 109, 110, 131, 170, 176, 177
    of Satan, 109, 170, 171
    paradigms, 84, 104, 203
    people, 103, 110, 114
    perspectives, 104, 107, 115, 203
Kluckhohn, Clyde, 27, 30
knees, 127, 160
knowledge, xi, 11, 31, 41, 44-46, 48, 65, 66, 73, 86, 87, 92, 93, 94, 111
    and worldview, 66, 67
    experiential, 94 (also see experience)
    intellectual, 32, 94, 95, 152
    observational, 94, 95, 97

Korea, 82
Kraft, Charles H., vii, viii
Kraft, Marguerite, xii
Kuhlman, Kathryn, 1, 2, 72

lame, 141
language, 182, 191, 195, 200
Latin America, 82, 107, 189
law, natural, 28, 39, 88, 89, 101, 102
law of self-preservation, 102
law, The, 105, 112
leading, 132, 150, 154
learning, 12, 58, 59, 79, 99, 114, 133, 134, 135, 142, 143, 156, 169, 176
    assimilated unconsciously, 59
    of worldview, 186
    through demonstration (see demonstration)
lecturing, 42
left-brained, 18, 52
left-hand taboo, 57
leg, 91, 138, 144, 148, 160
leg lengthening, 91
lenses, 19
leper, 150
liberalism, viii, 41
life, 11, 203
linguistics, 3
listening to God, 44, 46, 47, 49, 98, 99, 130, 135, 144, 153, 170, 176
literacy, 44, 45
live and let live, 33
logic, 105, 183, 195, 203
loneliness, 32
Lord's Supper, 131
love, 5, 84, 108, 112, 115, 121, 123, 128, 132, 133, 138, 139, 141, 149, 156, 158, 160, 161, 166, 167, 170, 177, 191, 197
    for self, 152
    of God, 108, 110, 120, 127, 166, 173
loyalties, 188
lust, 33, 128

Another Book of Interest by the Author

Defeating Dark Angels

Breaking Demonic Oppression in the Believer's Life

Charles H. Kraft

Ed's fourteen-year-old daughter had just told him, "There seems to be something inside me that takes over at times." He was nonplussed. What could he do?

In hundreds of desperate situations, Charles Kraft has seen God break demonic oppression in believers' lives as he and his ministry team have cast out demons in Jesus' name. For example, Ed's daughter has now regained full use of her faculties. But many times inner healing and even long-term counseling are necessary to resolve deep-seated problems that have intensified under demonic activity.

In *Defeating Dark Angels*, Charles Kraft explains how demons operate, how to resist their influence, and how to cast them out in Jesus' name. Here is the practical and spiritual help you need, both to defeat dark angels in your own life and to minister God's freedom and healing to others. **$8.99**

Available at your Christian bookstore or from:
Servant Publications • Dept. 209 • P.O. Box 7455
Ann Arbor, Michigan 48107
Please include payment plus $2.75 per book
for postage and handling.
Send for our FREE catalog of Christian books, music, and cassettes.